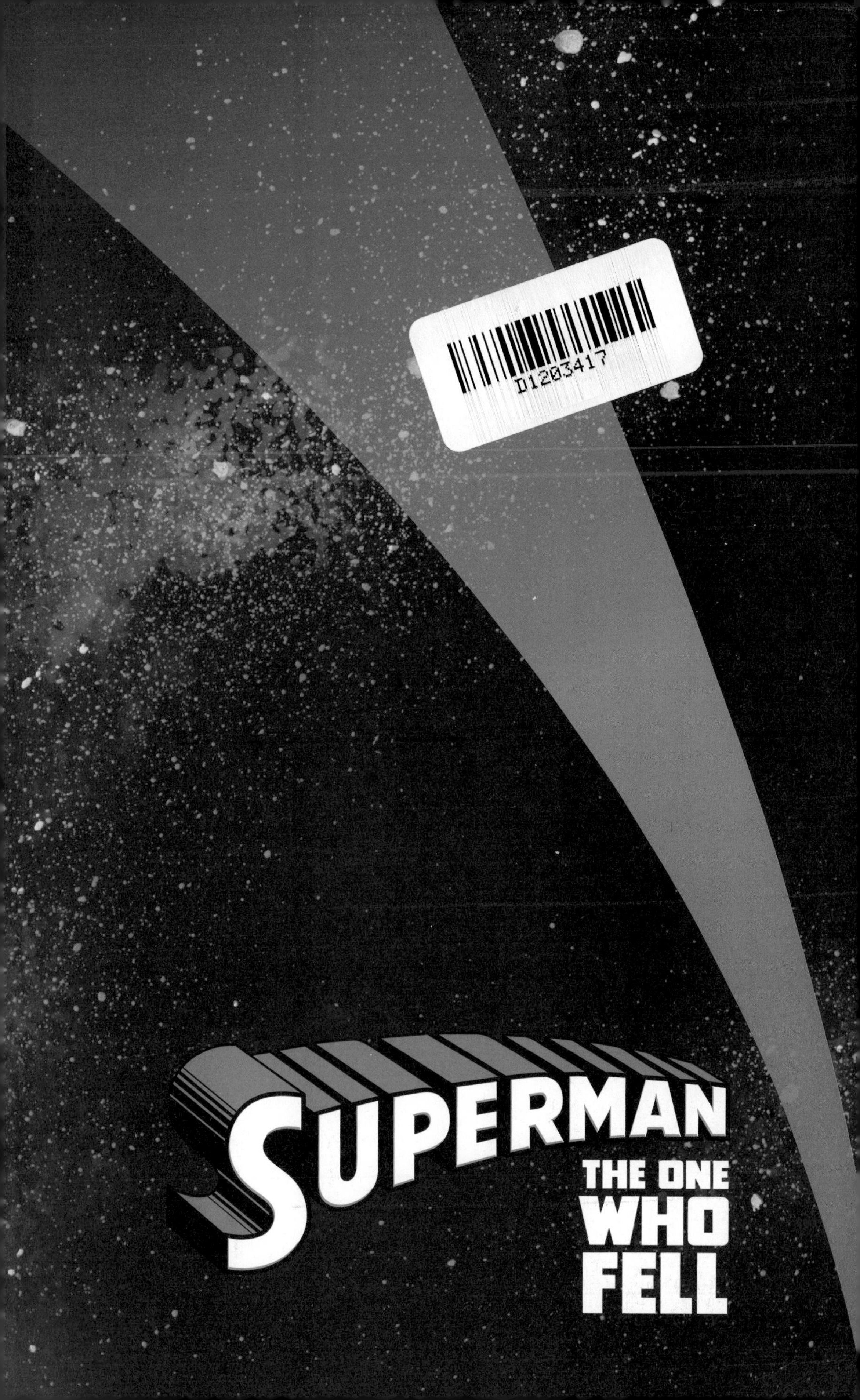
SUPERMAN
THE ONE WHO FELL

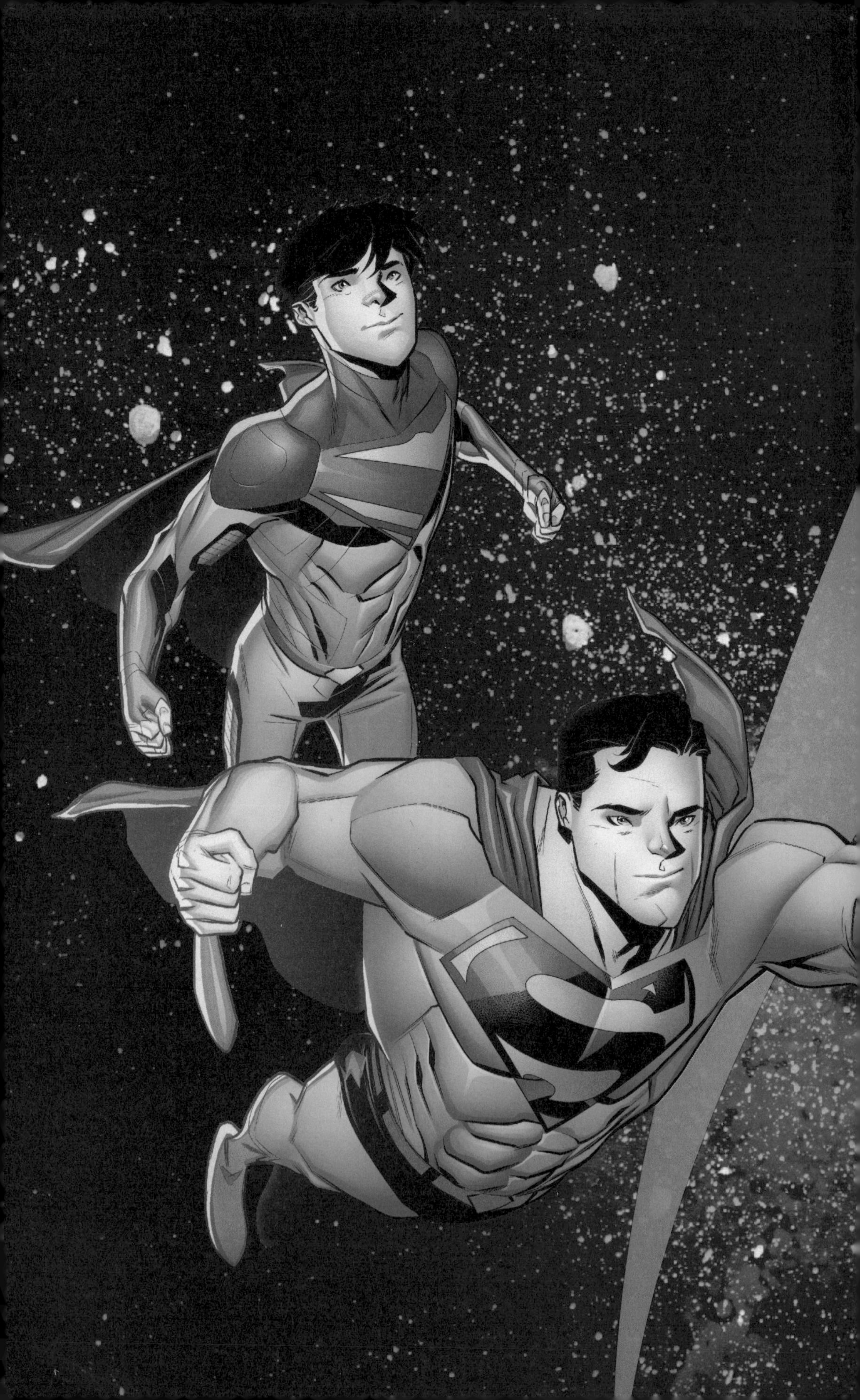

PHILLIP KENNEDY JOHNSON
writer

SCOTT GODLEWSKI
PHIL HESTER
pencillers

ERIC GAPSTUR
SCOTT GODLEWSKI
NORM RAPMUND
inkers

GABE ELTAEB
HI-FI
colorists

DAVE SHARPE
letterer

PHIL HESTER, ERIC GAPSTUR, HI-FI
collection cover artists

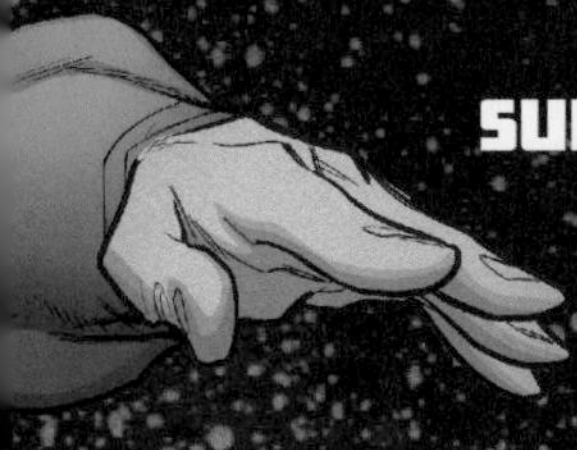

SUPERMAN created by **JERRY SIEGEL** and **JOE SHUSTER**.
SUPERBOY created by **JERRY SIEGEL**.
By special arrangement with the **JERRY SIEGEL** family.

SUPERMAN
THE ONE WHO FELL

JAMIE S. RICH
Editor – Original Series
DIEGO LOPEZ
Associate Editor – Original Series & Editor – Collected
Edition
STEVE COOK
Design Director – Books
DAMIAN RYLAND
Publication Design
ERIN VANOVER
Publication Production

MARIE JAVINS
Editor-in-Chief, DC Comics

DANIEL CHERRY III
Senior VP – General Manager
JIM LEE
Publisher & Chief Creative Officer
JOEN CHOE
VP – Global Brand & Creative Services
DON FALLETTI
VP – Manufacturing Operations & Workflow Management
LAWRENCE GANEM
VP – Talent Services
ALISON GILL
Senior VP – Manufacturing & Operations
NICK J. NAPOLITANO
VP – Manufacturing Administration & Design
NANCY SPEARS
VP – Revenue

SUPERMAN: THE ONE WHO FELL

DC Comics, 2900 West Alameda Ave., Burbank, CA 91505
Printed by LSC Communications, Owensville, MO, USA.
10/1/21. First Printing.
ISBN: 978-1-7951-264-2

Library of Congress Cataloging-in-Publication
Data is available.

PEFC Certified
This product is from
sustainably managed
forests and controlled
sources

PEFC/29-31-337   ● www.pefc.org

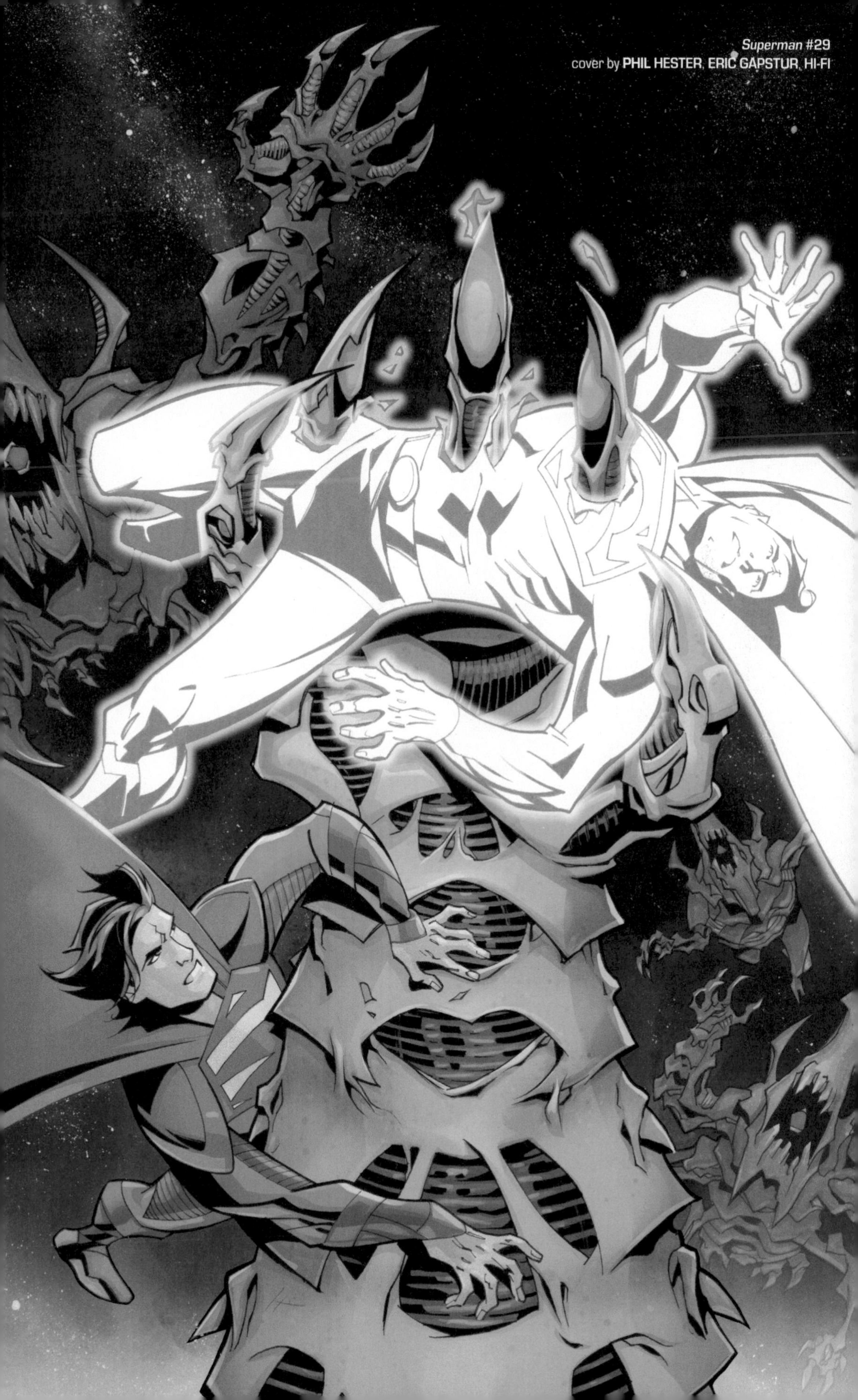

Superman #29
cover by **PHIL HESTER, ERIC GAPSTUR, HI-FI**

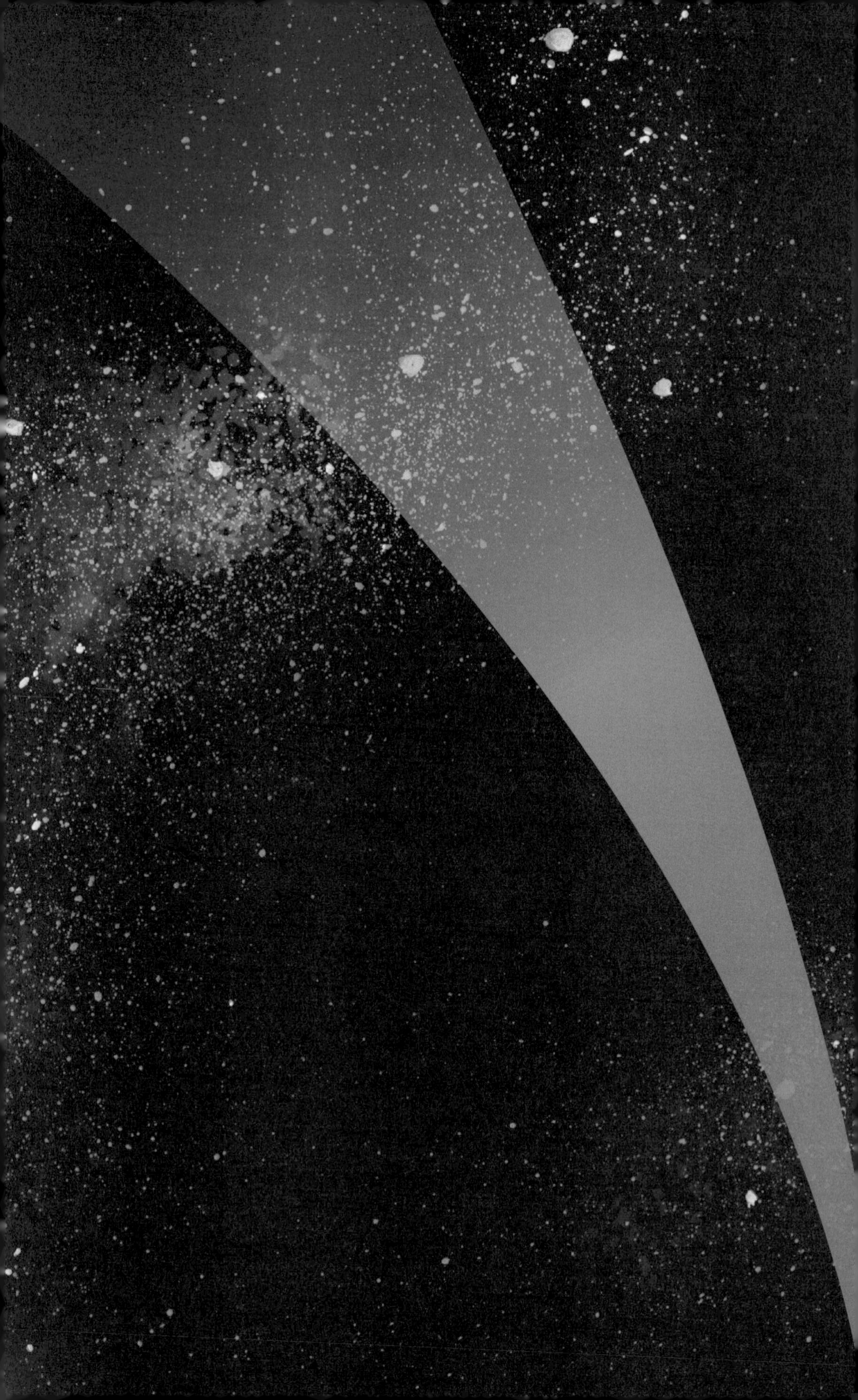

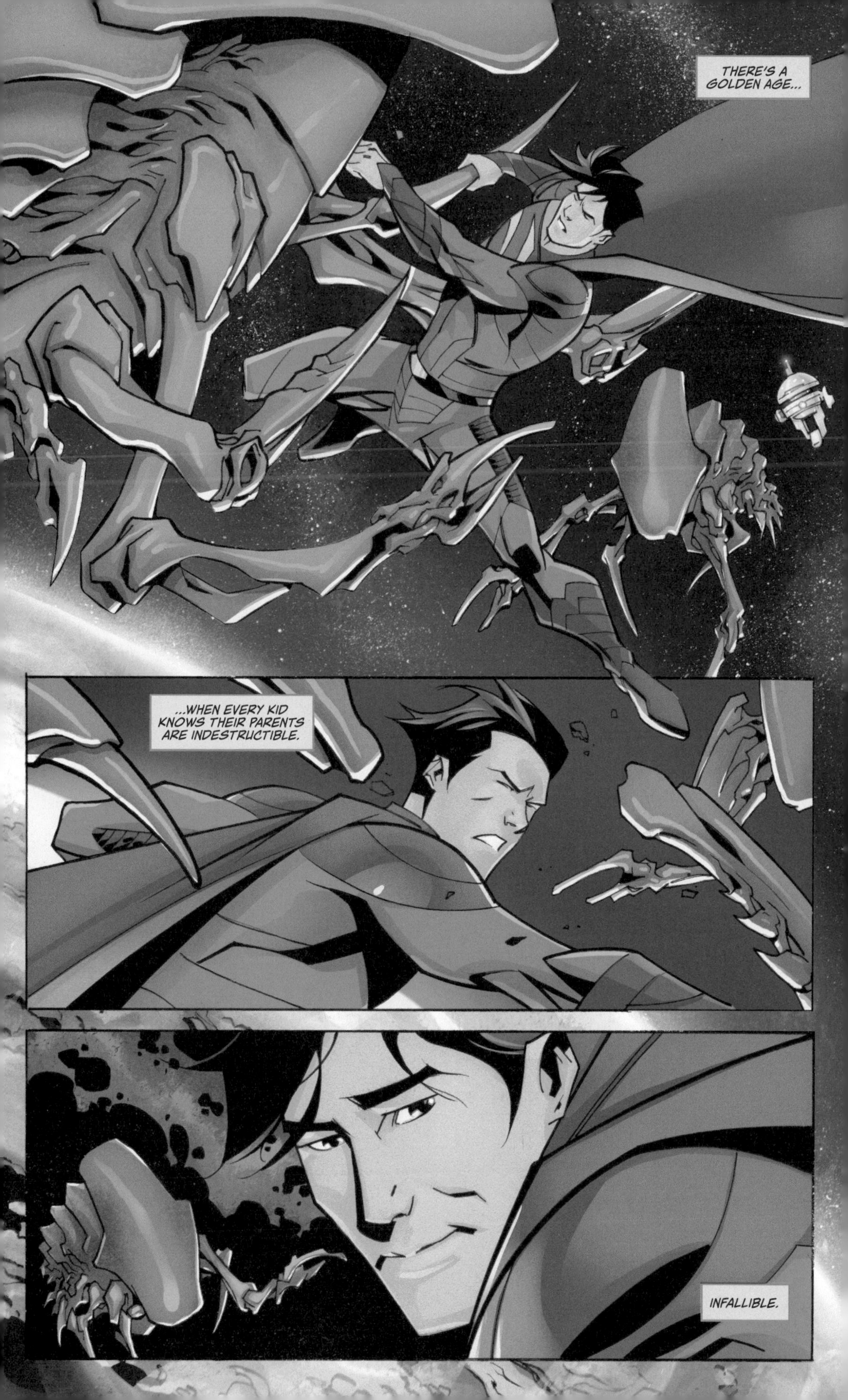
THERE'S A GOLDEN AGE...
...WHEN EVERY KID KNOWS THEIR PARENTS ARE INDESTRUCTIBLE.
INFALLIBLE.

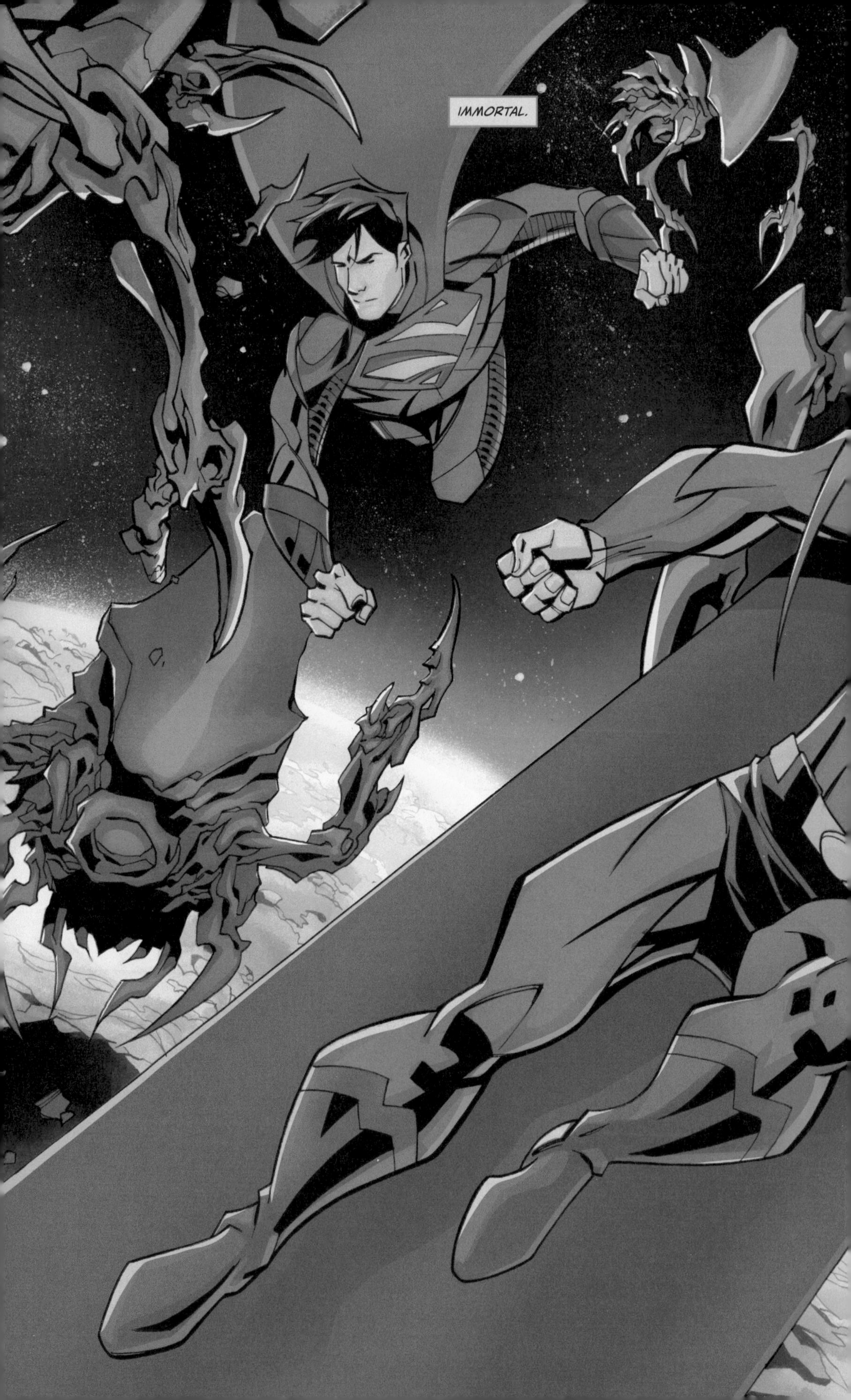
IMMORTAL.

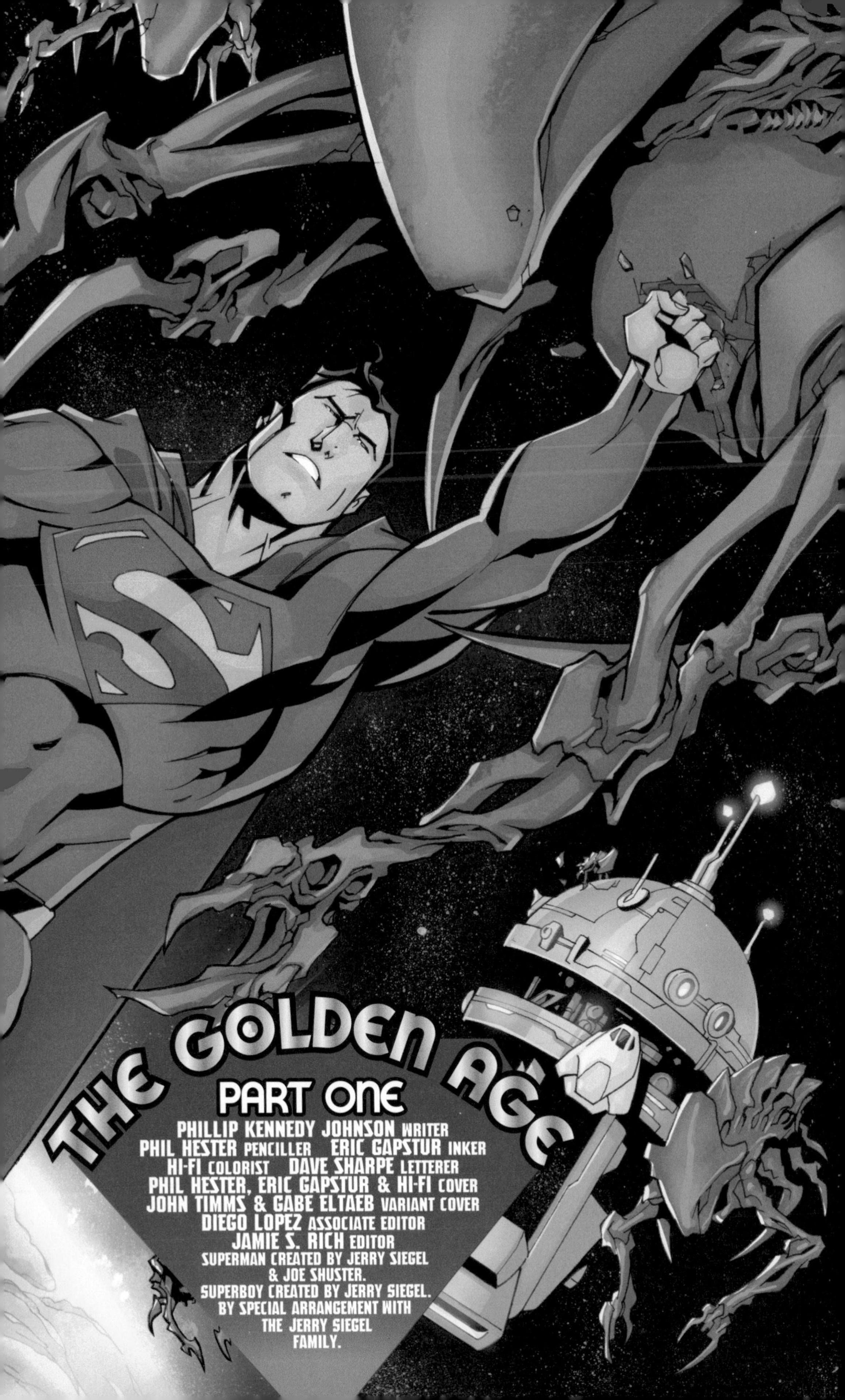
THE GOLDEN AGE
PART ONE
PHILLIP KENNEDY JOHNSON WRITER
PHIL HESTER PENCILLER ERIC GAPSTUR INKER
HI-FI COLORIST DAVE SHARPE LETTERER
PHIL HESTER, ERIC GAPSTUR & HI-FI COVER
JOHN TIMMS & GABE ELTAEB VARIANT COVER
DIEGO LOPEZ ASSOCIATE EDITOR
JAMIE S. RICH EDITOR
SUPERMAN CREATED BY JERRY SIEGEL & JOE SHUSTER.
SUPERBOY CREATED BY JERRY SIEGEL.
BY SPECIAL ARRANGEMENT WITH THE JERRY SIEGEL FAMILY.

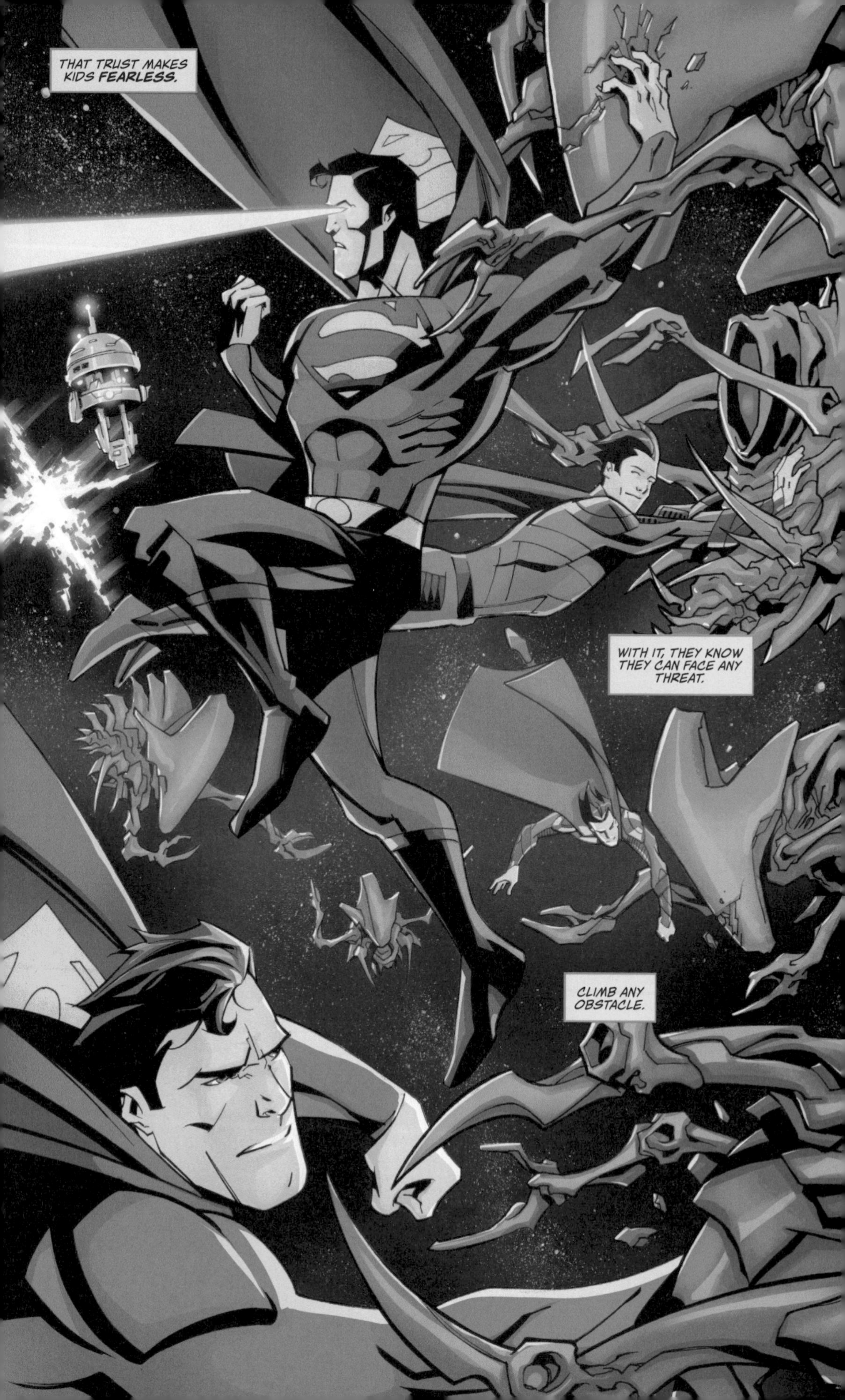
THAT TRUST MAKES KIDS FEARLESS.
WITH IT, THEY KNOW THEY CAN FACE ANY THREAT.
CLIMB ANY OBSTACLE.

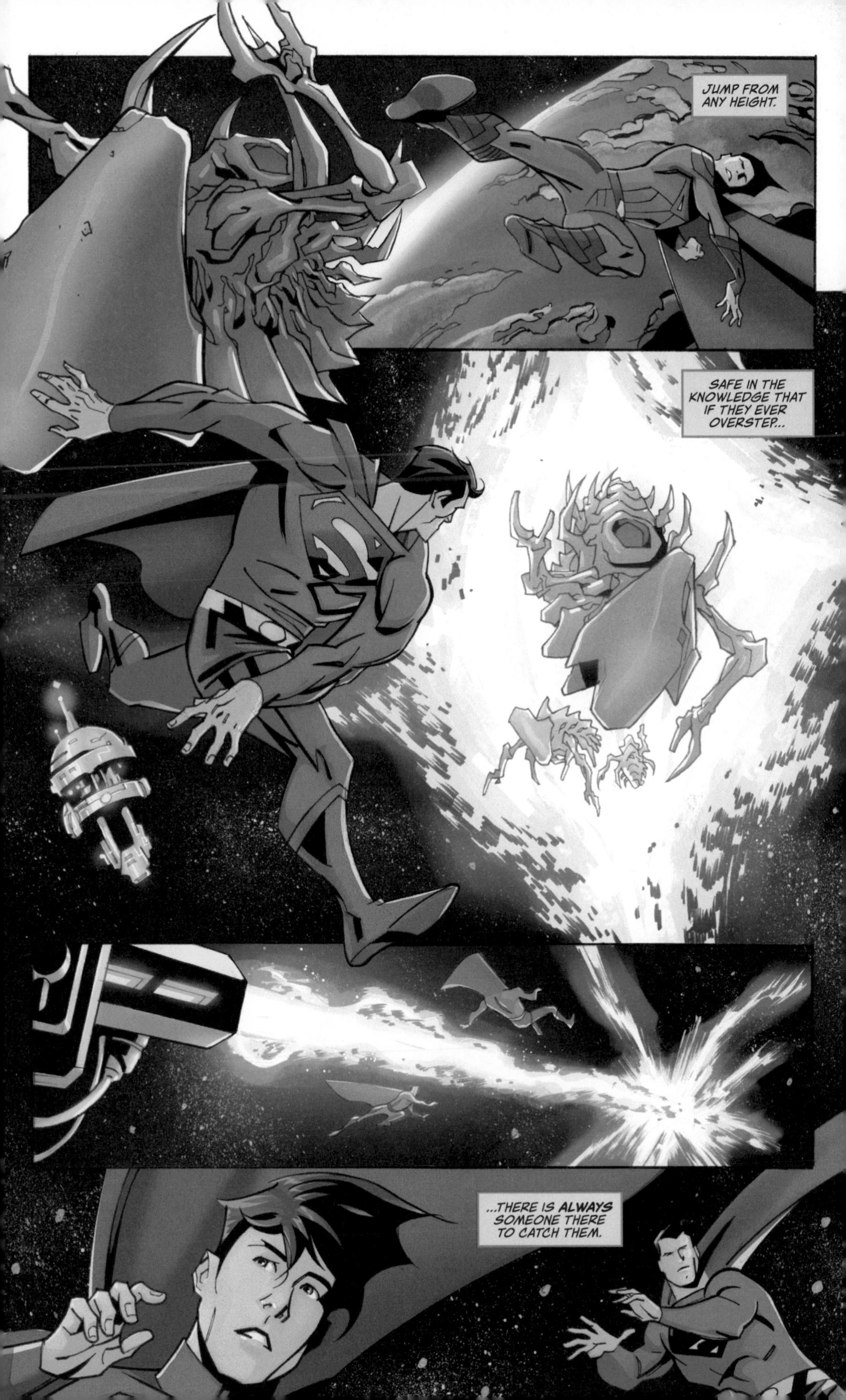
JUMP FROM ANY HEIGHT.
SAFE IN THE KNOWLEDGE THAT IF THEY EVER OVERSTEP...
...THERE IS ALWAYS SOMEONE THERE TO CATCH THEM.

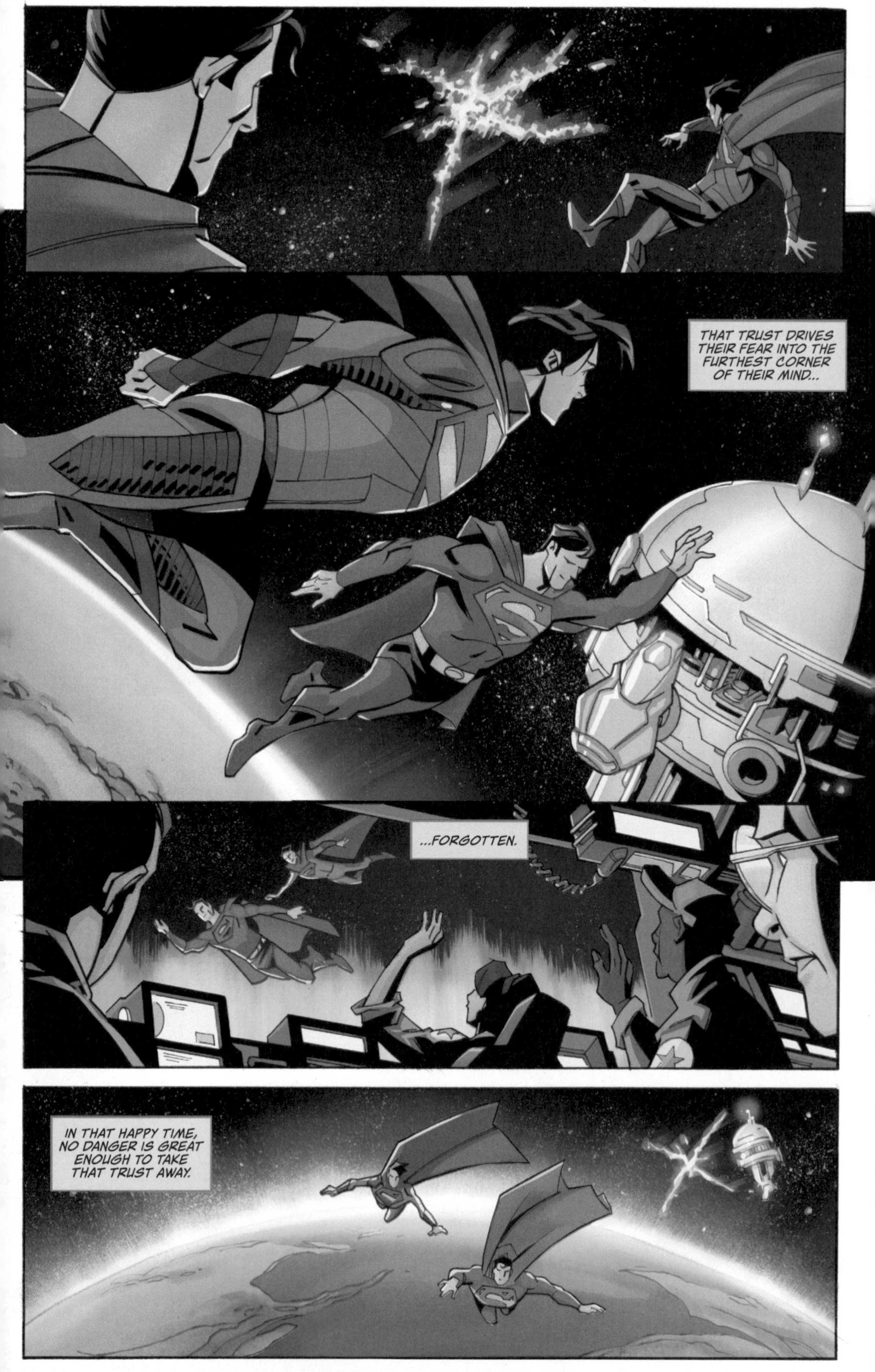
THAT TRUST DRIVES THEIR FEAR INTO THE FURTHEST CORNER OF THEIR MIND...
...FORGOTTEN.
IN THAT HAPPY TIME, NO DANGER IS GREAT ENOUGH TO TAKE THAT TRUST AWAY.

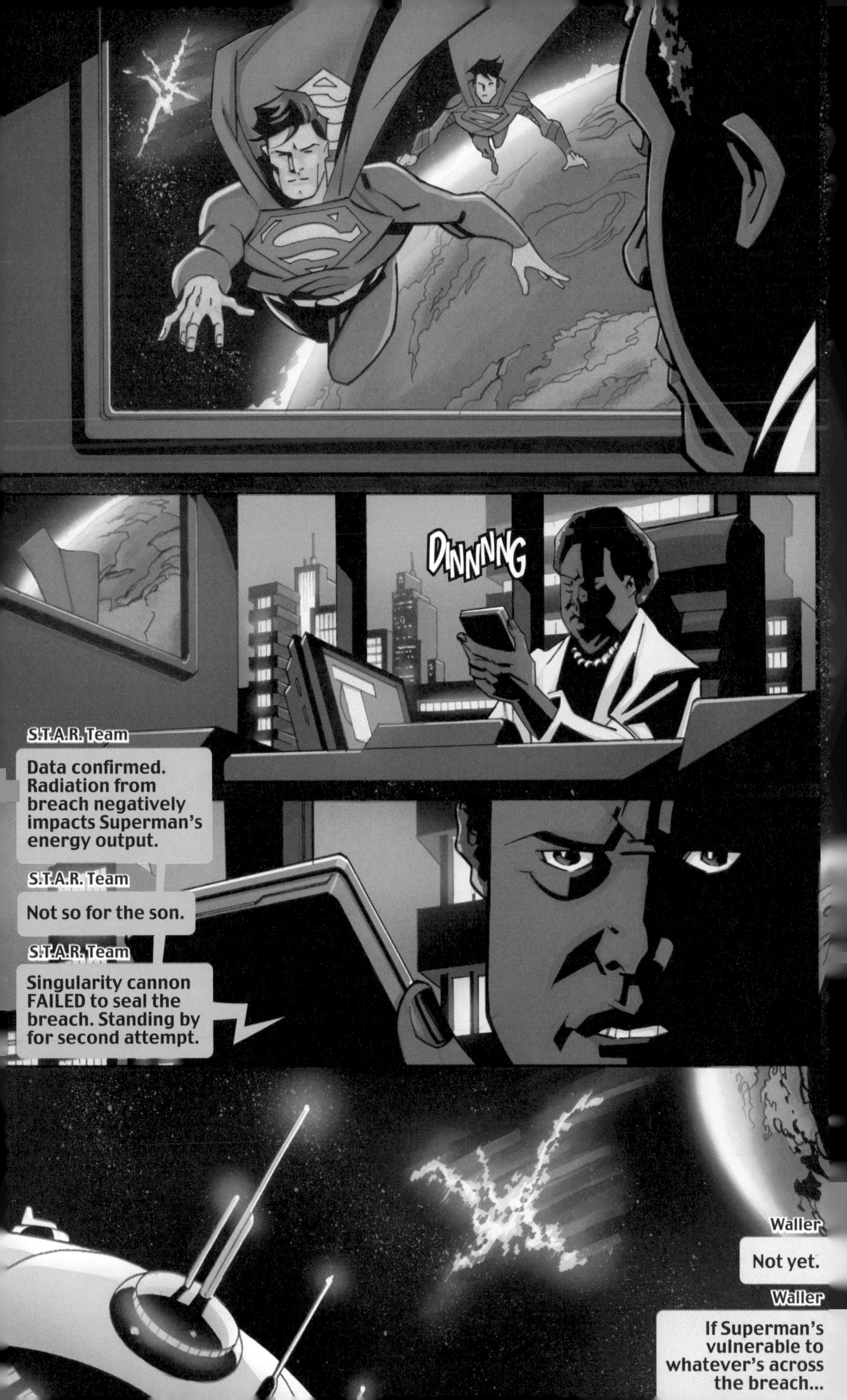
DINNNNG
S.T.A.R. Team
Data confirmed. Radiation from breach negatively impacts Superman's energy output.
S.T.A.R. Team
Not so for the son.
S.T.A.R. Team
Singularity cannon FAILED to seal the breach. Standing by for second attempt.
Waller
Not yet.
Waller
If Superman's vulnerable to whatever's across the breach...

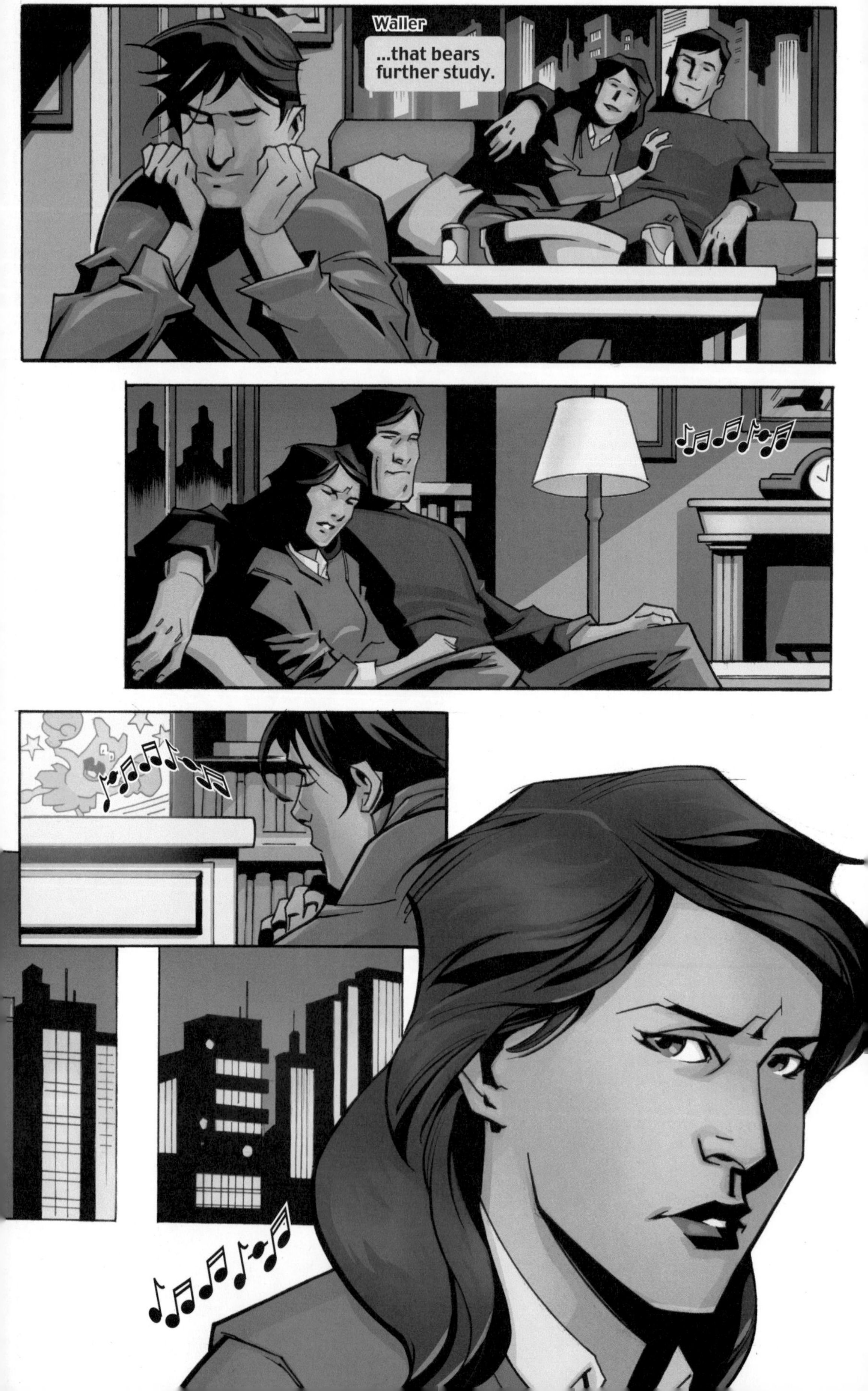
Waller
...that bears further study.

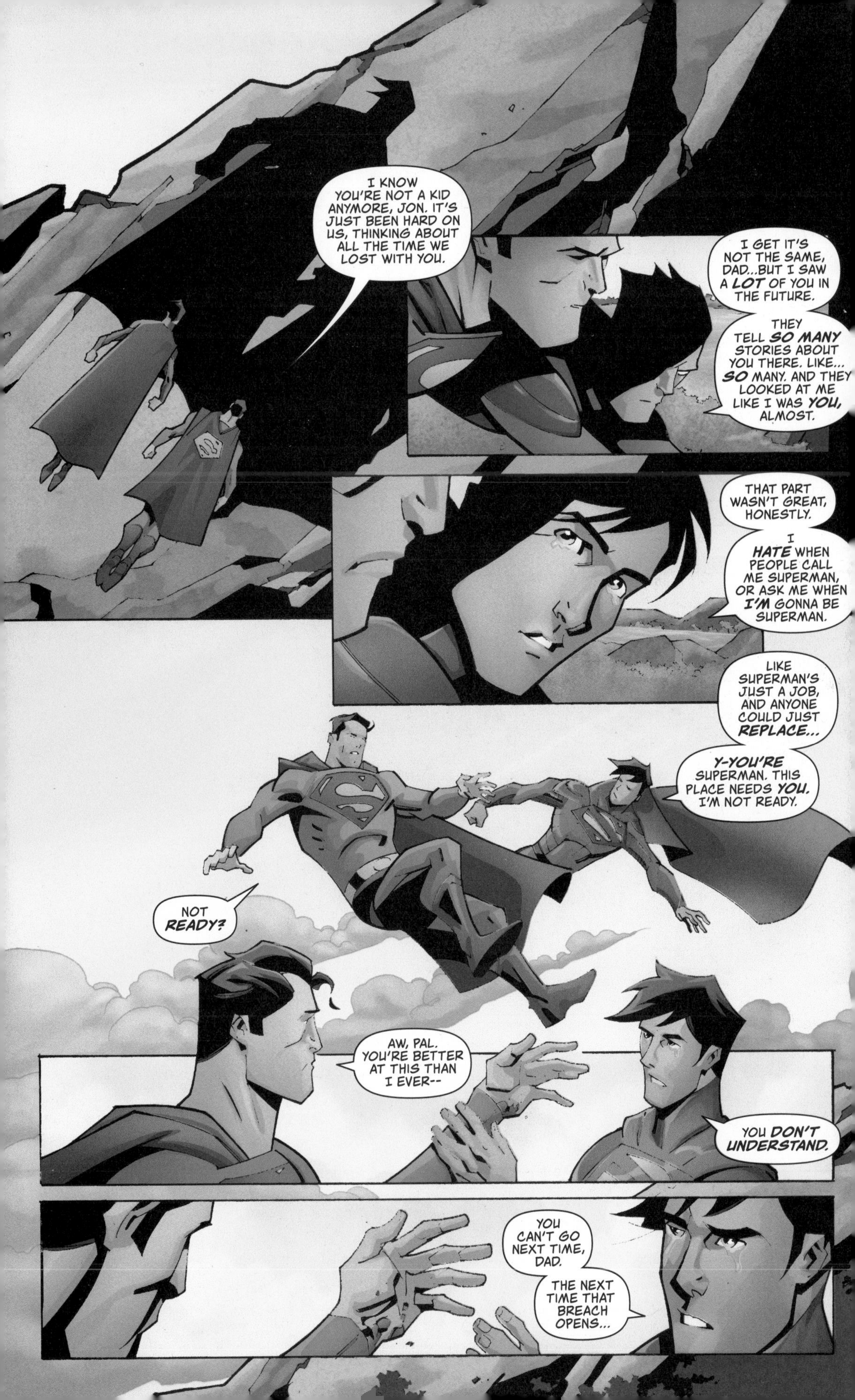
I KNOW YOU'RE NOT A KID ANYMORE, JON. IT'S JUST BEEN HARD ON US, THINKING ABOUT ALL THE TIME WE LOST WITH YOU.
I GET IT'S NOT THE SAME, DAD...BUT I SAW A LOT OF YOU IN THE FUTURE.
THEY TELL SO MANY STORIES ABOUT YOU THERE. LIKE... SO MANY. AND THEY LOOKED AT ME LIKE I WAS YOU, ALMOST.
THAT PART WASN'T GREAT, HONESTLY.
I HATE WHEN PEOPLE CALL ME SUPERMAN, OR ASK ME WHEN I'M GONNA BE SUPERMAN.
LIKE SUPERMAN'S JUST A JOB, AND ANYONE COULD JUST REPLACE...
Y-YOU'RE SUPERMAN. THIS PLACE NEEDS YOU. I'M NOT READY.
NOT READY?
AW, PAL. YOU'RE BETTER AT THIS THAN I EVER--
YOU DON'T UNDERSTAND.
YOU CAN'T GO NEXT TIME, DAD.
THE NEXT TIME THAT BREACH OPENS...

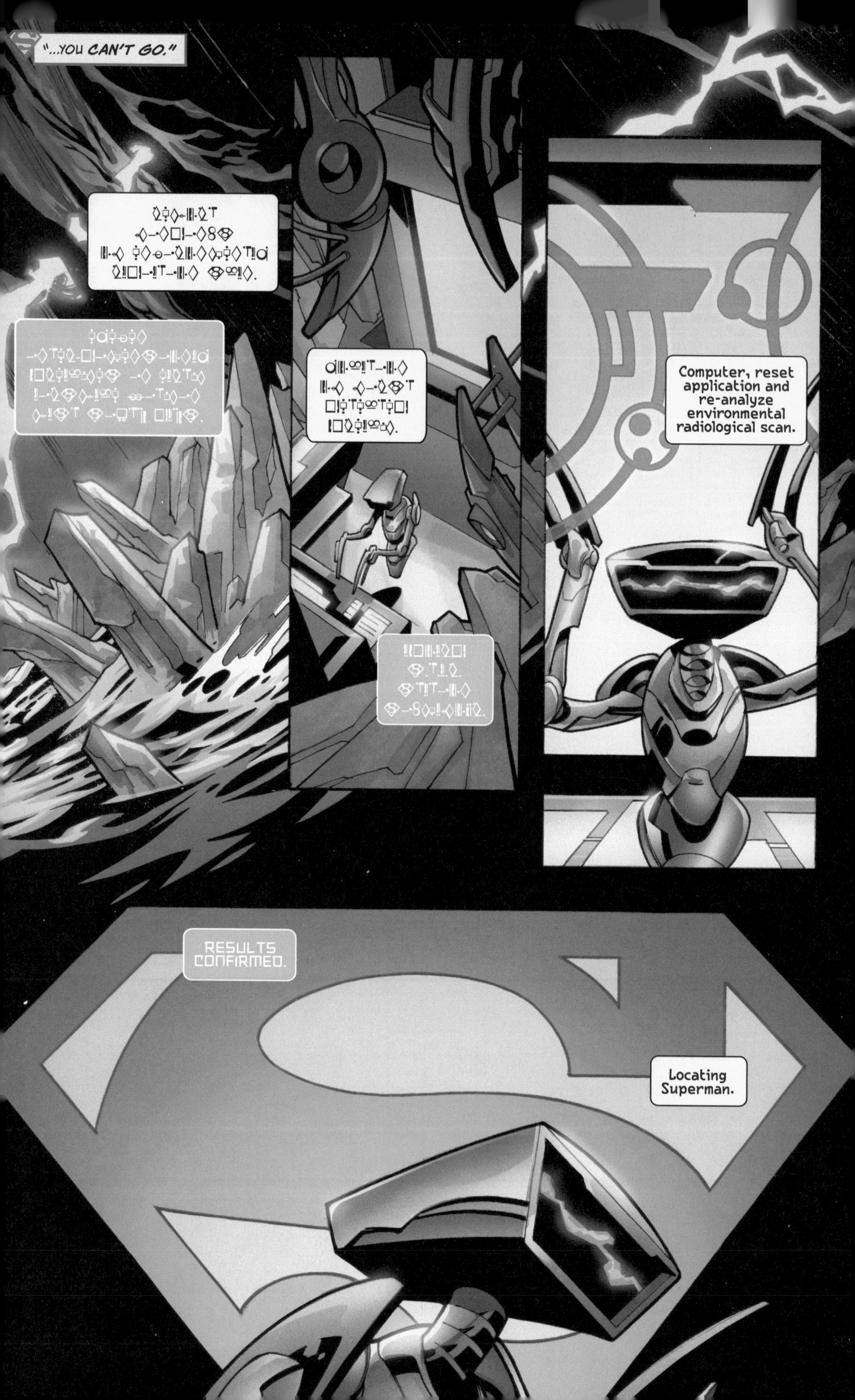
"...YOU CAN'T GO."
Computer, reset application and re-analyze environmental radiological scan.
RESULTS CONFIRMED.
Locating Superman.

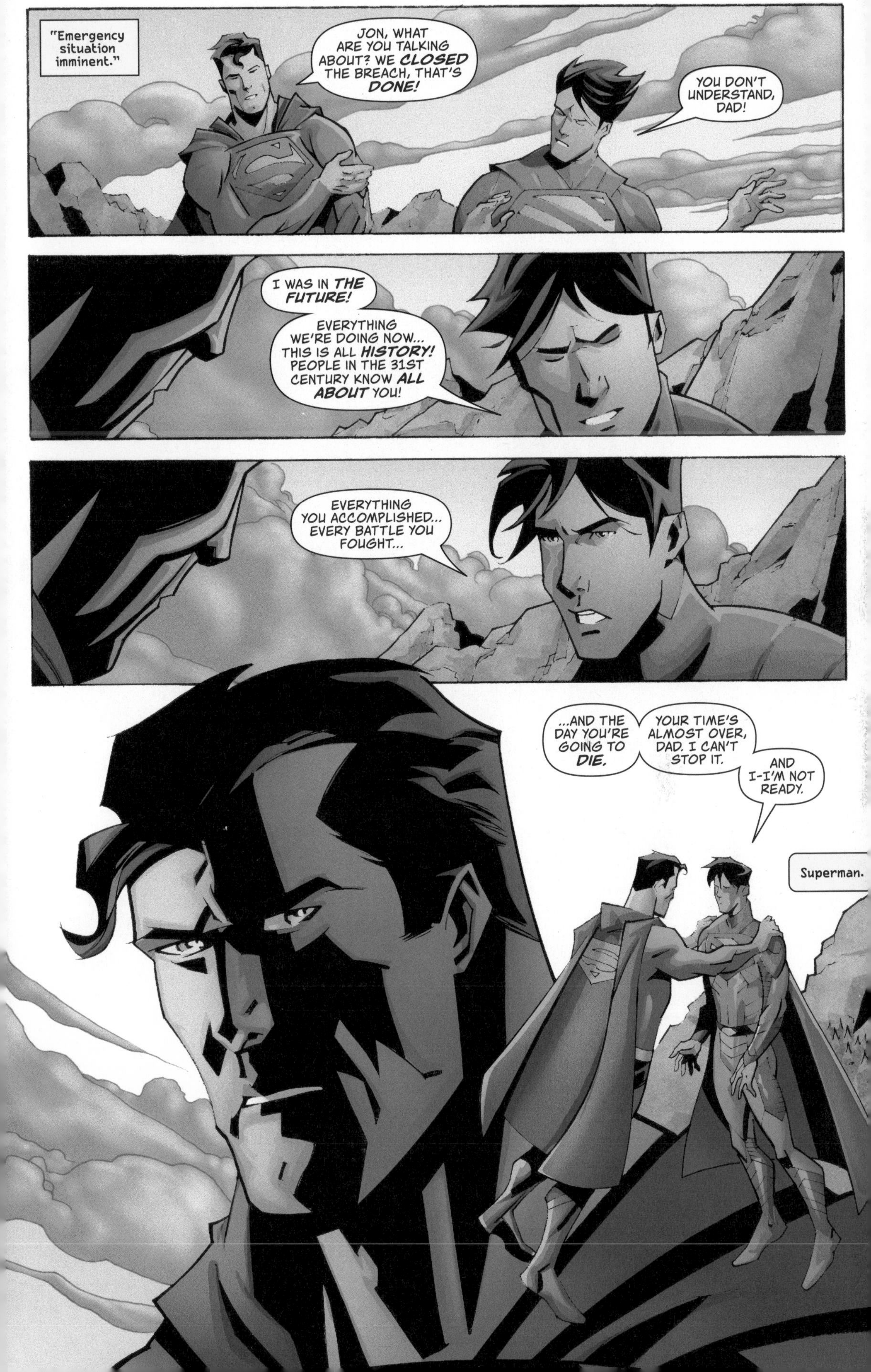
"Emergency situation imminent."
JON, WHAT ARE YOU TALKING ABOUT? WE CLOSED THE BREACH, THAT'S DONE!
YOU DON'T UNDERSTAND, DAD!
I WAS IN THE FUTURE!
EVERYTHING WE'RE DOING NOW... THIS IS ALL HISTORY! PEOPLE IN THE 31ST CENTURY KNOW ALL ABOUT YOU!
EVERYTHING YOU ACCOMPLISHED... EVERY BATTLE YOU FOUGHT...
...AND THE DAY YOU'RE GOING TO DIE.
YOUR TIME'S ALMOST OVER, DAD. I CAN'T STOP IT.
AND I-I'M NOT READY.
Superman.

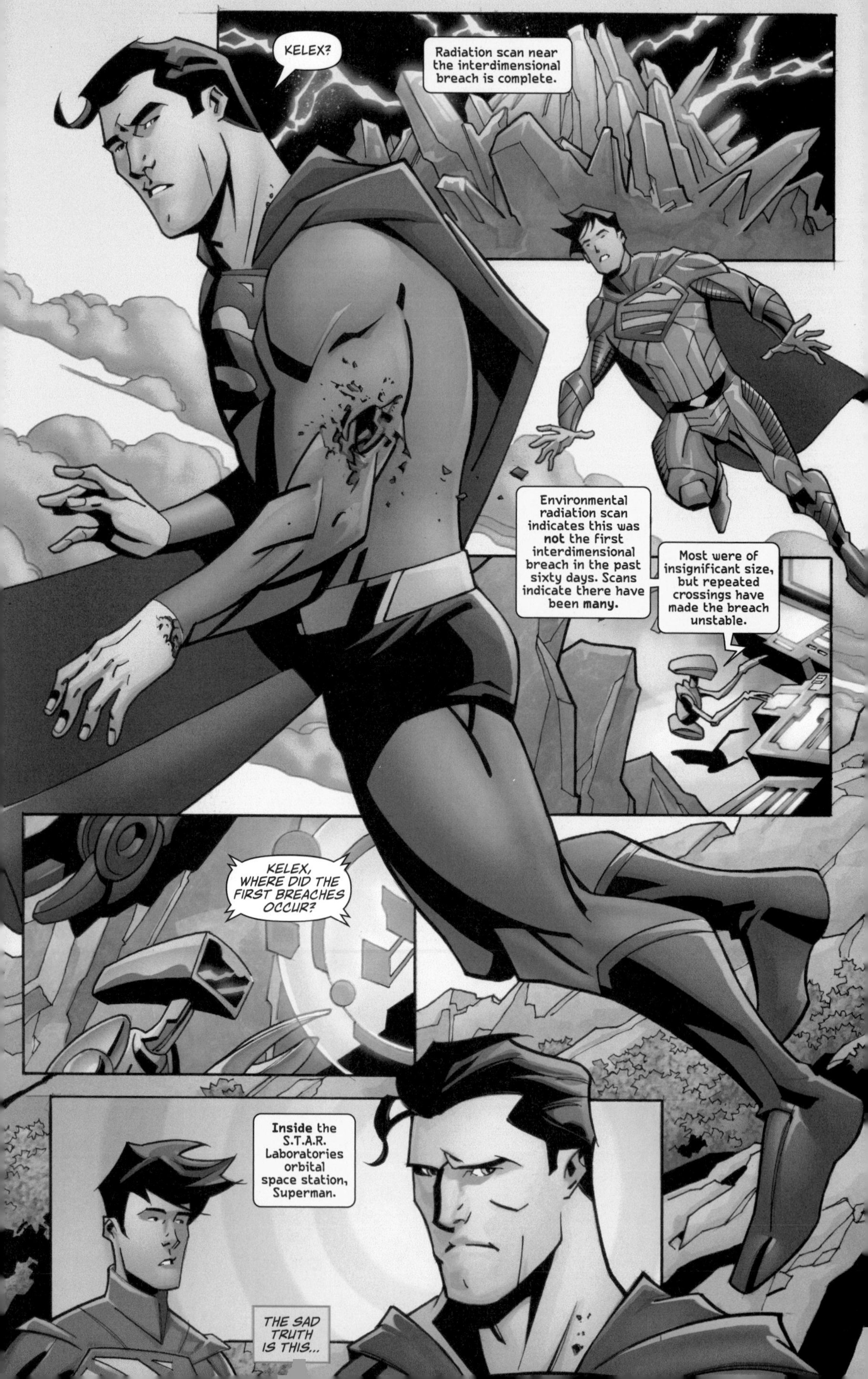
KELEX?
Radiation scan near the interdimensional breach is complete.
Environmental radiation scan indicates this was **not** the first interdimensional breach in the past sixty days. Scans indicate there have been **many**.
Most were of insignificant size, but repeated crossings have made the breach unstable.
KELEX, WHERE DID THE FIRST BREACHES OCCUR?
Inside the S.T.A.R. Laboratories orbital space station, Superman.
THE SAD TRUTH IS THIS...

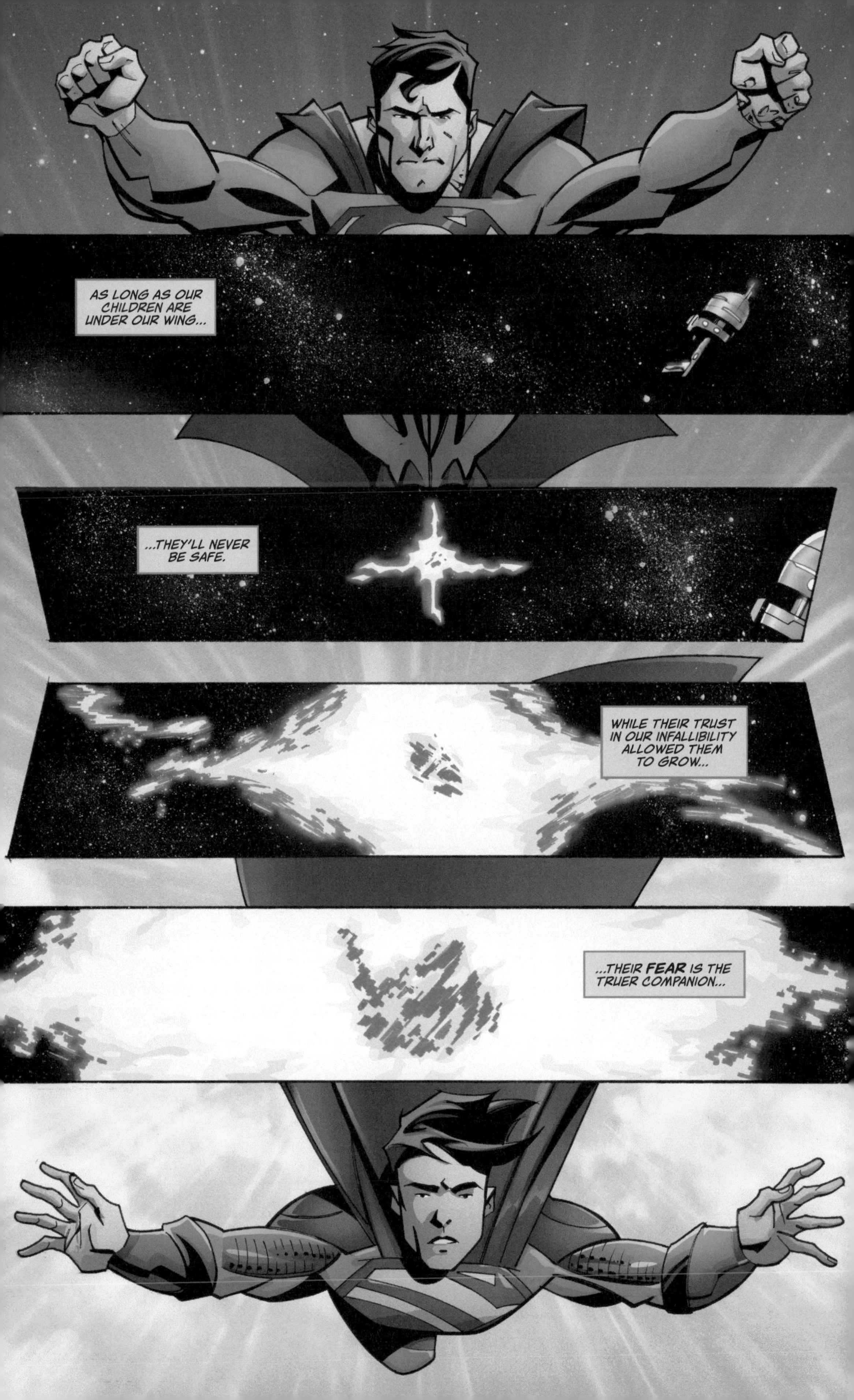
AS LONG AS OUR CHILDREN ARE UNDER OUR WING...
...THEY'LL NEVER BE SAFE.
WHILE THEIR TRUST IN OUR INFALLIBILITY ALLOWED THEM TO GROW...
...THEIR **FEAR** IS THE TRUER COMPANION...

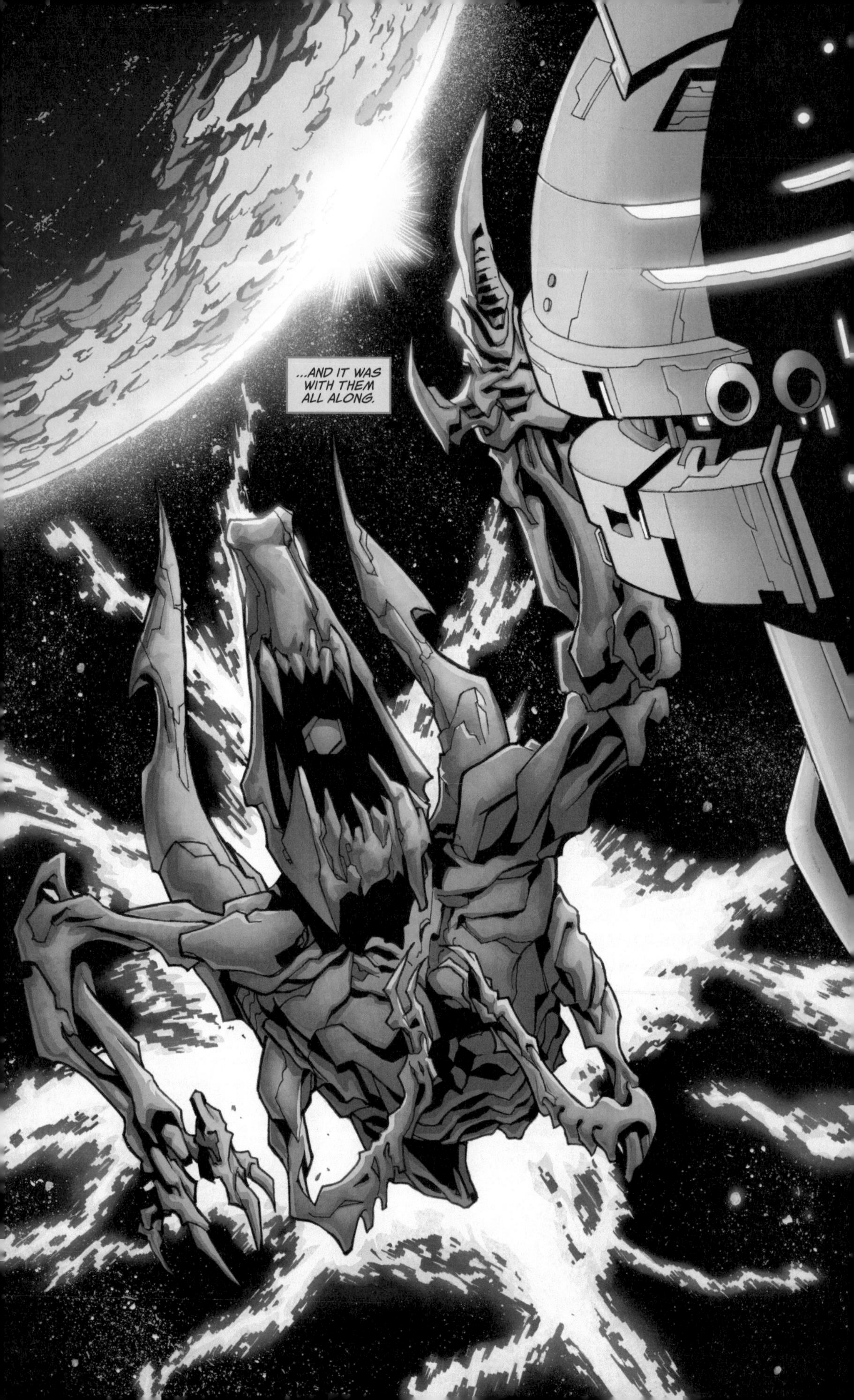
...AND IT WAS
WITH THEM
ALL ALONG.

Action Comics #1029 cover by **PHIL HESTER, ERIC GAPSTUR, HI-FI**

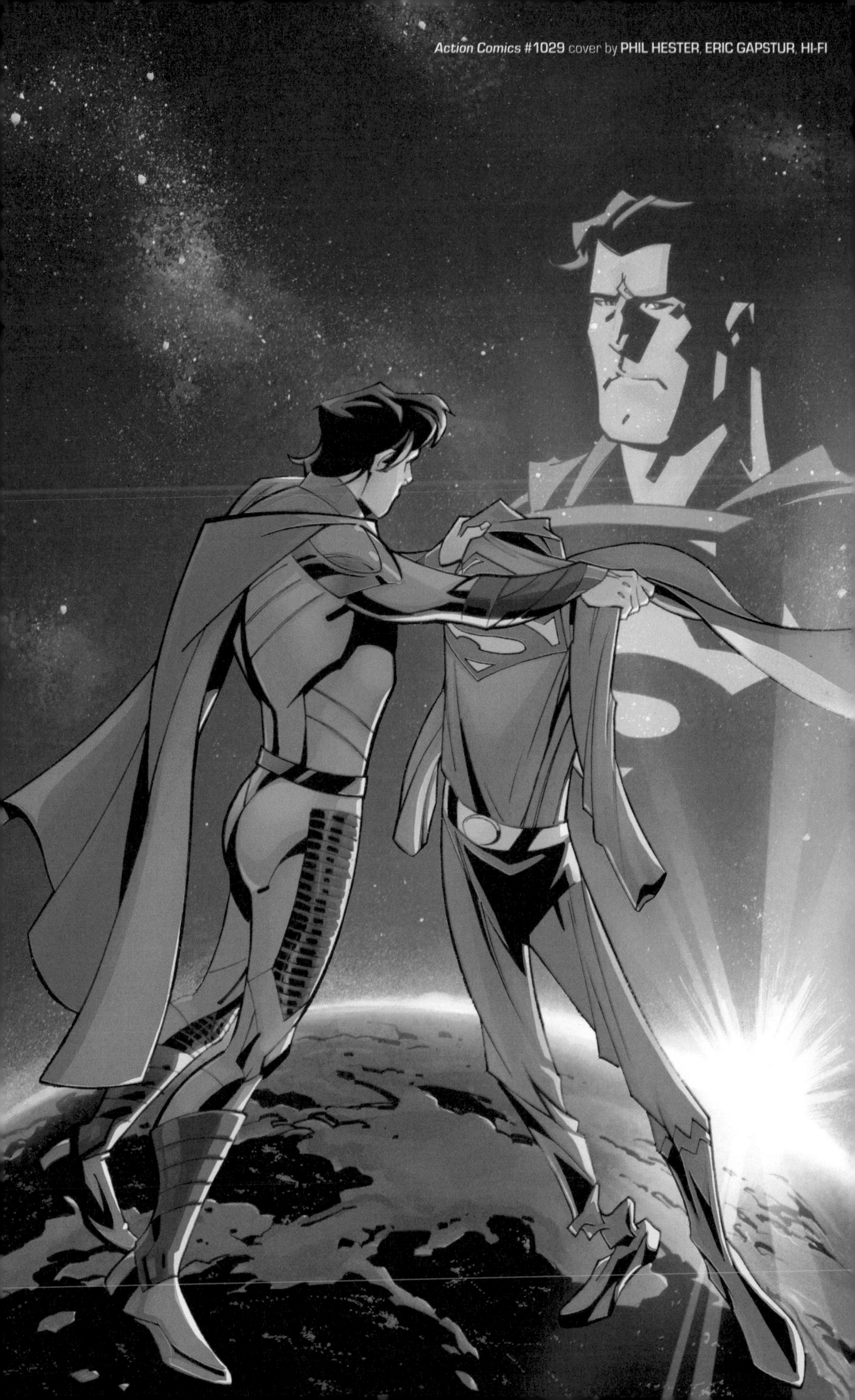

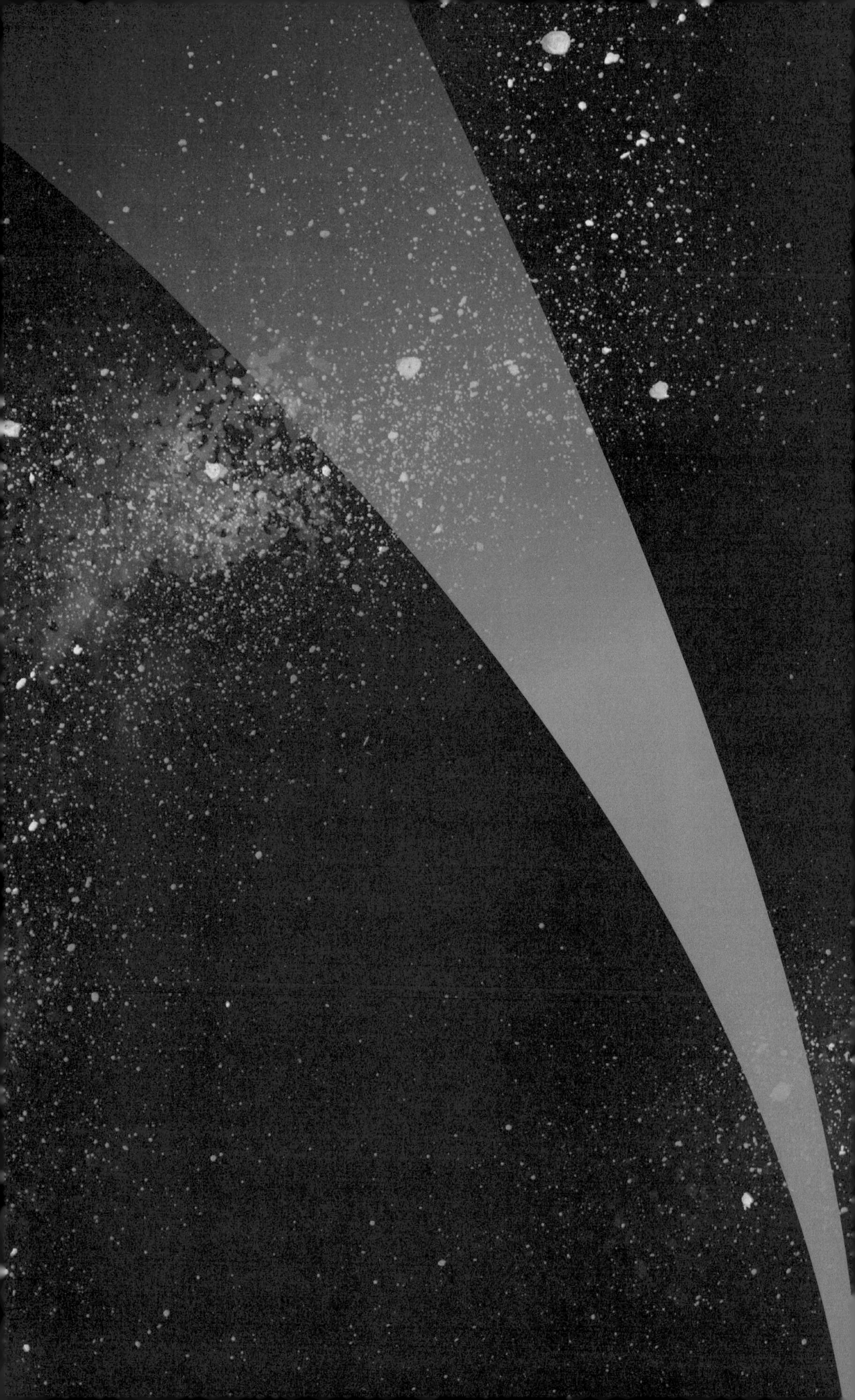

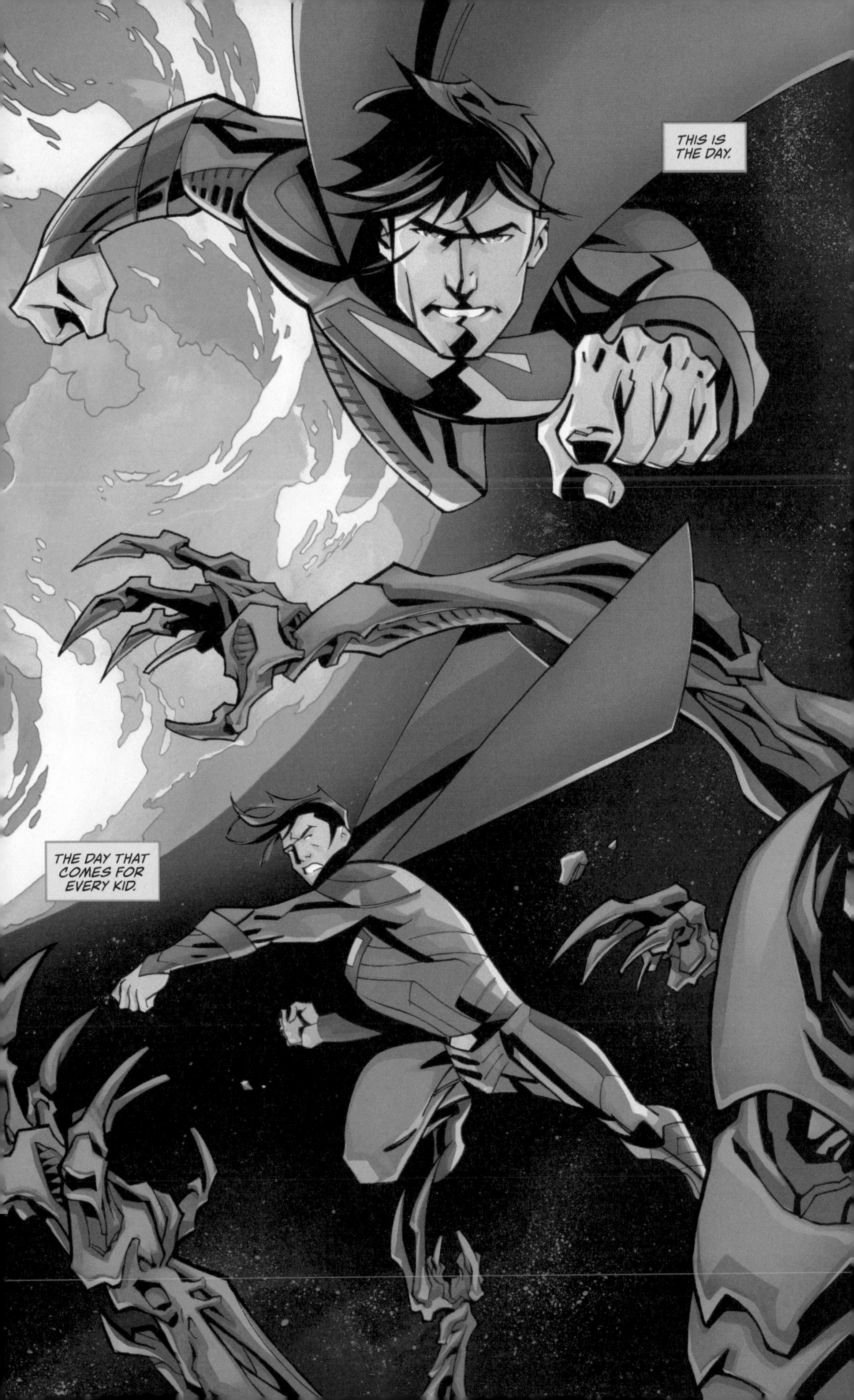
THIS IS THE DAY.
THE DAY THAT COMES FOR EVERY KID.

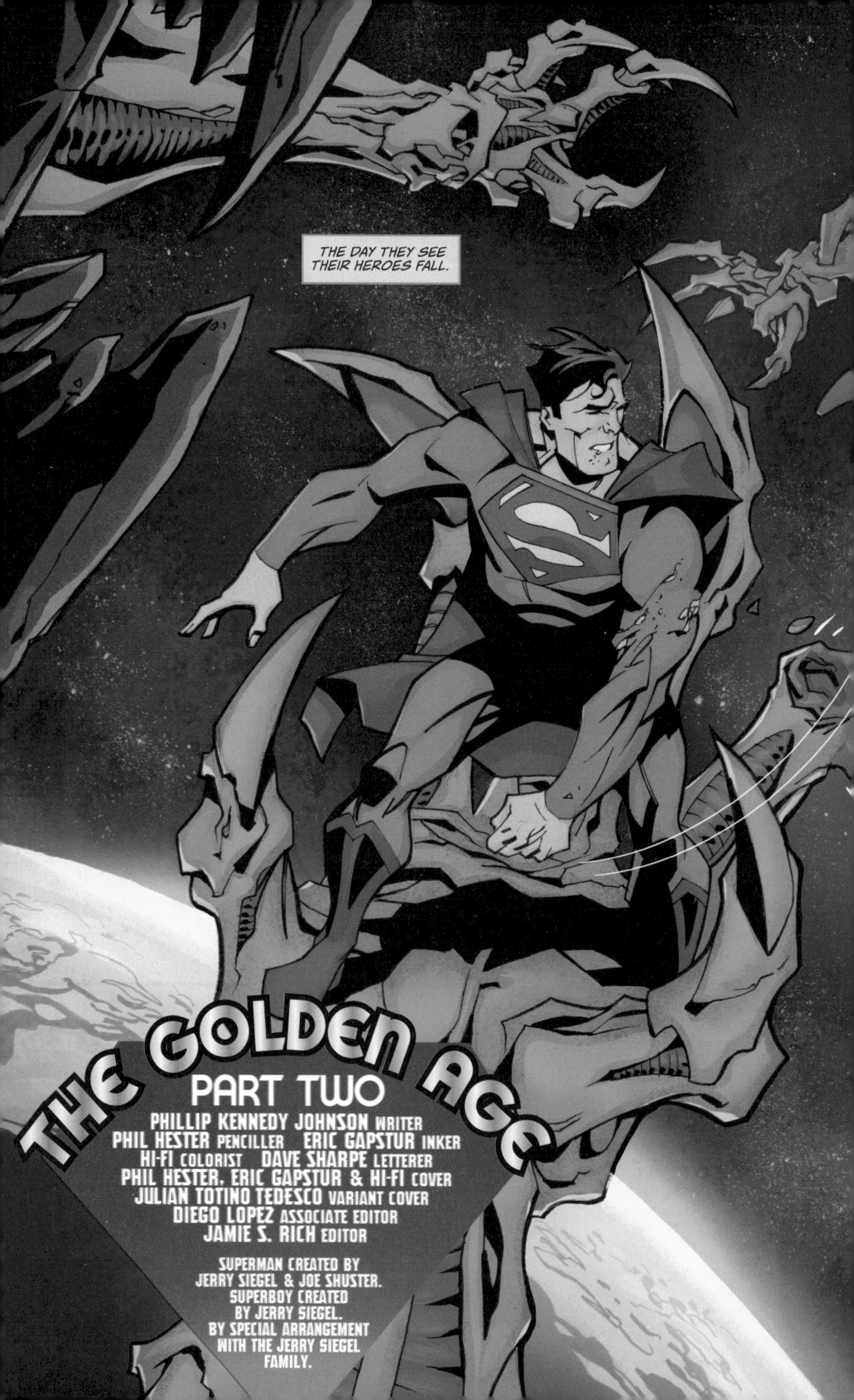
THE DAY THEY SEE
THEIR HEROES FALL.
THE GOLDEN AGE
PART TWO
PHILLIP KENNEDY JOHNSON WRITER
PHIL HESTER PENCILLER ERIC GAPSTUR INKER
HI-FI COLORIST DAVE SHARPE LETTERER
PHIL HESTER, ERIC GAPSTUR & HI-FI COVER
JULIAN TOTINO TEDESCO VARIANT COVER
DIEGO LOPEZ ASSOCIATE EDITOR
JAMIE S. RICH EDITOR
SUPERMAN CREATED BY
JERRY SIEGEL & JOE SHUSTER.
SUPERBOY CREATED
BY JERRY SIEGEL.
BY SPECIAL ARRANGEMENT
WITH THE JERRY SIEGEL
FAMILY.

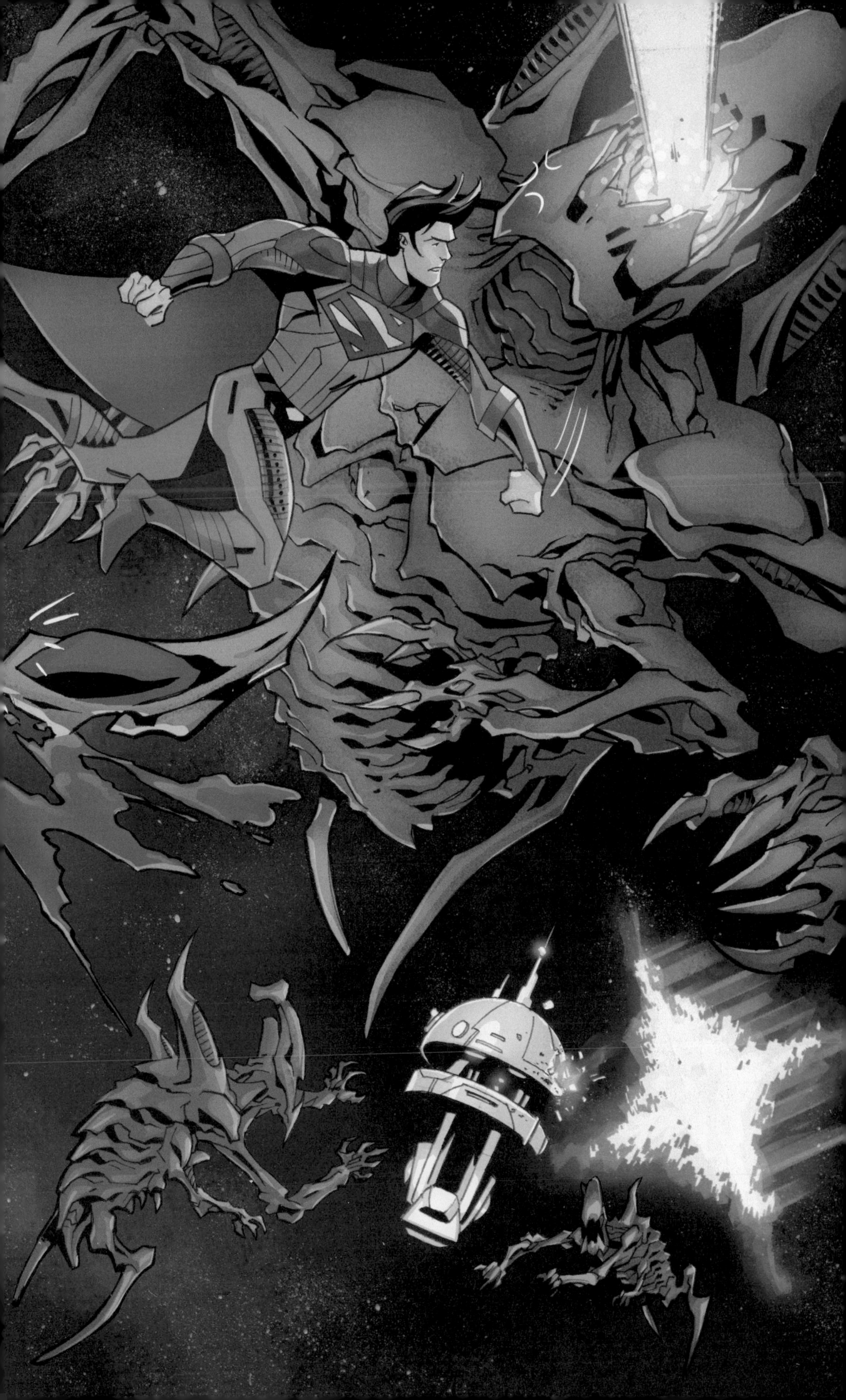

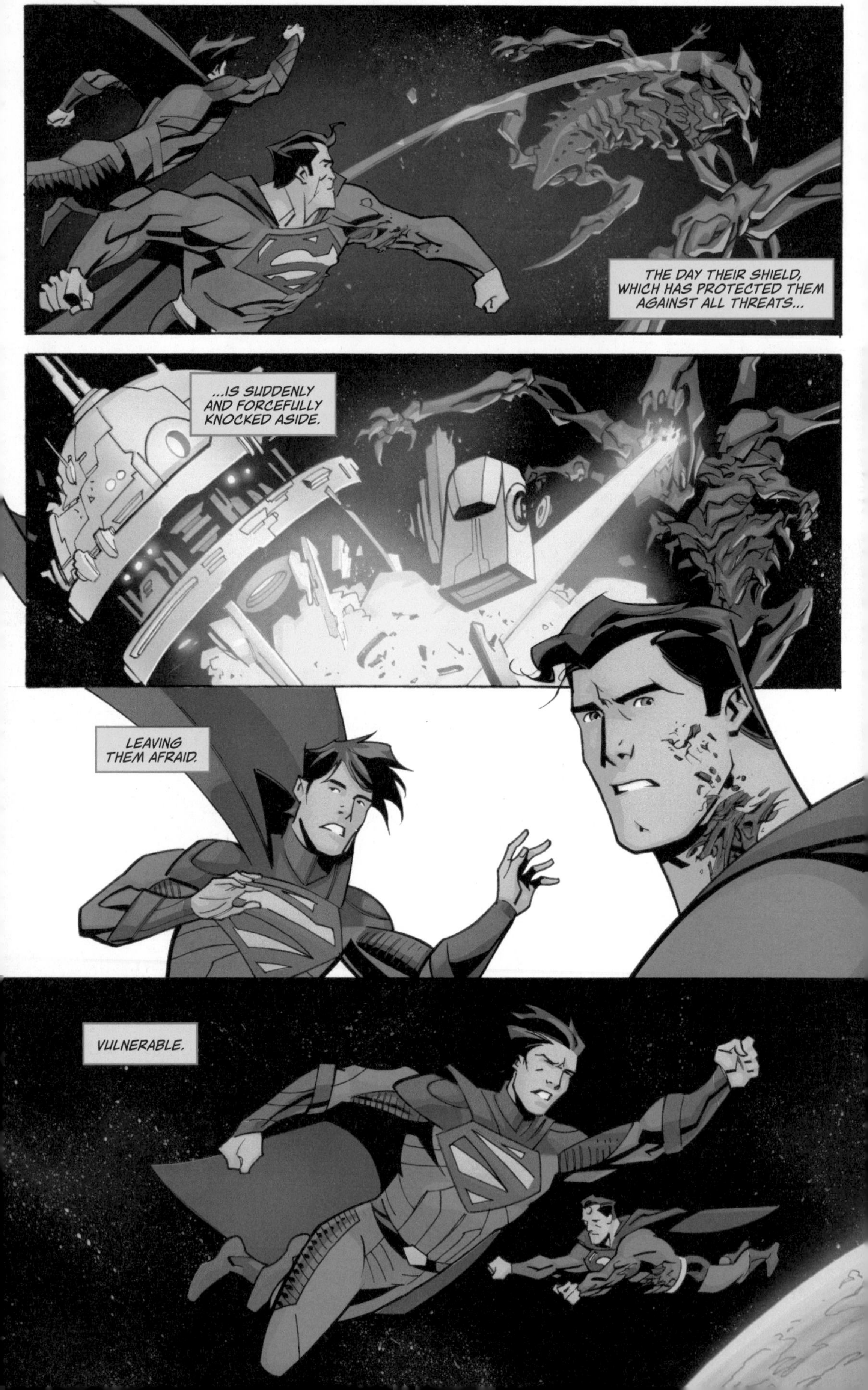
THE DAY THEIR SHIELD, WHICH HAS PROTECTED THEM AGAINST ALL THREATS...
...IS SUDDENLY AND FORCEFULLY KNOCKED ASIDE.
LEAVING THEM AFRAID.
VULNERABLE.

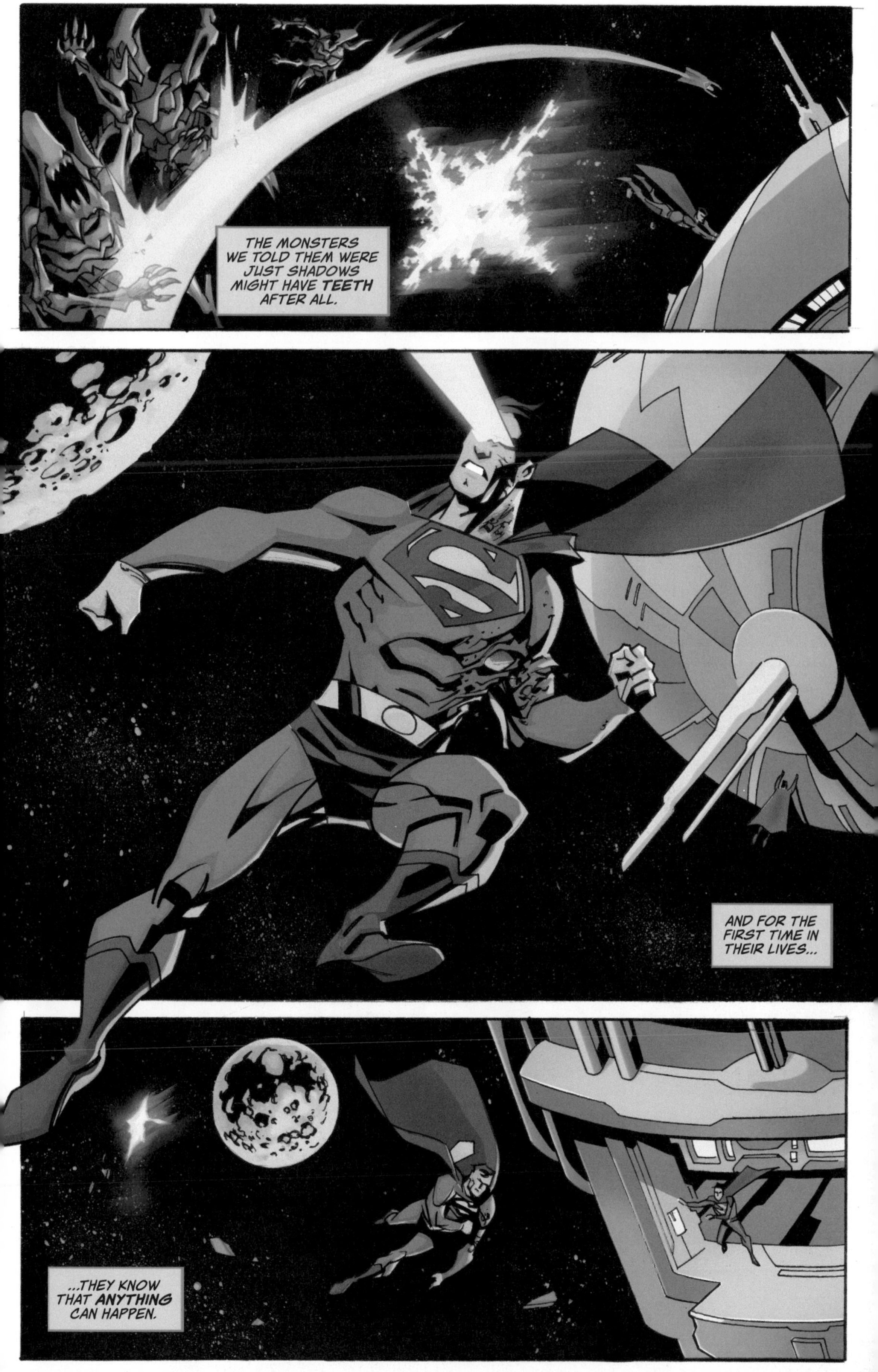
THE MONSTERS WE TOLD THEM WERE JUST SHADOWS MIGHT HAVE TEETH AFTER ALL.
AND FOR THE FIRST TIME IN THEIR LIVES...
...THEY KNOW THAT ANYTHING CAN HAPPEN.

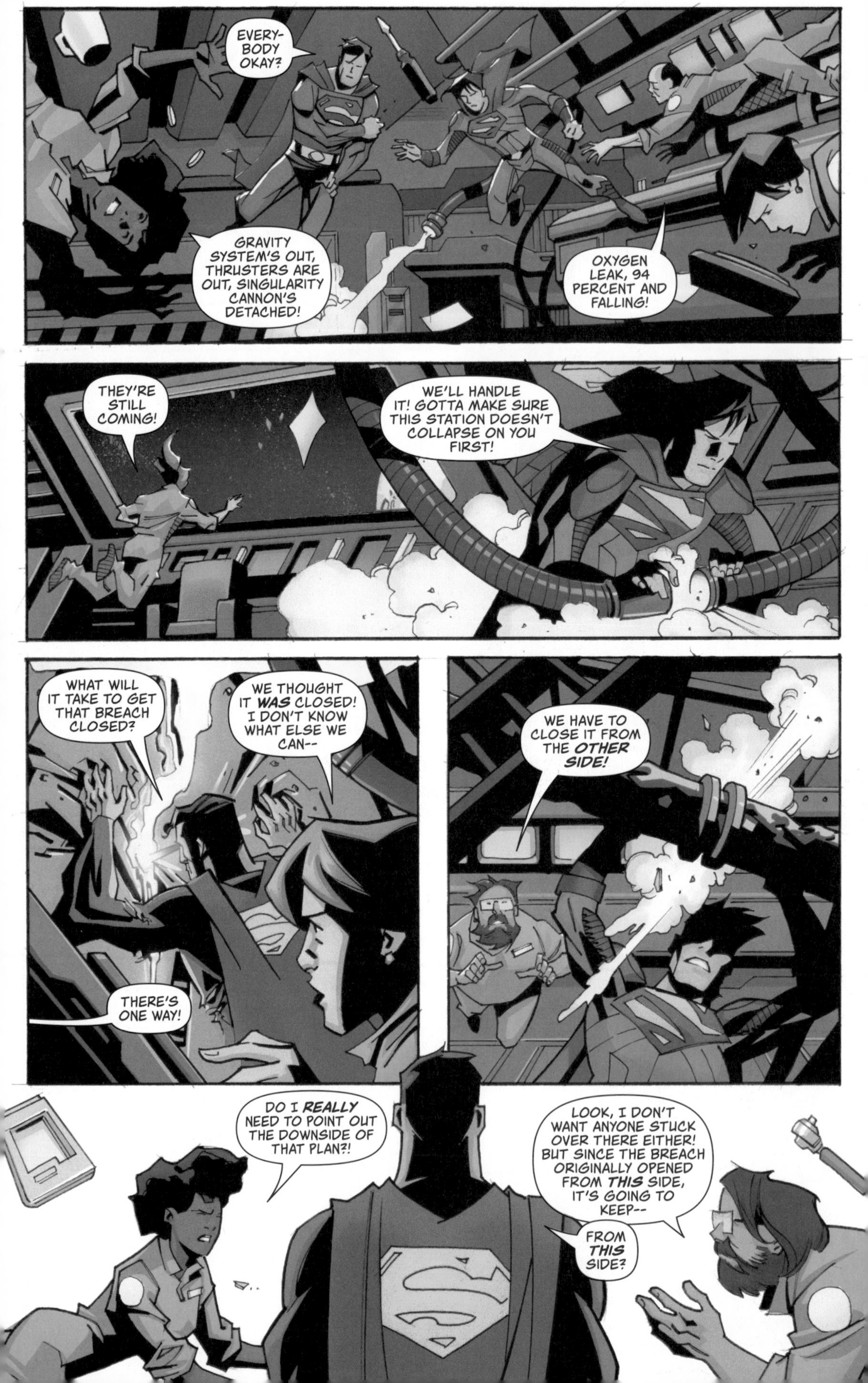
EVERY-BODY OKAY?
GRAVITY SYSTEM'S OUT, THRUSTERS ARE OUT, SINGULARITY CANNON'S DETACHED!
OXYGEN LEAK, 94 PERCENT AND FALLING!
THEY'RE STILL COMING!
WE'LL HANDLE IT! GOTTA MAKE SURE THIS STATION DOESN'T COLLAPSE ON YOU FIRST!
WHAT WILL IT TAKE TO GET THAT BREACH CLOSED?
WE THOUGHT IT WAS CLOSED! I DON'T KNOW WHAT ELSE WE CAN--
THERE'S ONE WAY!
WE HAVE TO CLOSE IT FROM THE OTHER SIDE!
DO I REALLY NEED TO POINT OUT THE DOWNSIDE OF THAT PLAN?!
LOOK, I DON'T WANT ANYONE STUCK OVER THERE EITHER! BUT SINCE THE BREACH ORIGINALLY OPENED FROM THIS SIDE, IT'S GOING TO KEEP--
FROM THIS SIDE?

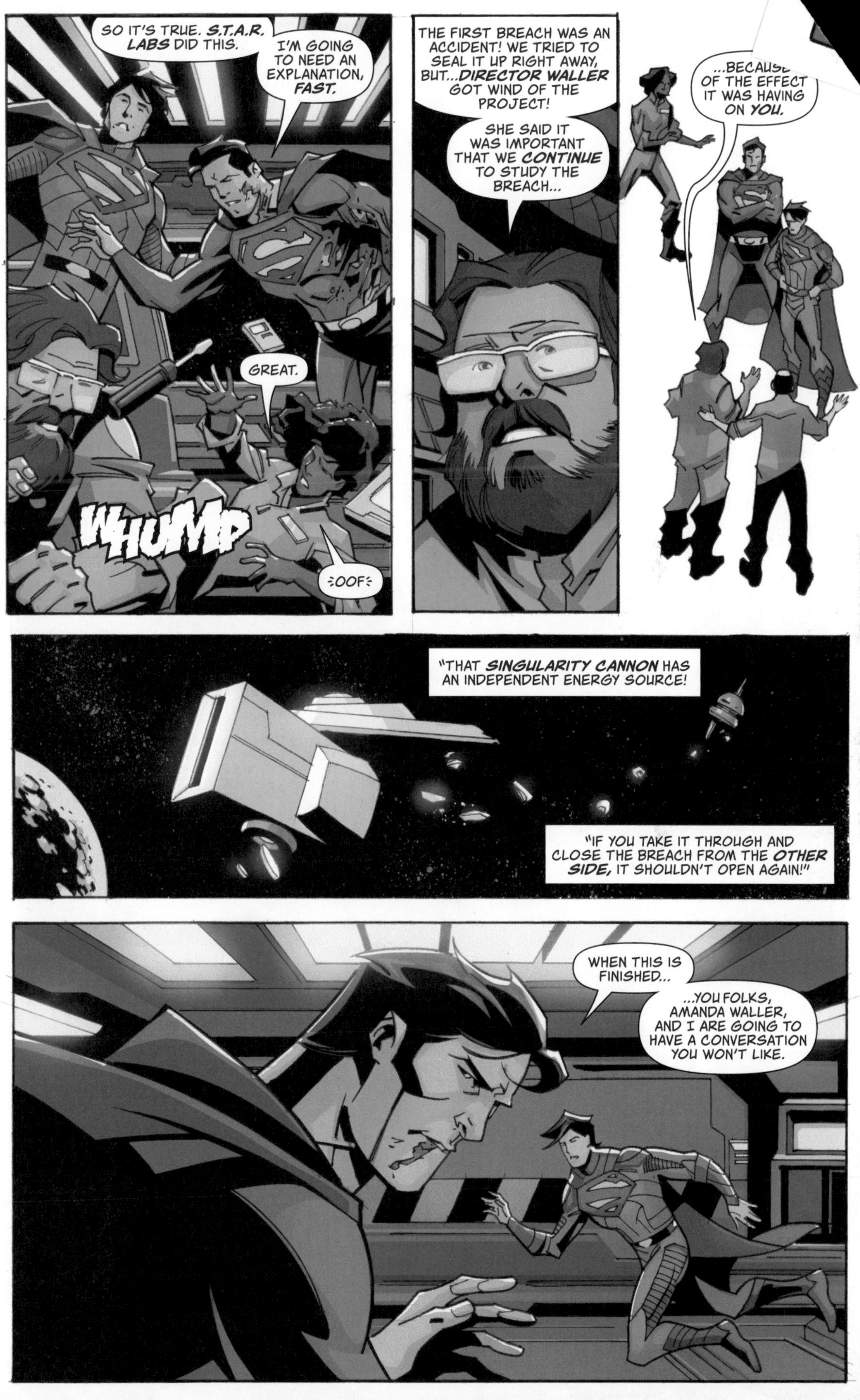

SO IT'S TRUE. S.T.A.R. LABS DID THIS.
I'M GOING TO NEED AN EXPLANATION, FAST.
GREAT.
WHUMP
OOF
THE FIRST BREACH WAS AN ACCIDENT! WE TRIED TO SEAL IT UP RIGHT AWAY, BUT...DIRECTOR WALLER GOT WIND OF THE PROJECT!
SHE SAID IT WAS IMPORTANT THAT WE CONTINUE TO STUDY THE BREACH...
...BECAUSE OF THE EFFECT IT WAS HAVING ON YOU.
"THAT SINGULARITY CANNON HAS AN INDEPENDENT ENERGY SOURCE!
"IF YOU TAKE IT THROUGH AND CLOSE THE BREACH FROM THE OTHER SIDE, IT SHOULDN'T OPEN AGAIN!"
WHEN THIS IS FINISHED...
...YOU FOLKS, AMANDA WALLER, AND I ARE GOING TO HAVE A CONVERSATION YOU WON'T LIKE.

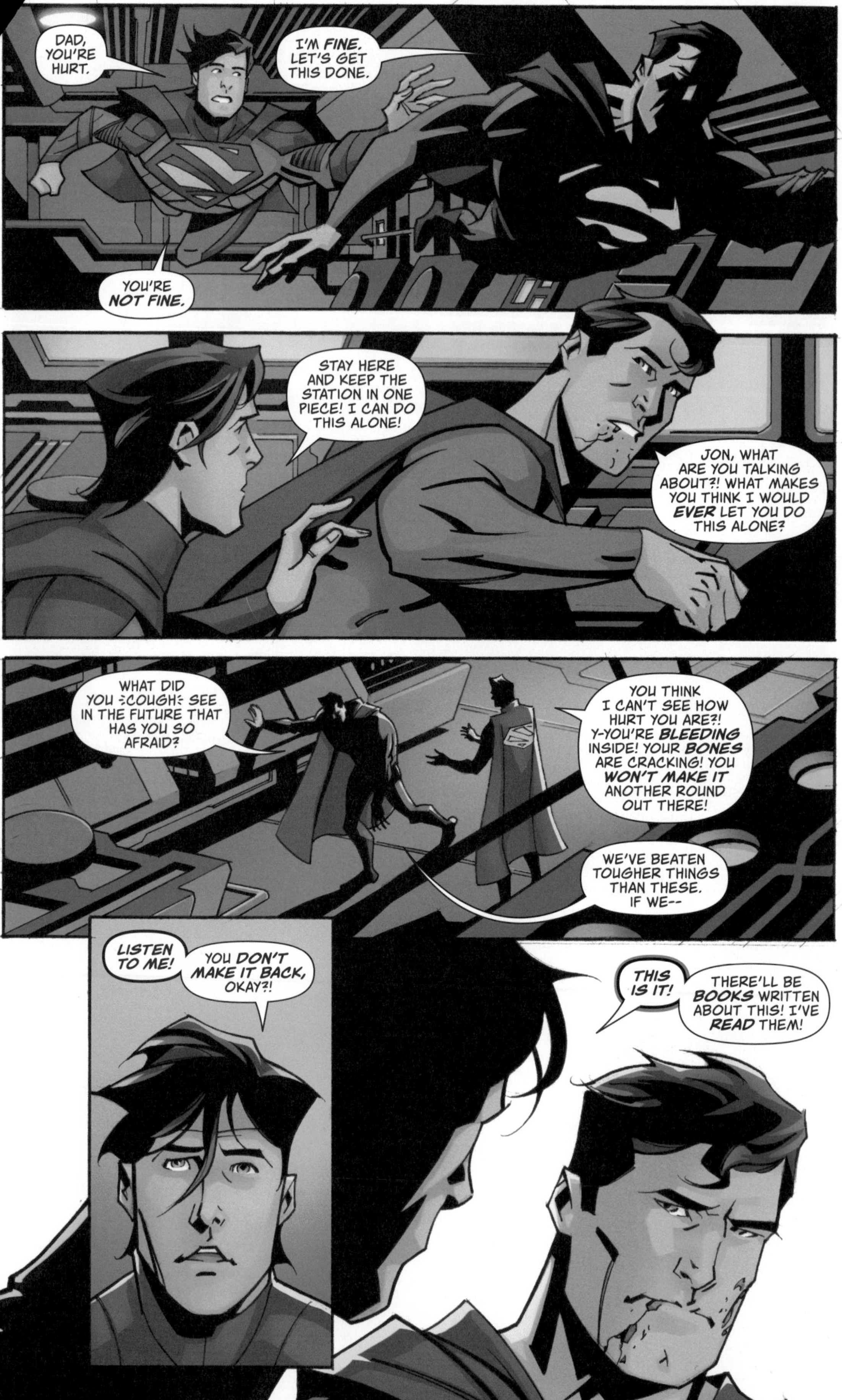
DAD, YOU'RE HURT.
I'M FINE. LET'S GET THIS DONE.
YOU'RE NOT FINE.
STAY HERE AND KEEP THE STATION IN ONE PIECE! I CAN DO THIS ALONE!
JON, WHAT ARE YOU TALKING ABOUT?! WHAT MAKES YOU THINK I WOULD EVER LET YOU DO THIS ALONE?
WHAT DID YOU ~COUGH~ SEE IN THE FUTURE THAT HAS YOU SO AFRAID?
YOU THINK I CAN'T SEE HOW HURT YOU ARE?! Y-YOU'RE BLEEDING INSIDE! YOUR BONES ARE CRACKING! YOU WON'T MAKE IT ANOTHER ROUND OUT THERE!
WE'VE BEATEN TOUGHER THINGS THAN THESE. IF WE--
LISTEN TO ME!
YOU DON'T MAKE IT BACK, OKAY?!
THIS IS IT!
THERE'LL BE BOOKS WRITTEN ABOUT THIS! I'VE READ THEM!

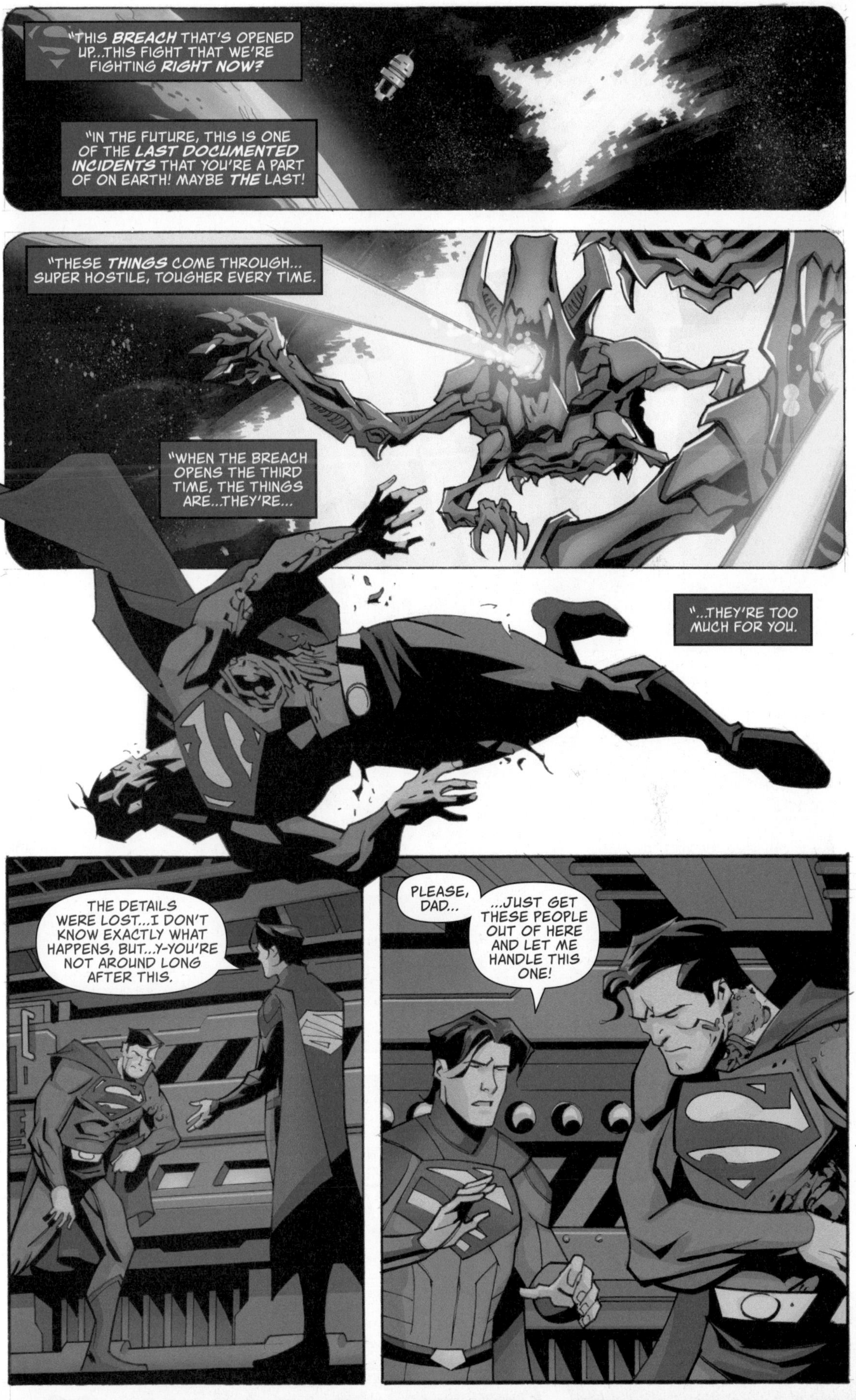
"THIS BREACH THAT'S OPENED UP...THIS FIGHT THAT WE'RE FIGHTING RIGHT NOW?
"IN THE FUTURE, THIS IS ONE OF THE LAST DOCUMENTED INCIDENTS THAT YOU'RE A PART OF ON EARTH! MAYBE THE LAST!
"THESE THINGS COME THROUGH... SUPER HOSTILE, TOUGHER EVERY TIME.
"WHEN THE BREACH OPENS THE THIRD TIME, THE THINGS ARE...THEY'RE...
"...THEY'RE TOO MUCH FOR YOU.
THE DETAILS WERE LOST...I DON'T KNOW EXACTLY WHAT HAPPENS, BUT...Y-YOU'RE NOT AROUND LONG AFTER THIS.
PLEASE, DAD...
...JUST GET THESE PEOPLE OUT OF HERE AND LET ME HANDLE THIS ONE!

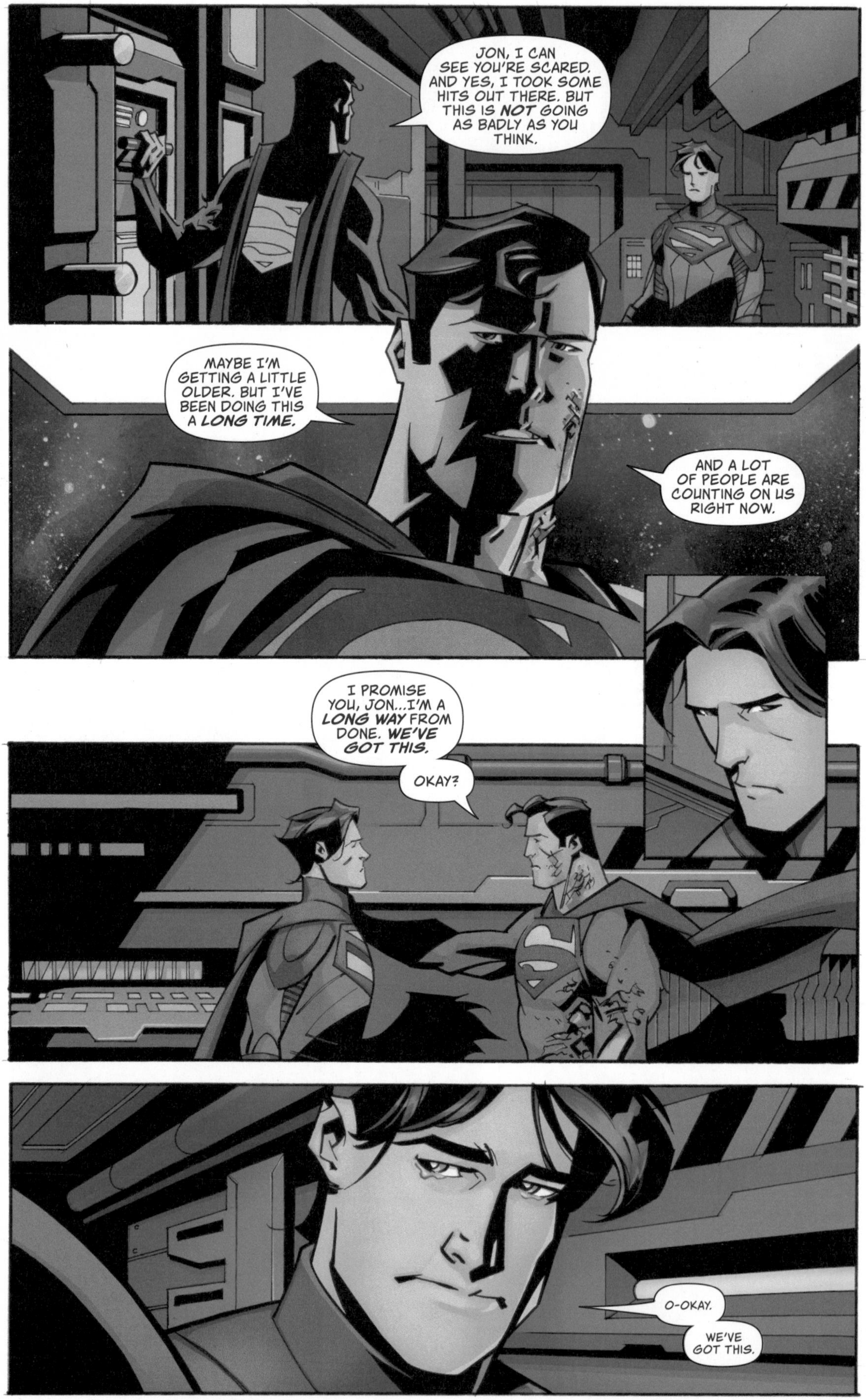
JON, I CAN SEE YOU'RE SCARED. AND YES, I TOOK SOME HITS OUT THERE. BUT THIS IS NOT GOING AS BADLY AS YOU THINK.
MAYBE I'M GETTING A LITTLE OLDER. BUT I'VE BEEN DOING THIS A LONG TIME.
AND A LOT OF PEOPLE ARE COUNTING ON US RIGHT NOW.
I PROMISE YOU, JON...I'M A LONG WAY FROM DONE. WE'VE GOT THIS.
OKAY?
O-OKAY.
WE'VE GOT THIS.

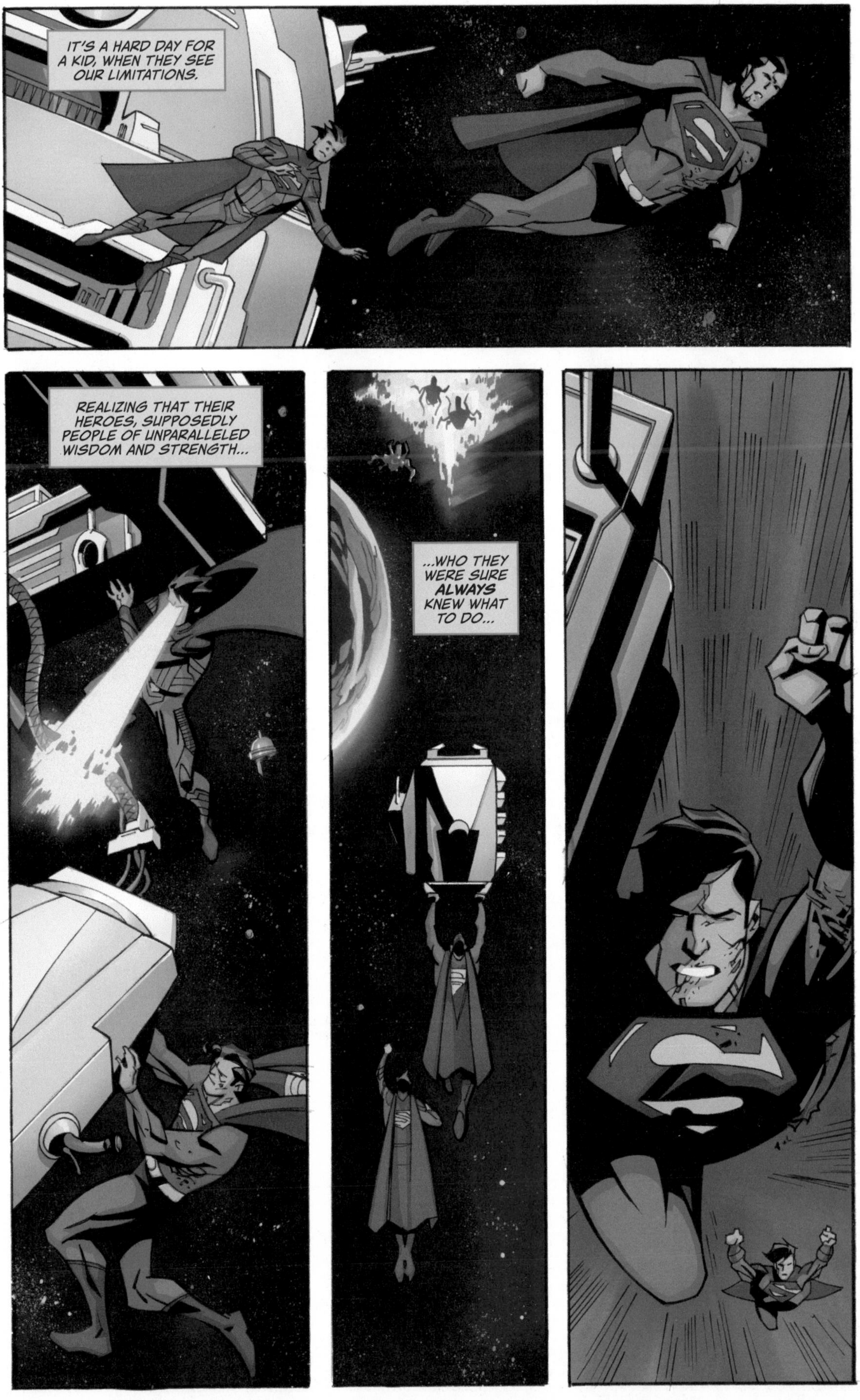

IT'S A HARD DAY FOR A KID, WHEN THEY SEE OUR LIMITATIONS.
REALIZING THAT THEIR HEROES, SUPPOSEDLY PEOPLE OF UNPARALLELED WISDOM AND STRENGTH...
...WHO THEY WERE SURE ALWAYS KNEW WHAT TO DO...

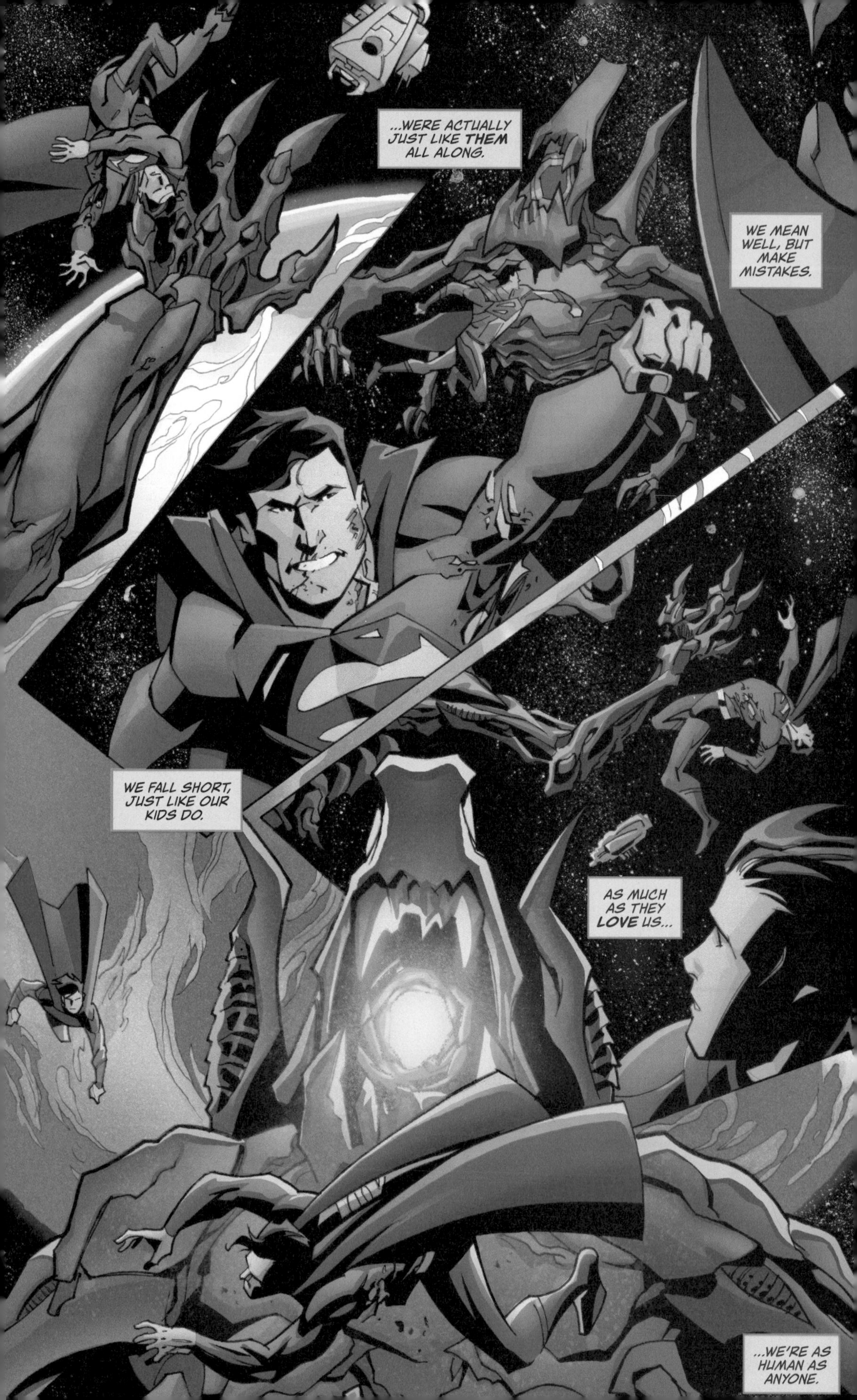
...WERE ACTUALLY JUST LIKE THEM ALL ALONG.
WE MEAN WELL, BUT MAKE MISTAKES.
WE FALL SHORT, JUST LIKE OUR KIDS DO.
AS MUCH AS THEY LOVE US...
...WE'RE AS HUMAN AS ANYONE.

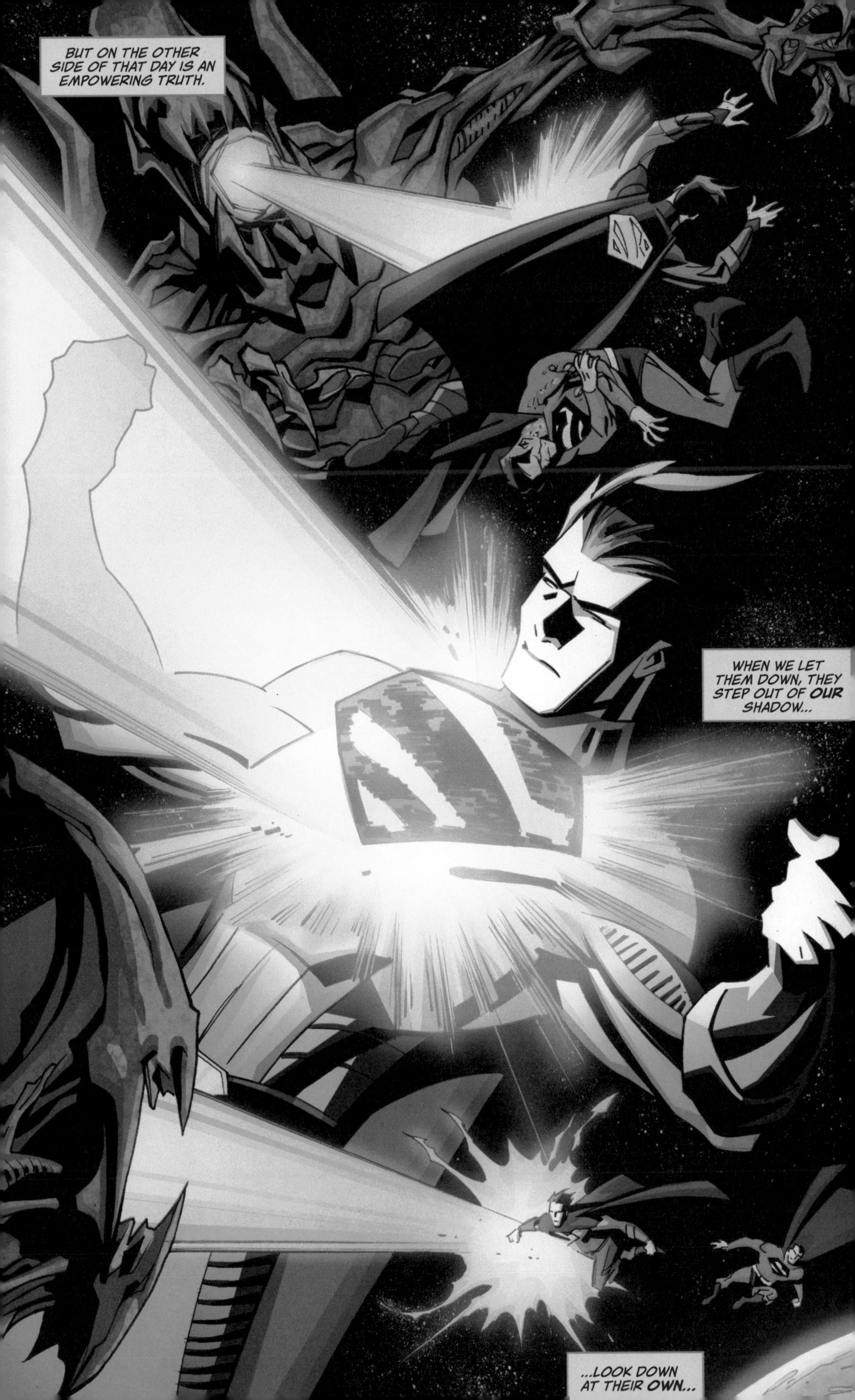
BUT ON THE OTHER SIDE OF THAT DAY IS AN EMPOWERING TRUTH.
WHEN WE LET THEM DOWN, THEY STEP OUT OF OUR SHADOW...
...LOOK DOWN AT THEIR OWN...

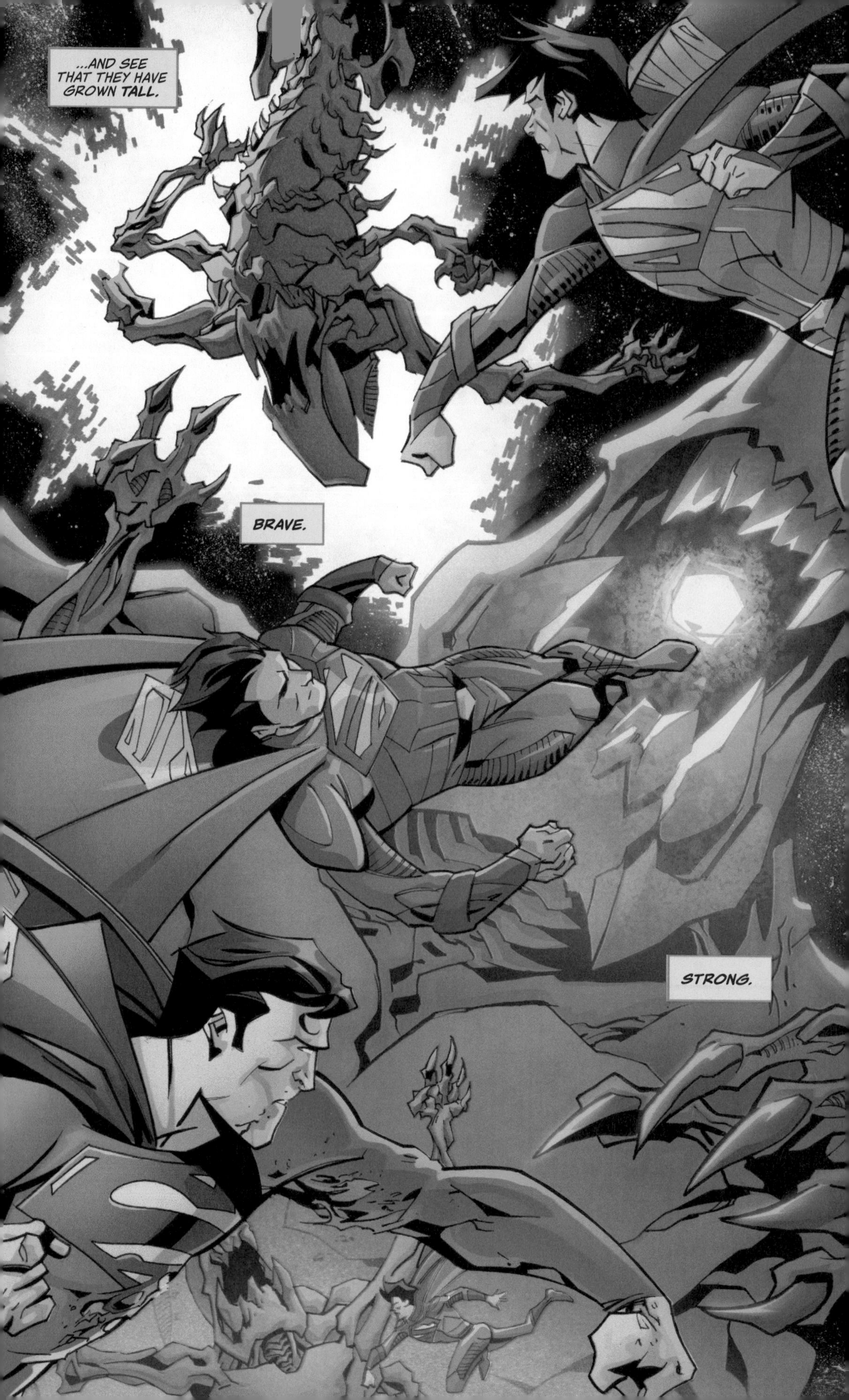
...AND SEE THAT THEY HAVE GROWN TALL.
BRAVE.
STRONG.

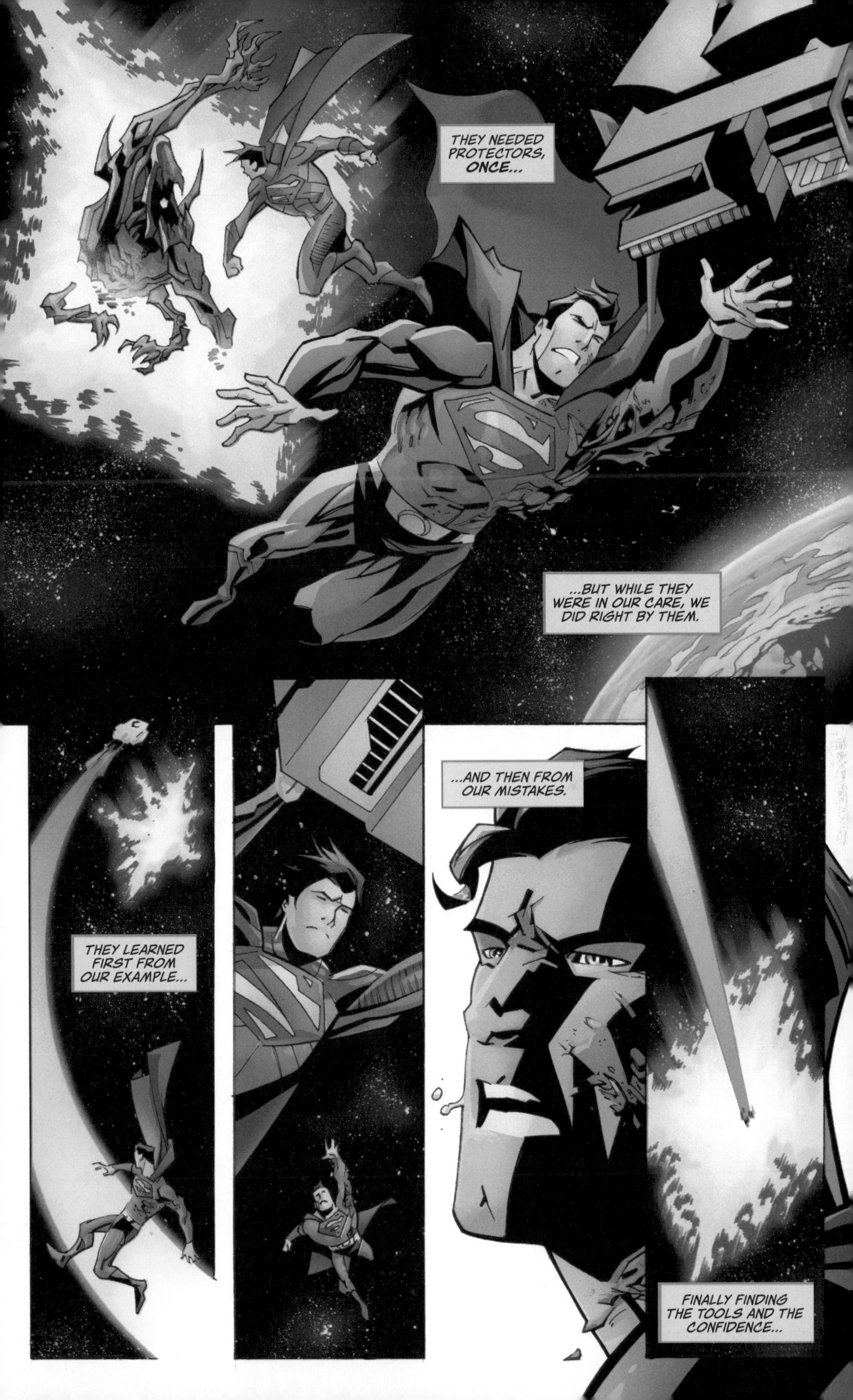

THEY NEEDED PROTECTORS, ONCE...
...BUT WHILE THEY WERE IN OUR CARE, WE DID RIGHT BY THEM.
THEY LEARNED FIRST FROM OUR EXAMPLE...
...AND THEN FROM OUR MISTAKES.
FINALLY FINDING THE TOOLS AND THE CONFIDENCE...

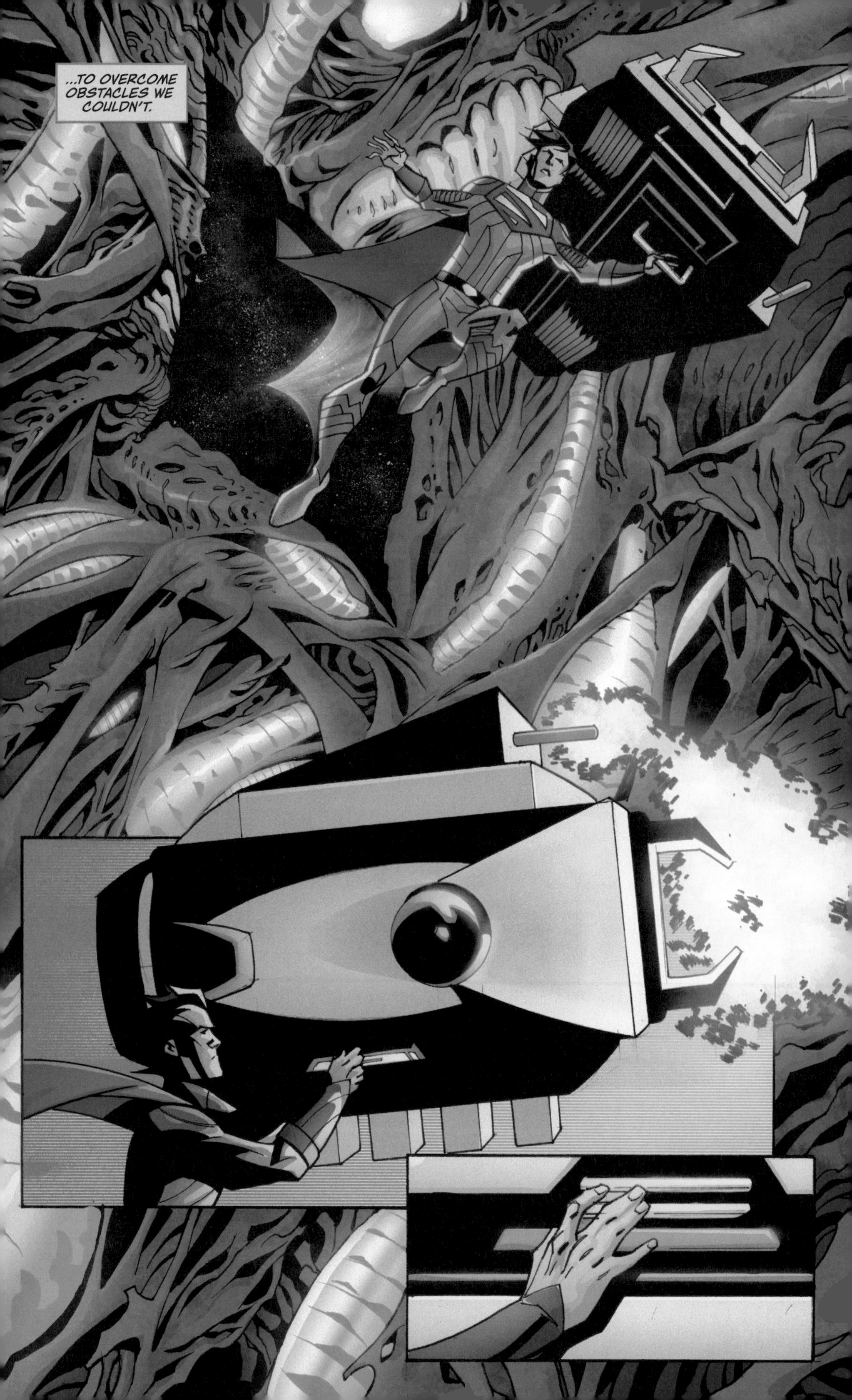
...TO OVERCOME OBSTACLES WE COULDN'T.

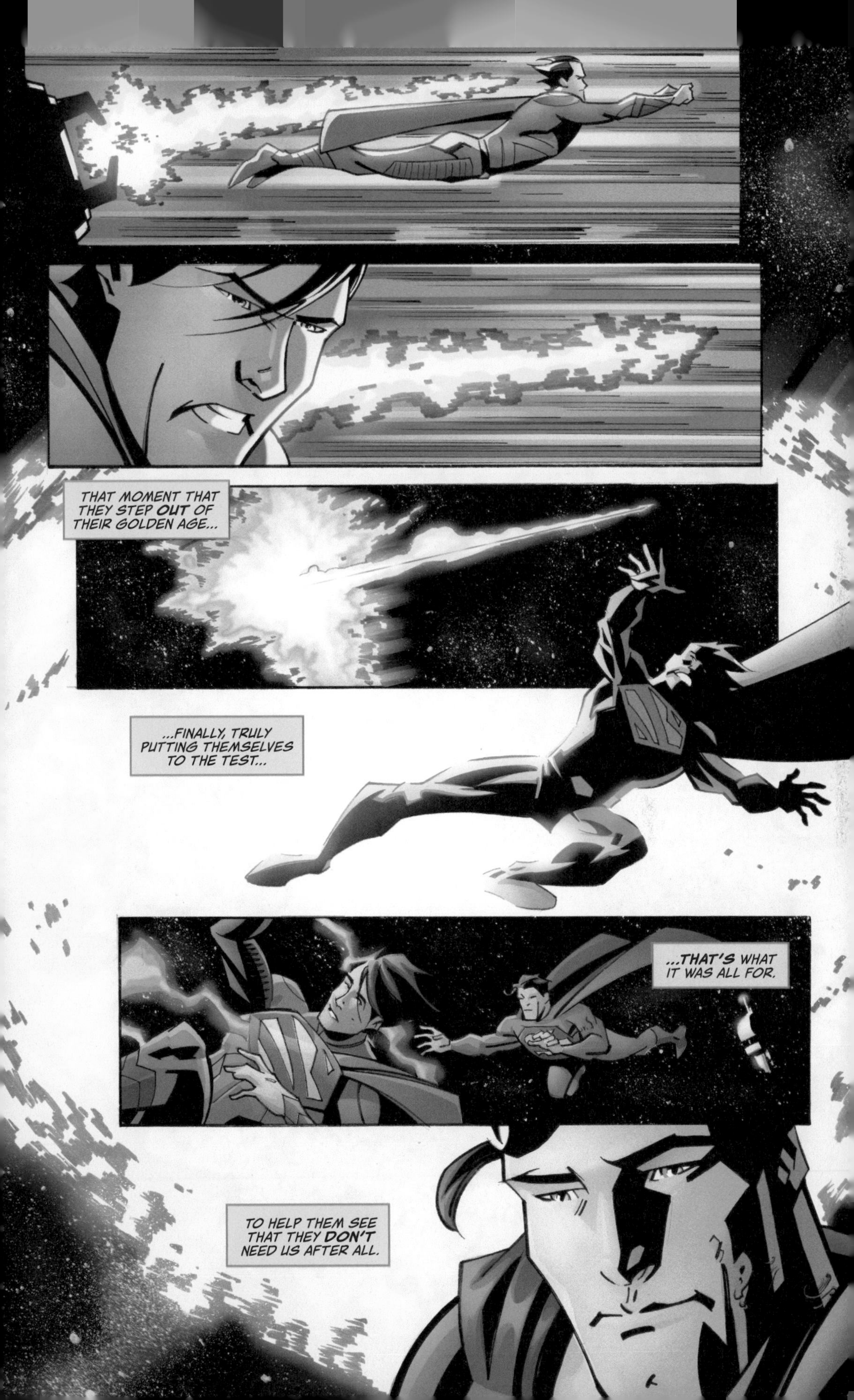
THAT MOMENT THAT THEY STEP OUT OF THEIR GOLDEN AGE...
...FINALLY, TRULY PUTTING THEMSELVES TO THE TEST...
...THAT'S WHAT IT WAS ALL FOR.
TO HELP THEM SEE THAT THEY DON'T NEED US AFTER ALL.

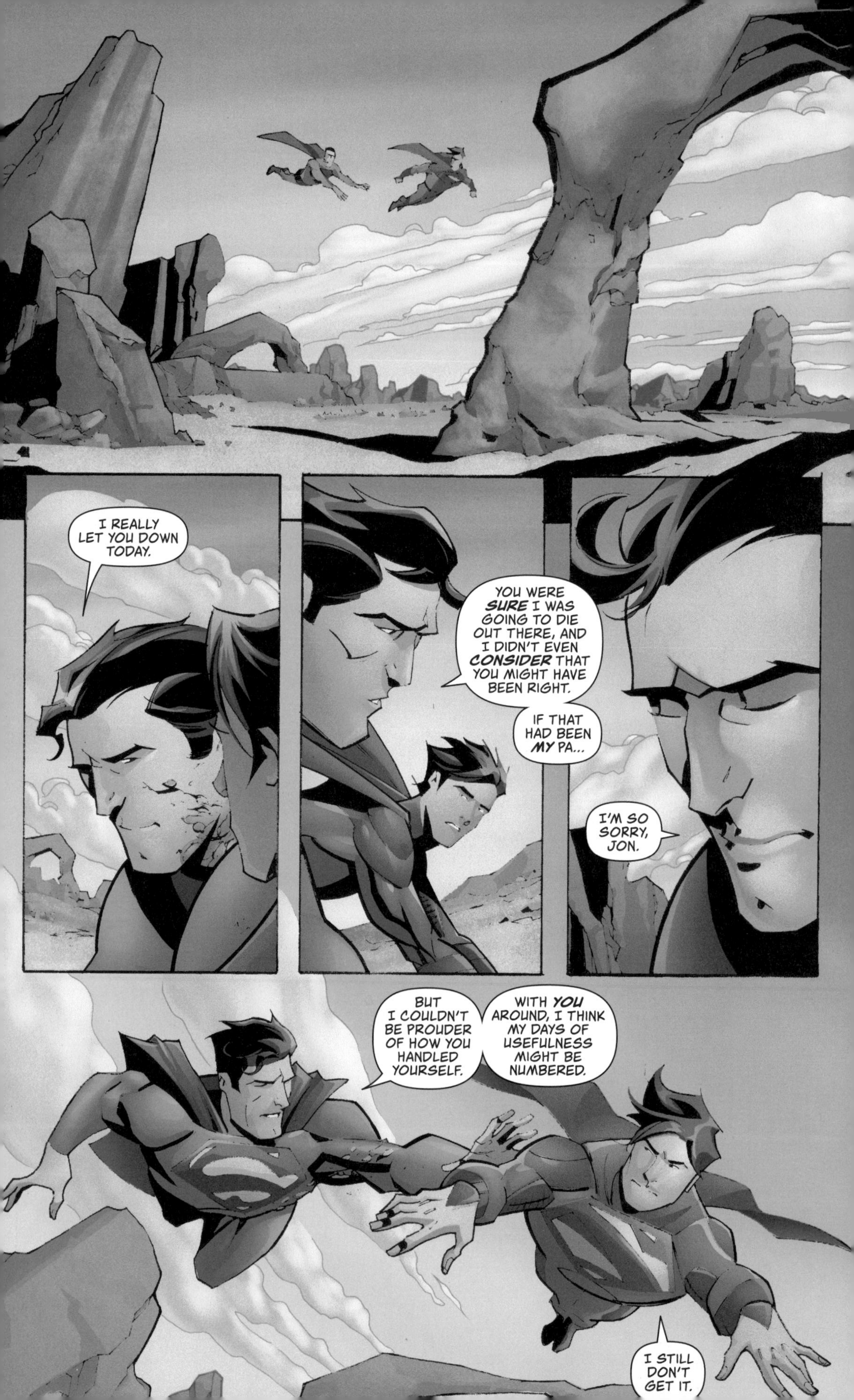

I REALLY LET YOU DOWN TODAY.
YOU WERE SURE I WAS GOING TO DIE OUT THERE, AND I DIDN'T EVEN CONSIDER THAT YOU MIGHT HAVE BEEN RIGHT.
IF THAT HAD BEEN MY PA...
I'M SO SORRY, JON.
BUT I COULDN'T BE PROUDER OF HOW YOU HANDLED YOURSELF.
WITH YOU AROUND, I THINK MY DAYS OF USEFULNESS MIGHT BE NUMBERED.
I STILL DON'T GET IT.

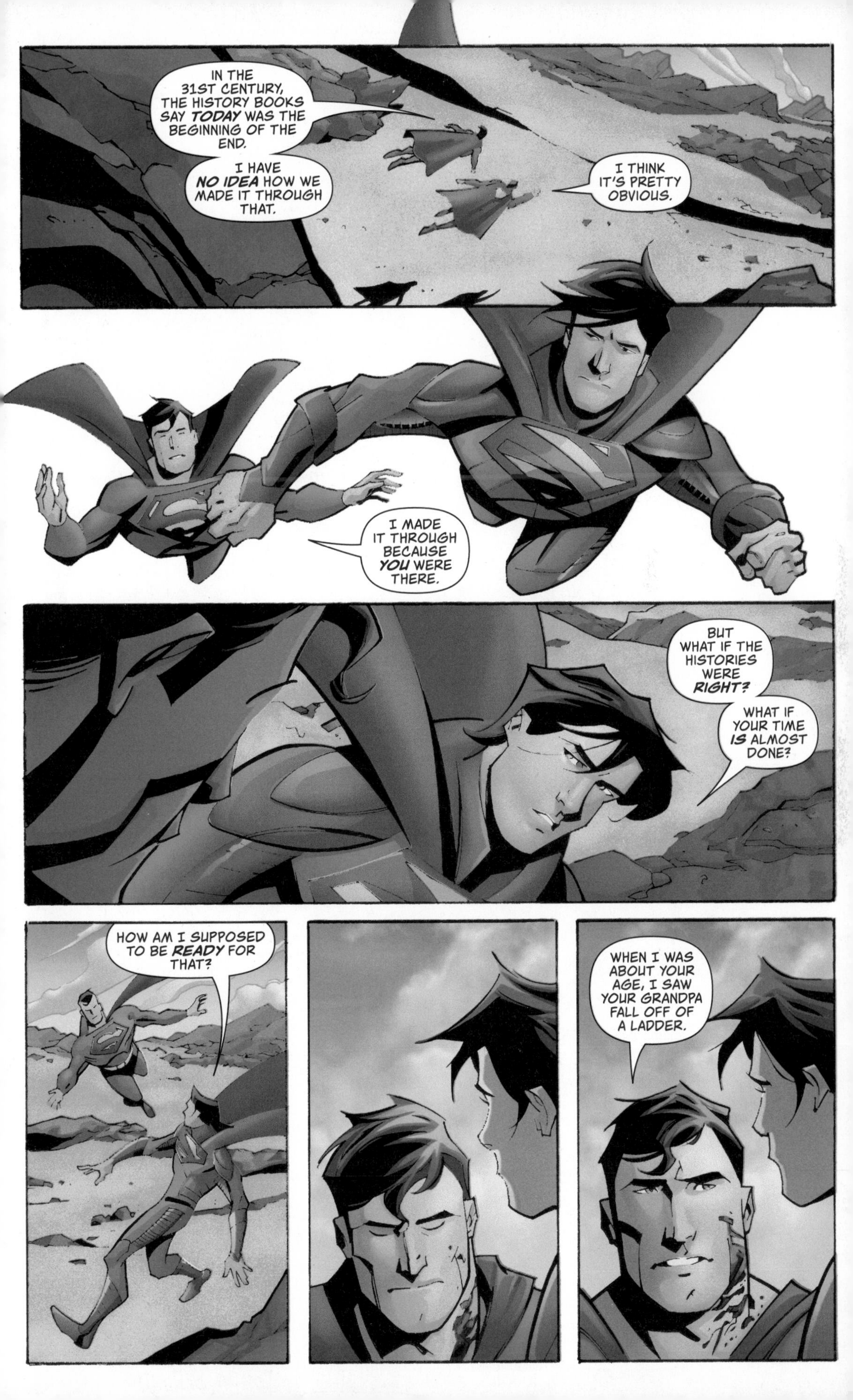
IN THE 31ST CENTURY, THE HISTORY BOOKS SAY TODAY WAS THE BEGINNING OF THE END.
I HAVE NO IDEA HOW WE MADE IT THROUGH THAT.
I THINK IT'S PRETTY OBVIOUS.
I MADE IT THROUGH BECAUSE YOU WERE THERE.
BUT WHAT IF THE HISTORIES WERE RIGHT?
WHAT IF YOUR TIME IS ALMOST DONE?
HOW AM I SUPPOSED TO BE READY FOR THAT?
WHEN I WAS ABOUT YOUR AGE, I SAW YOUR GRANDPA FALL OFF OF A LADDER.

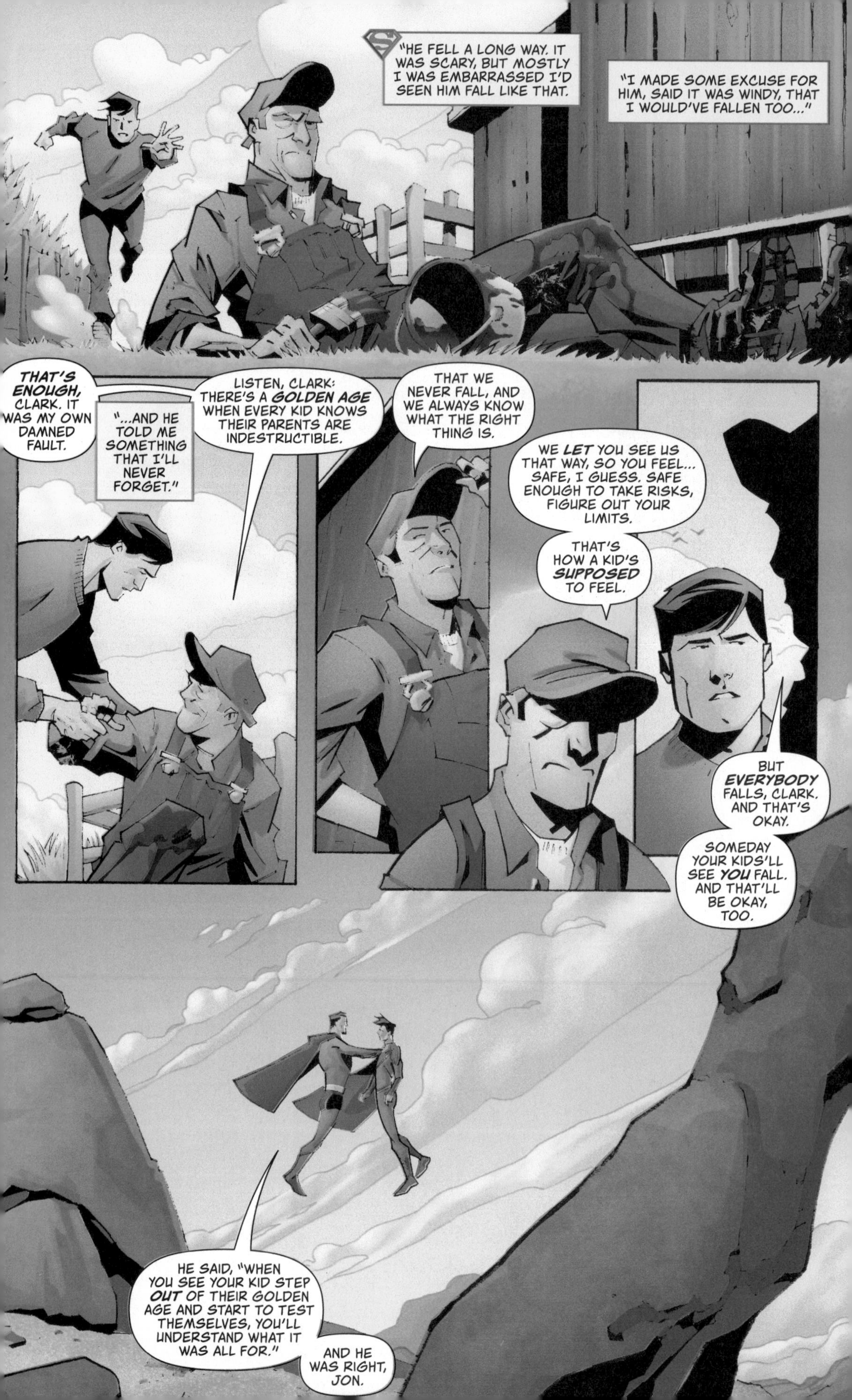
"HE FELL A LONG WAY. IT WAS SCARY, BUT MOSTLY I WAS EMBARRASSED I'D SEEN HIM FALL LIKE THAT.
"I MADE SOME EXCUSE FOR HIM, SAID IT WAS WINDY, THAT I WOULD'VE FALLEN TOO..."
THAT'S ENOUGH, CLARK. IT WAS MY OWN DAMNED FAULT.
"...AND HE TOLD ME SOMETHING THAT I'LL NEVER FORGET."
LISTEN, CLARK: THERE'S A GOLDEN AGE WHEN EVERY KID KNOWS THEIR PARENTS ARE INDESTRUCTIBLE.
THAT WE NEVER FALL, AND WE ALWAYS KNOW WHAT THE RIGHT THING IS.
WE LET YOU SEE US THAT WAY, SO YOU FEEL... SAFE, I GUESS. SAFE... SAFE ENOUGH TO TAKE RISKS, FIGURE OUT YOUR LIMITS.
THAT'S HOW A KID'S SUPPOSED TO FEEL.
BUT EVERYBODY FALLS, CLARK. AND THAT'S OKAY.
SOMEDAY YOUR KIDS'LL SEE YOU FALL. AND THAT'LL BE OKAY, TOO.
HE SAID, "WHEN YOU SEE YOUR KID STEP OUT OF THEIR GOLDEN AGE AND START TO TEST THEMSELVES, YOU'LL UNDERSTAND WHAT IT WAS ALL FOR."
AND HE WAS RIGHT, JON.

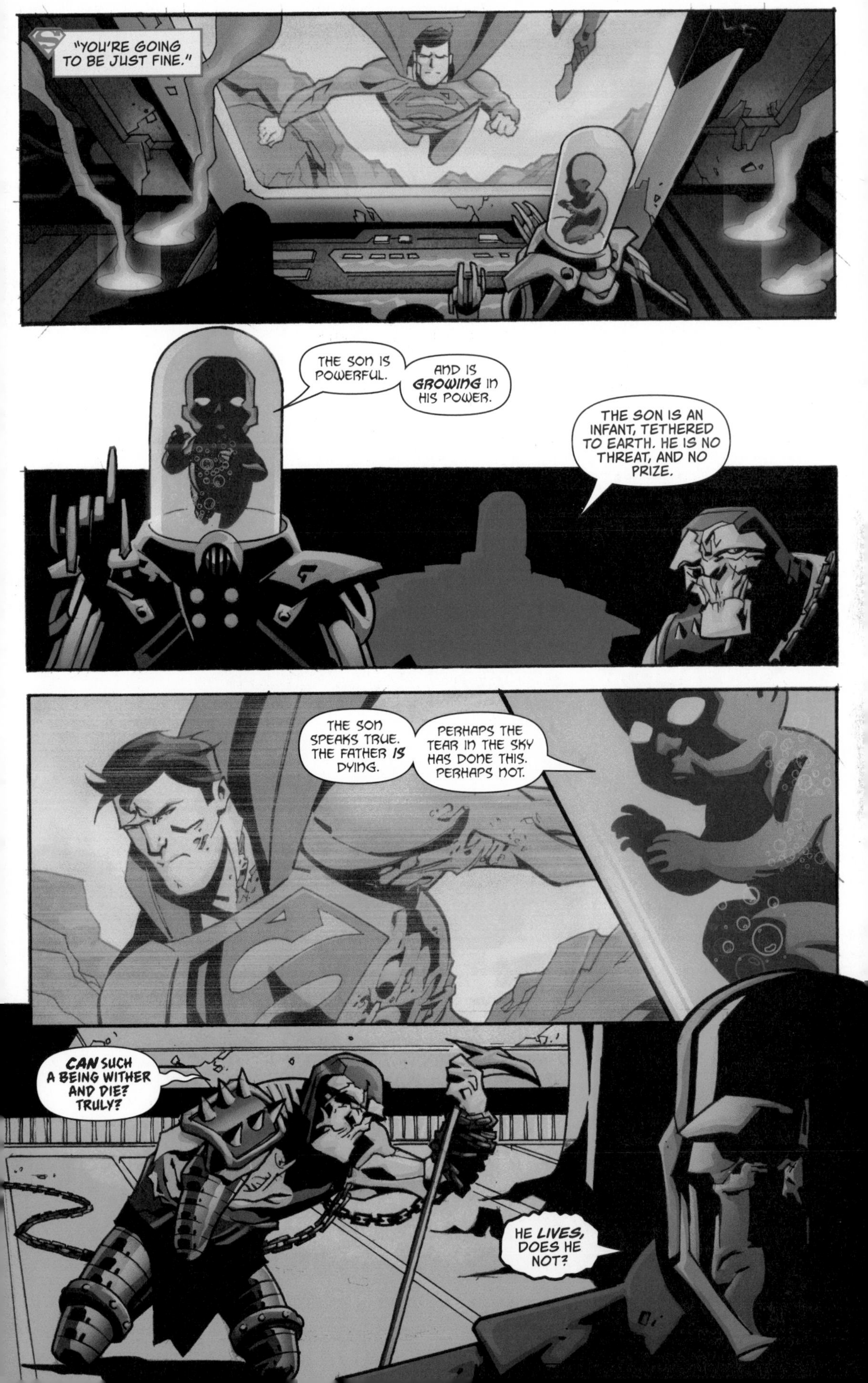
"YOU'RE GOING TO BE JUST FINE."
THE SON IS POWERFUL.
AND IS GROWING IN HIS POWER.
THE SON IS AN INFANT, TETHERED TO EARTH. HE IS NO THREAT, AND NO PRIZE.
THE SON SPEAKS TRUE. THE FATHER IS DYING.
PERHAPS THE TEAR IN THE SKY HAS DONE THIS. PERHAPS NOT.
CAN SUCH A BEING WITHER AND DIE? TRULY?
HE LIVES, DOES HE NOT?

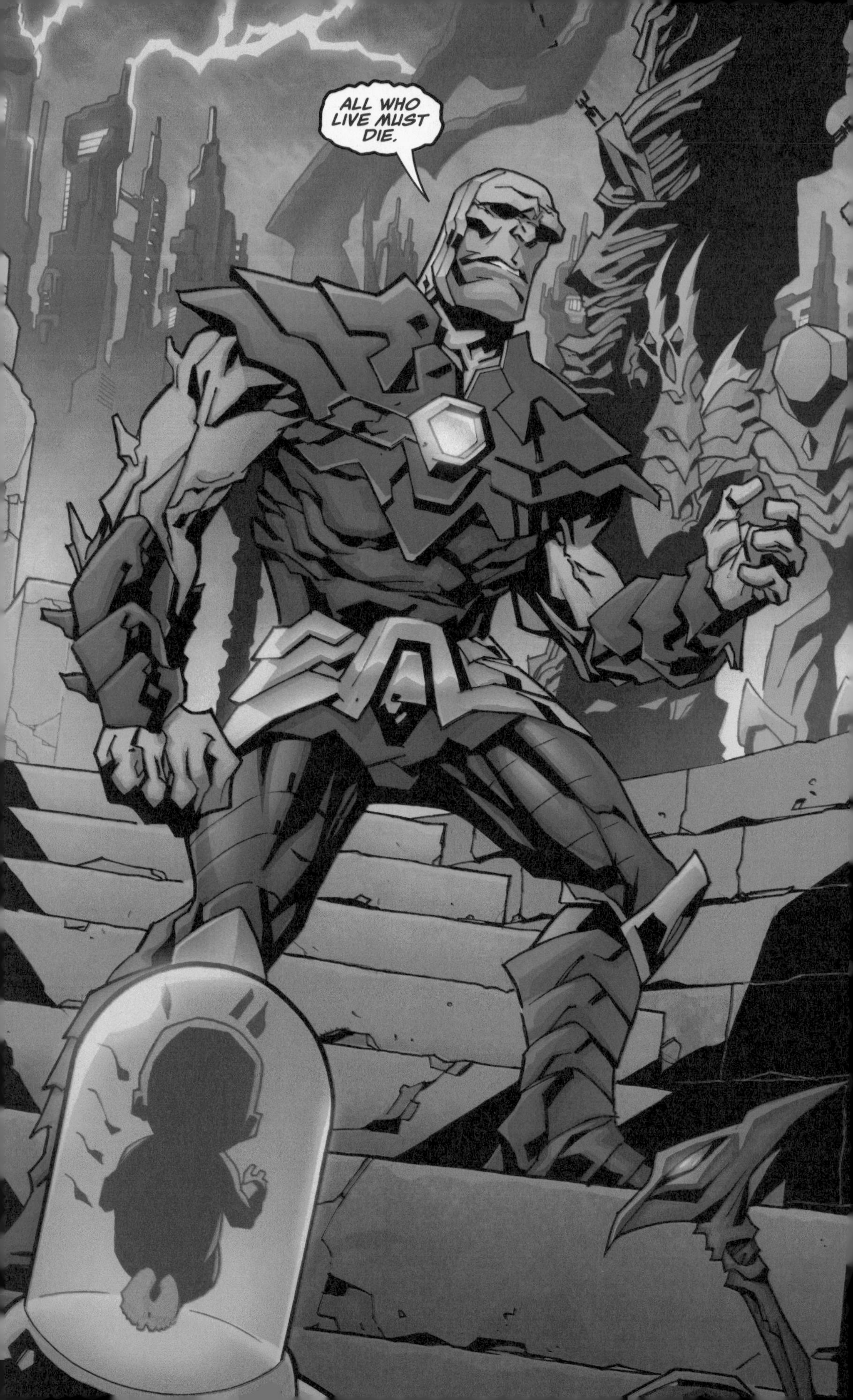
ALL WHO LIVE MUST DIE.

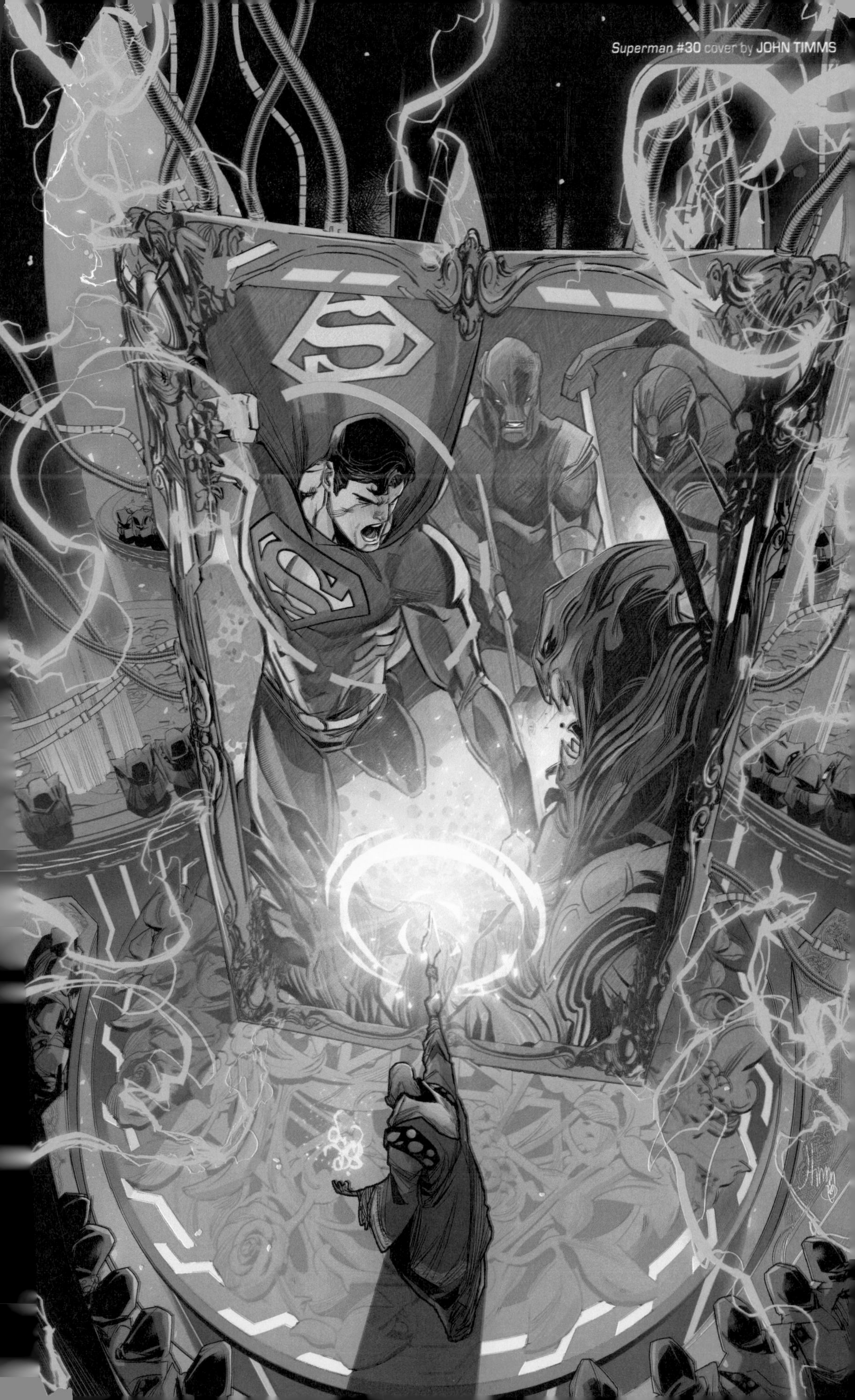

Superman #30 cover by JOHN TIMMS

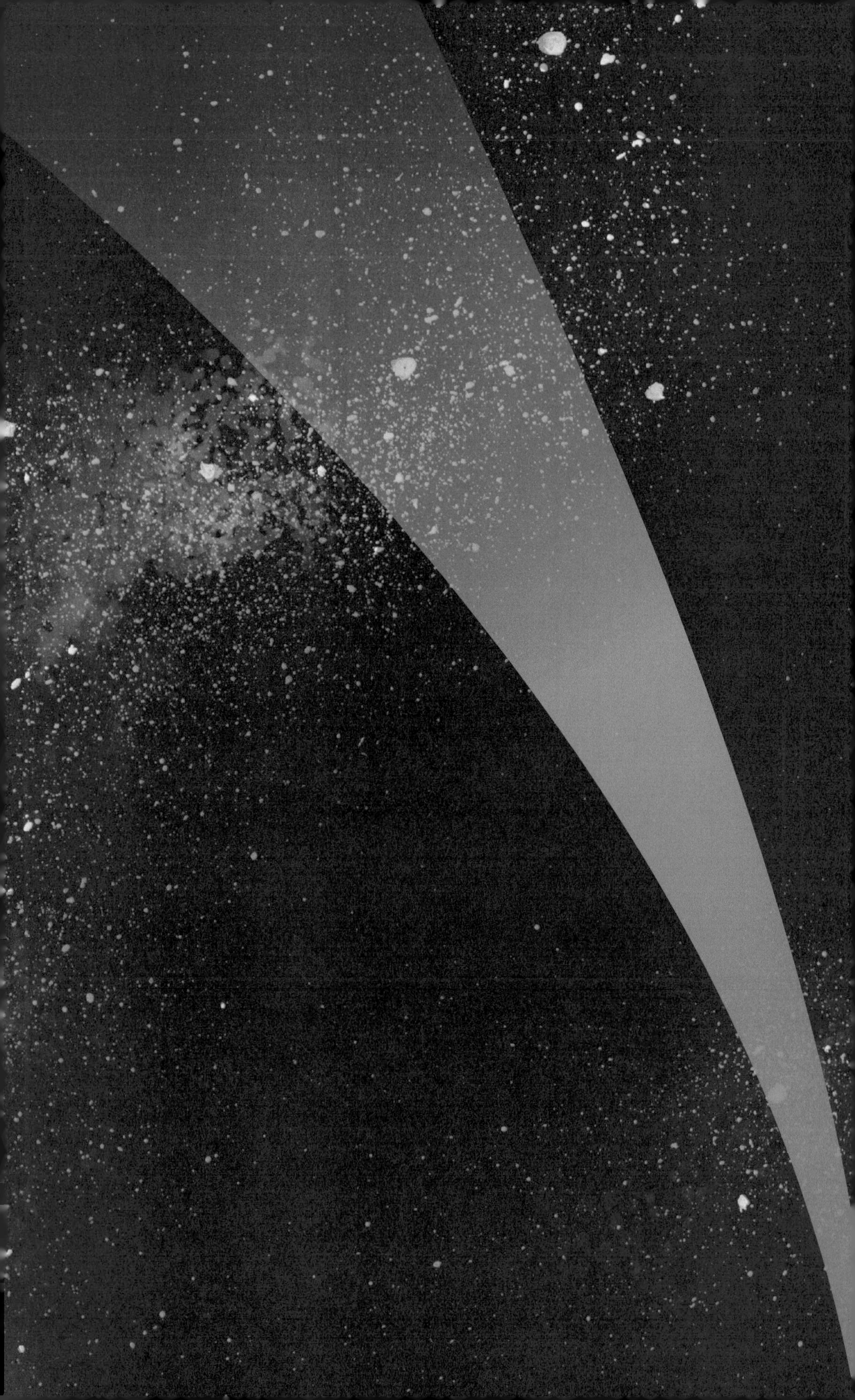

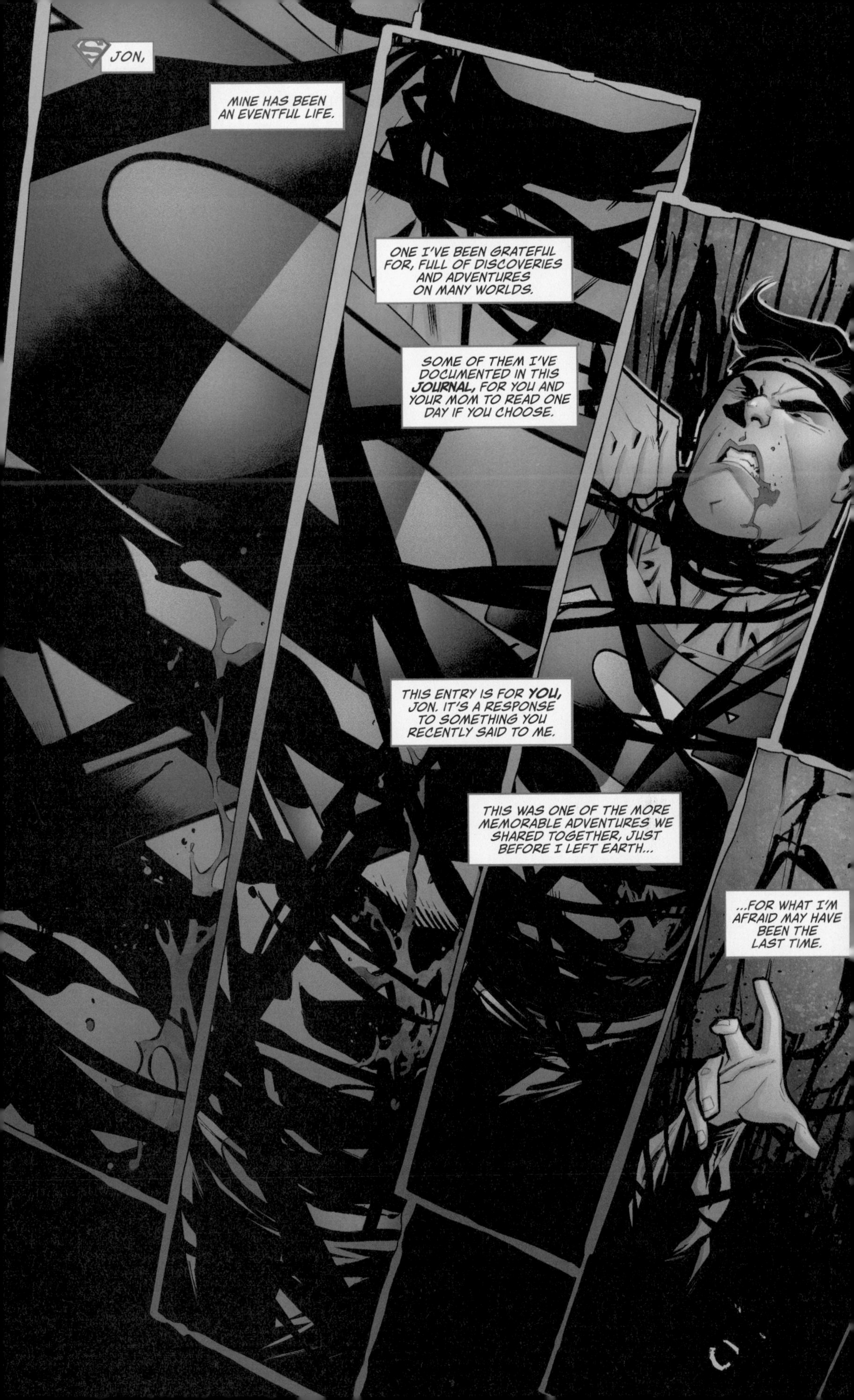
JON,
MINE HAS BEEN AN EVENTFUL LIFE.
ONE I'VE BEEN GRATEFUL FOR, FULL OF DISCOVERIES AND ADVENTURES ON MANY WORLDS.
SOME OF THEM I'VE DOCUMENTED IN THIS JOURNAL, FOR YOU AND YOUR MOM TO READ ONE DAY IF YOU CHOOSE.
THIS ENTRY IS FOR YOU, JON. IT'S A RESPONSE TO SOMETHING YOU RECENTLY SAID TO ME.
THIS WAS ONE OF THE MORE MEMORABLE ADVENTURES WE SHARED TOGETHER, JUST BEFORE I LEFT EARTH...
...FOR WHAT I'M AFRAID MAY HAVE BEEN THE LAST TIME.

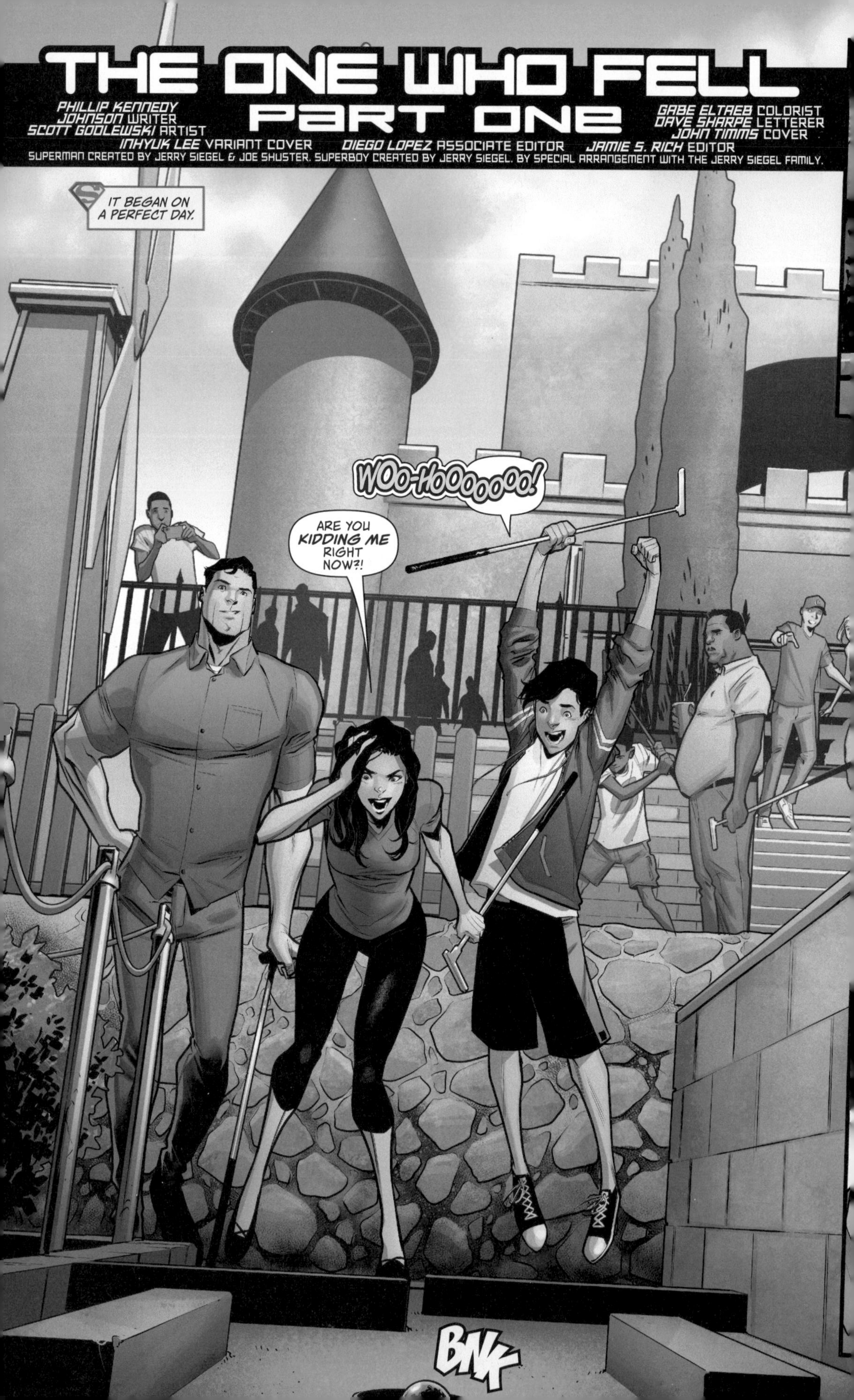
THE ONE WHO FELL
PART ONE
PHILLIP KENNEDY JOHNSON WRITER
SCOTT GODLEWSKI ARTIST
GABE ELTAEB COLORIST
DAVE SHARPE LETTERER
JOHN TIMMS COVER
INHYUK LEE VARIANT COVER
DIEGO LOPEZ ASSOCIATE EDITOR
JAMIE S. RICH EDITOR
SUPERMAN CREATED BY JERRY SIEGEL & JOE SHUSTER. SUPERBOY CREATED BY JERRY SIEGEL. BY SPECIAL ARRANGEMENT WITH THE JERRY SIEGEL FAMILY.
IT BEGAN ON A PERFECT DAY.
WOO-HOOOOOOOO!
ARE YOU KIDDING ME RIGHT NOW?!
BNK

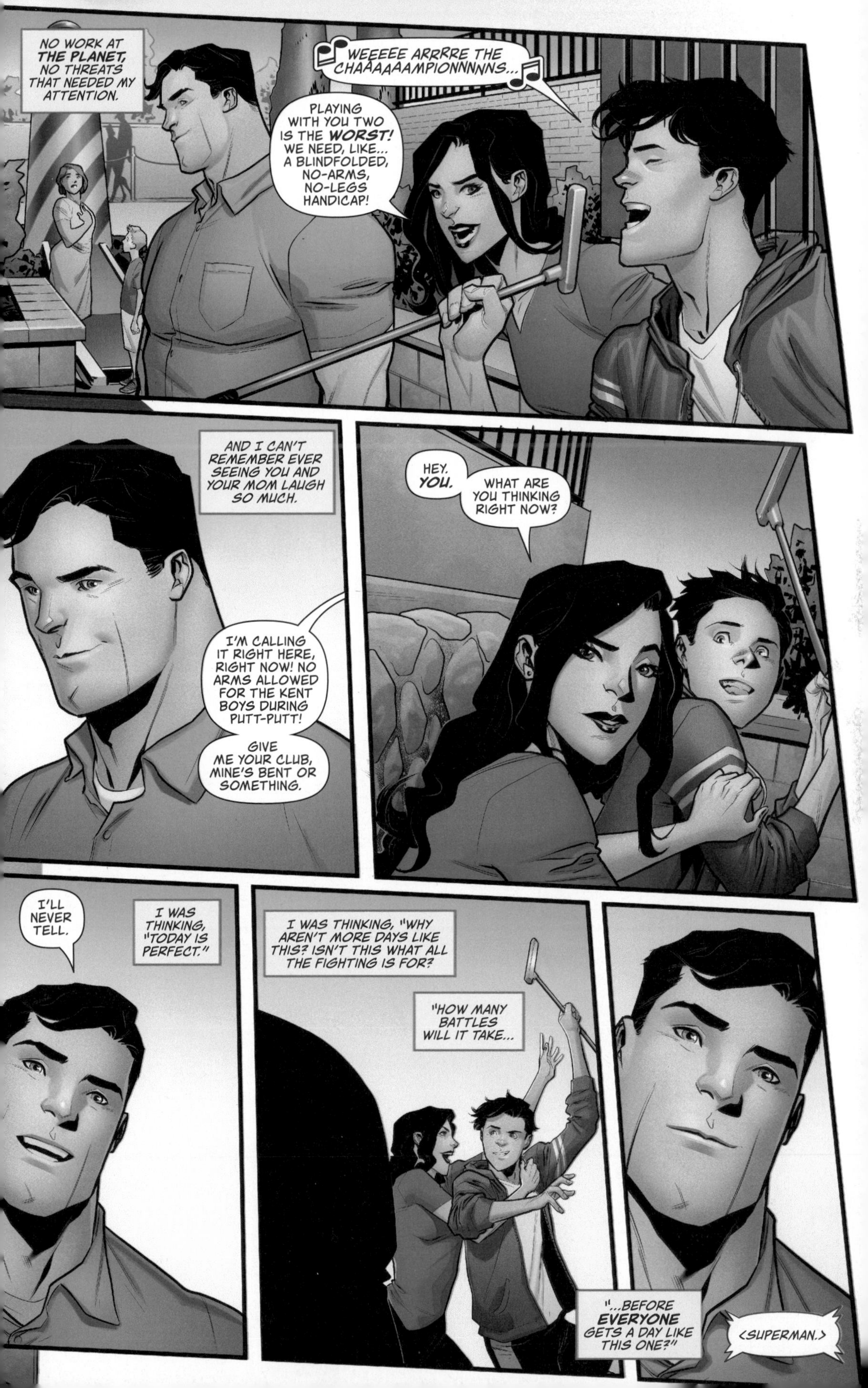

NO WORK AT THE PLANET, NO THREATS THAT NEEDED MY ATTENTION.
WEEEEE ARRRRE THE CHAAAAAAMPIONNNNNS...
PLAYING WITH YOU TWO IS THE WORST! WE NEED, LIKE... A BLINDFOLDED, NO-ARMS, NO-LEGS HANDICAP!
AND I CAN'T REMEMBER EVER SEEING YOU AND YOUR MOM LAUGH SO MUCH.
I'M CALLING IT RIGHT HERE, RIGHT NOW! NO ARMS ALLOWED FOR THE KENT BOYS DURING PUTT-PUTT!
GIVE ME YOUR CLUB, MINE'S BENT OR SOMETHING.
HEY. YOU.
WHAT ARE YOU THINKING RIGHT NOW?
I'LL NEVER TELL.
I WAS THINKING, "TODAY IS PERFECT."
I WAS THINKING, "WHY AREN'T MORE DAYS LIKE THIS? ISN'T THIS WHAT ALL THE FIGHTING IS FOR?
"HOW MANY BATTLES WILL IT TAKE...
"...BEFORE EVERYONE GETS A DAY LIKE THIS ONE?"
<SUPERMAN.>

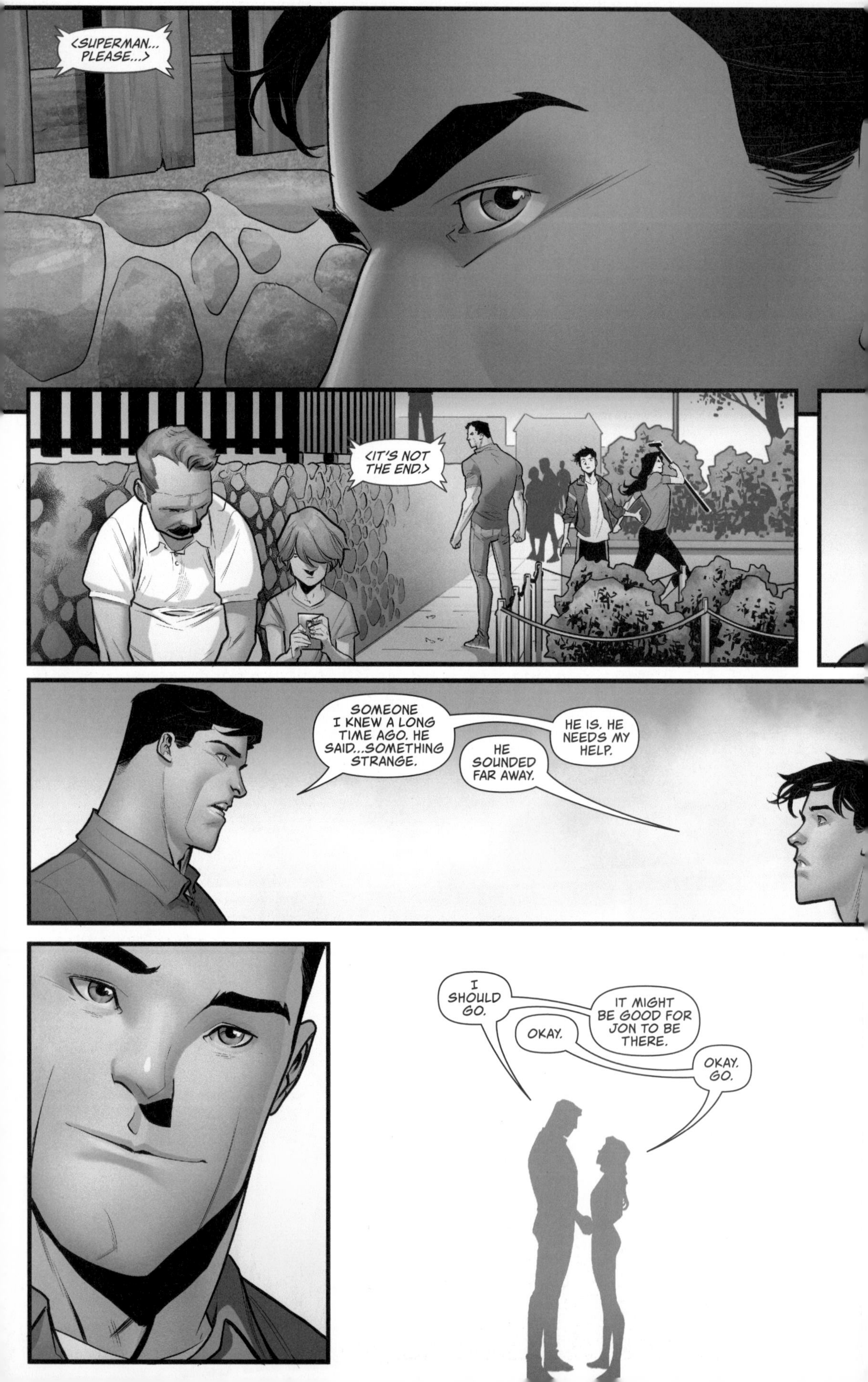
<SUPERMAN... PLEASE...>
<IT'S NOT THE END.>
SOMEONE I KNEW A LONG TIME AGO. HE SAID...SOMETHING STRANGE.
HE IS. HE NEEDS MY HELP.
HE SOUNDED FAR AWAY.
I SHOULD GO.
IT MIGHT BE GOOD FOR JON TO BE THERE.
OKAY.
OKAY. GO.

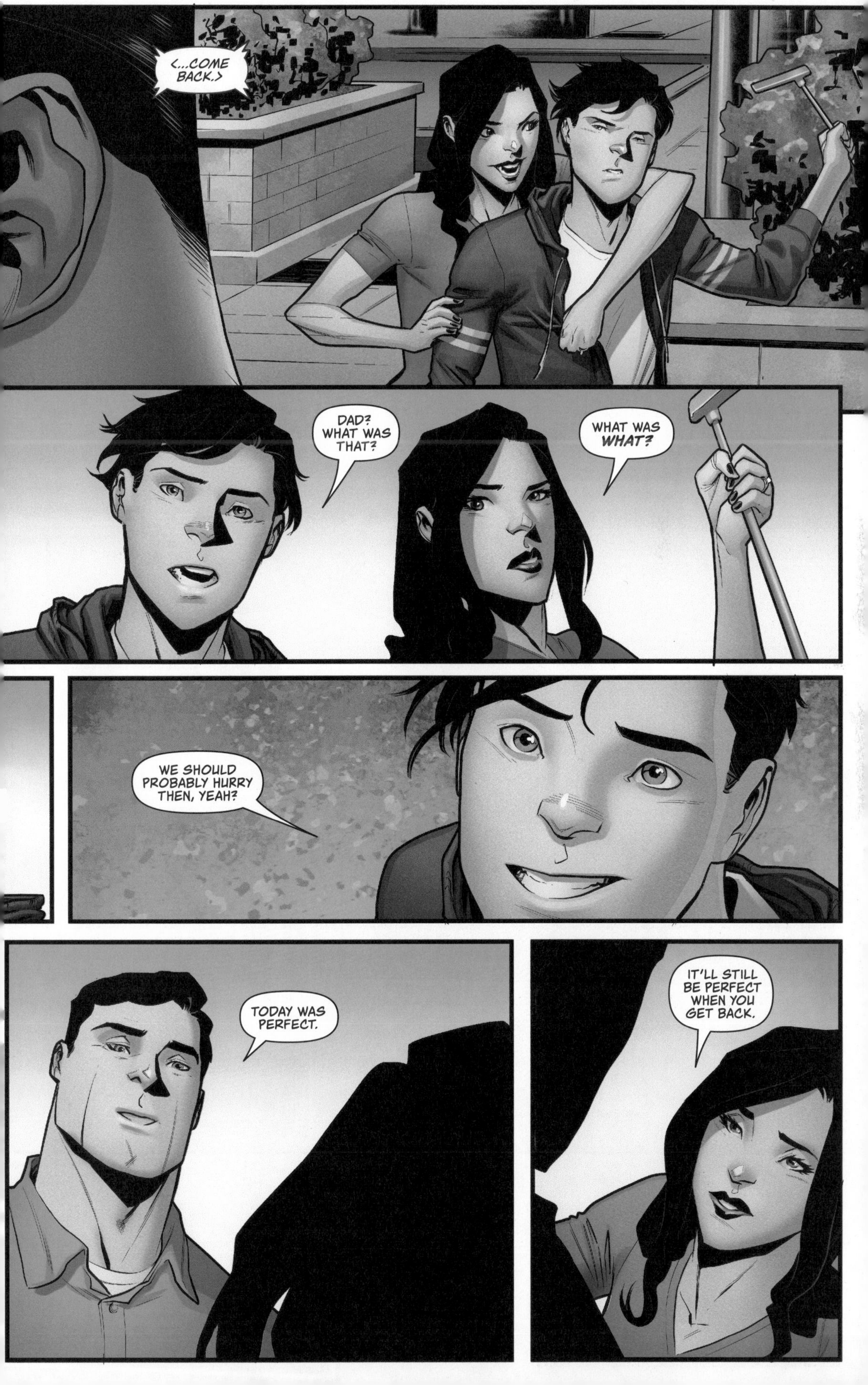
<...COME BACK.>
DAD? WHAT WAS THAT?
WHAT WAS *WHAT?*
WE SHOULD PROBABLY HURRY THEN, YEAH?
TODAY WAS PERFECT.
IT'LL STILL BE PERFECT WHEN YOU GET BACK.

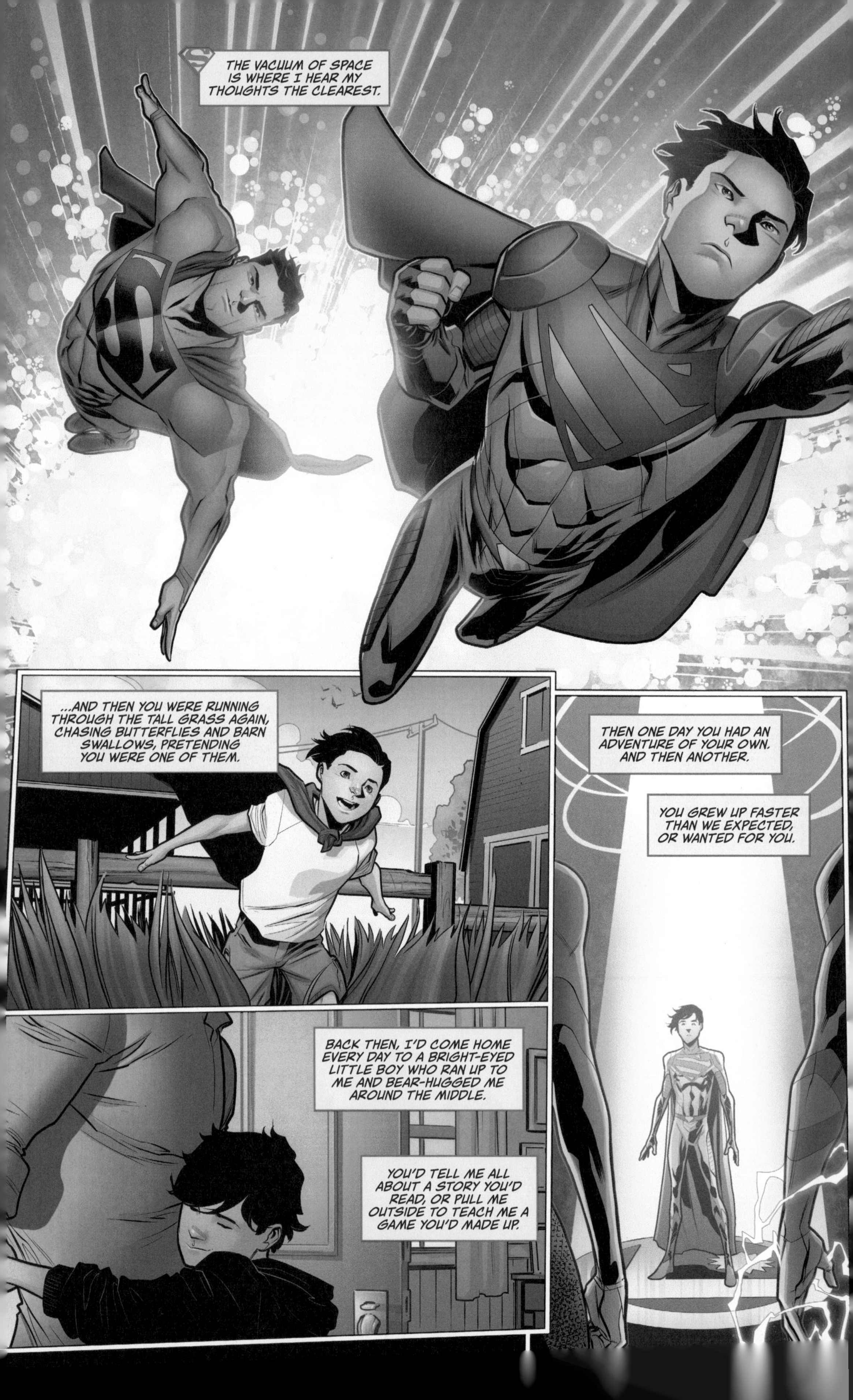
THE VACUUM OF SPACE IS WHERE I HEAR MY THOUGHTS THE CLEAREST.
...AND THEN YOU WERE RUNNING THROUGH THE TALL GRASS AGAIN, CHASING BUTTERFLIES AND BARN SWALLOWS, PRETENDING YOU WERE ONE OF THEM.
BACK THEN, I'D COME HOME EVERY DAY TO A BRIGHT-EYED LITTLE BOY WHO RAN UP TO ME AND BEAR-HUGGED ME AROUND THE MIDDLE.
YOU'D TELL ME ALL ABOUT A STORY YOU'D READ, OR PULL ME OUTSIDE TO TEACH ME A GAME YOU'D MADE UP.
THEN ONE DAY YOU HAD AN ADVENTURE OF YOUR OWN. AND THEN ANOTHER.
YOU GREW UP FASTER THAN WE EXPECTED, OR WANTED FOR YOU.

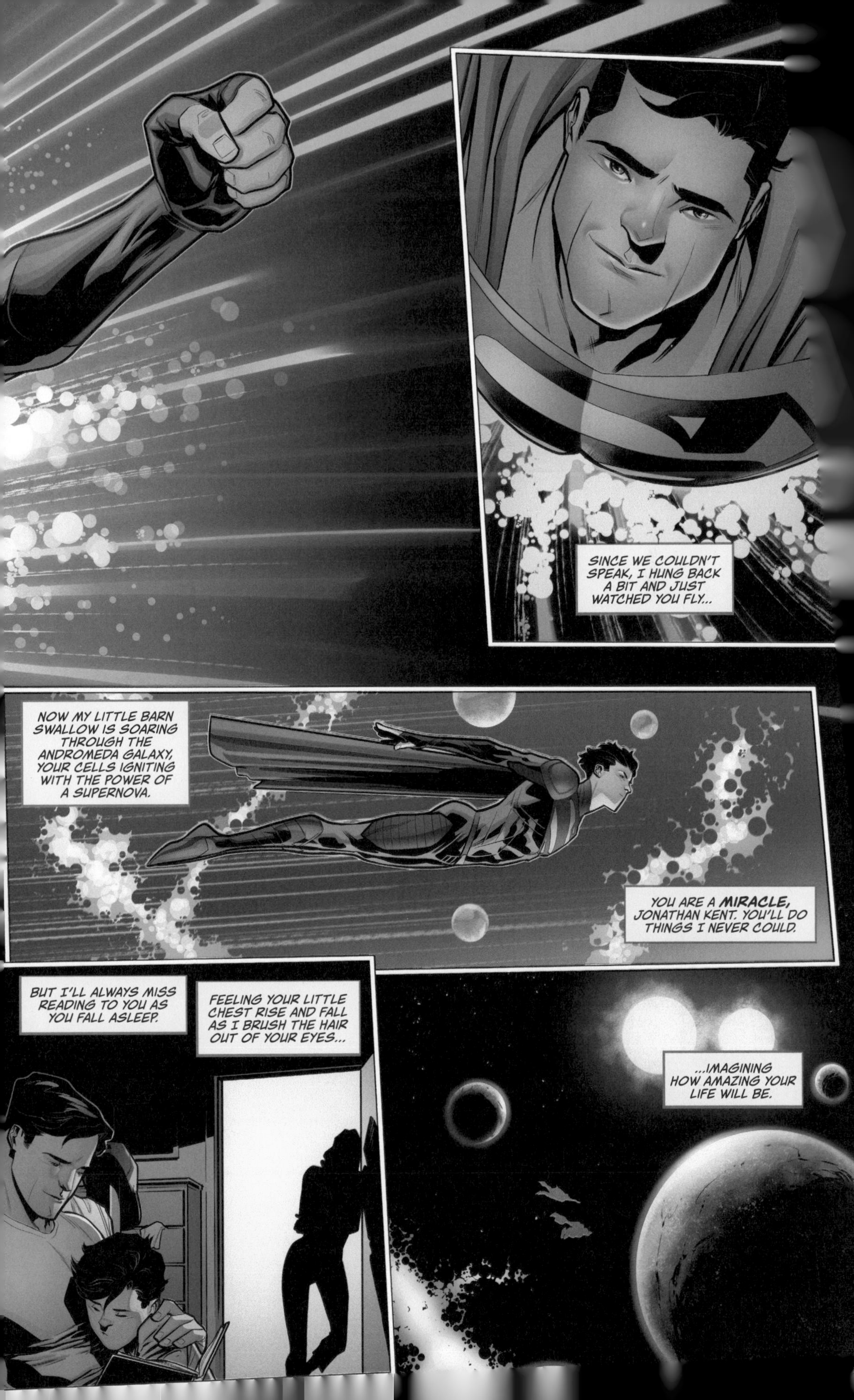
SINCE WE COULDN'T SPEAK, I HUNG BACK A BIT AND JUST WATCHED YOU FLY...
NOW MY LITTLE BARN SWALLOW IS SOARING THROUGH THE ANDROMEDA GALAXY, YOUR CELLS IGNITING WITH THE POWER OF A SUPERNOVA.
YOU ARE A **MIRACLE,** JONATHAN KENT. YOU'LL DO THINGS I NEVER COULD.
BUT I'LL ALWAYS MISS READING TO YOU AS YOU FALL ASLEEP.
FEELING YOUR LITTLE CHEST RISE AND FALL AS I BRUSH THE HAIR OUT OF YOUR EYES...
...IMAGINING HOW AMAZING YOUR LIFE WILL BE.

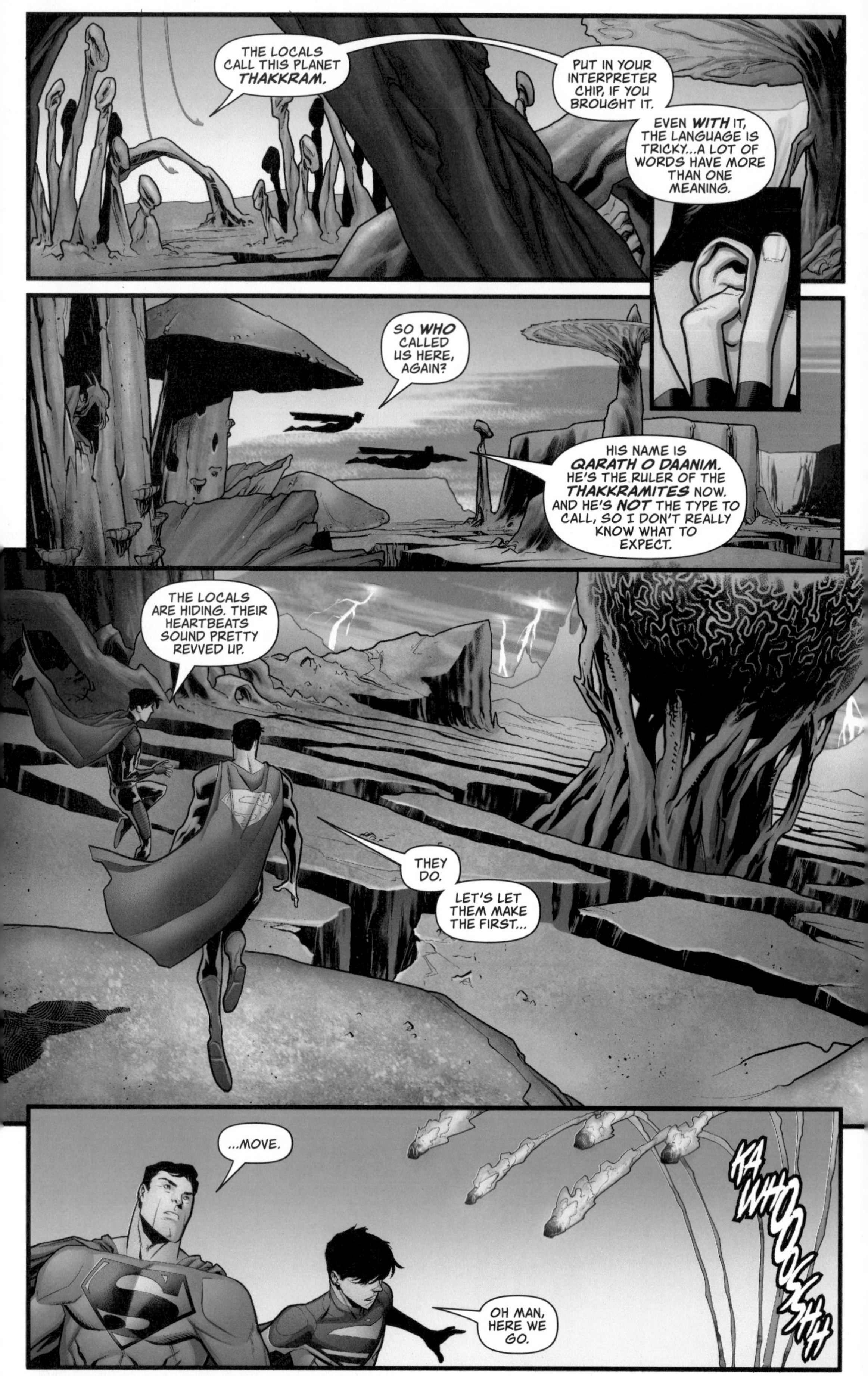

THE LOCALS CALL THIS PLANET THAKKRAM.
PUT IN YOUR INTERPRETER CHIP, IF YOU BROUGHT IT.
EVEN WITH IT, THE LANGUAGE IS TRICKY...A LOT OF WORDS HAVE MORE THAN ONE MEANING.
SO WHO CALLED US HERE, AGAIN?
HIS NAME IS QARATH O DAANIM. HE'S THE RULER OF THE THAKKRAMITES NOW. AND HE'S NOT THE TYPE TO CALL, SO I DON'T REALLY KNOW WHAT TO EXPECT.
THE LOCALS ARE HIDING. THEIR HEARTBEATS SOUND PRETTY REVVED UP.
THEY DO.
LET'S LET THEM MAKE THE FIRST...
...MOVE.
OH MAN, HERE WE GO.
KA WHOOOSHH

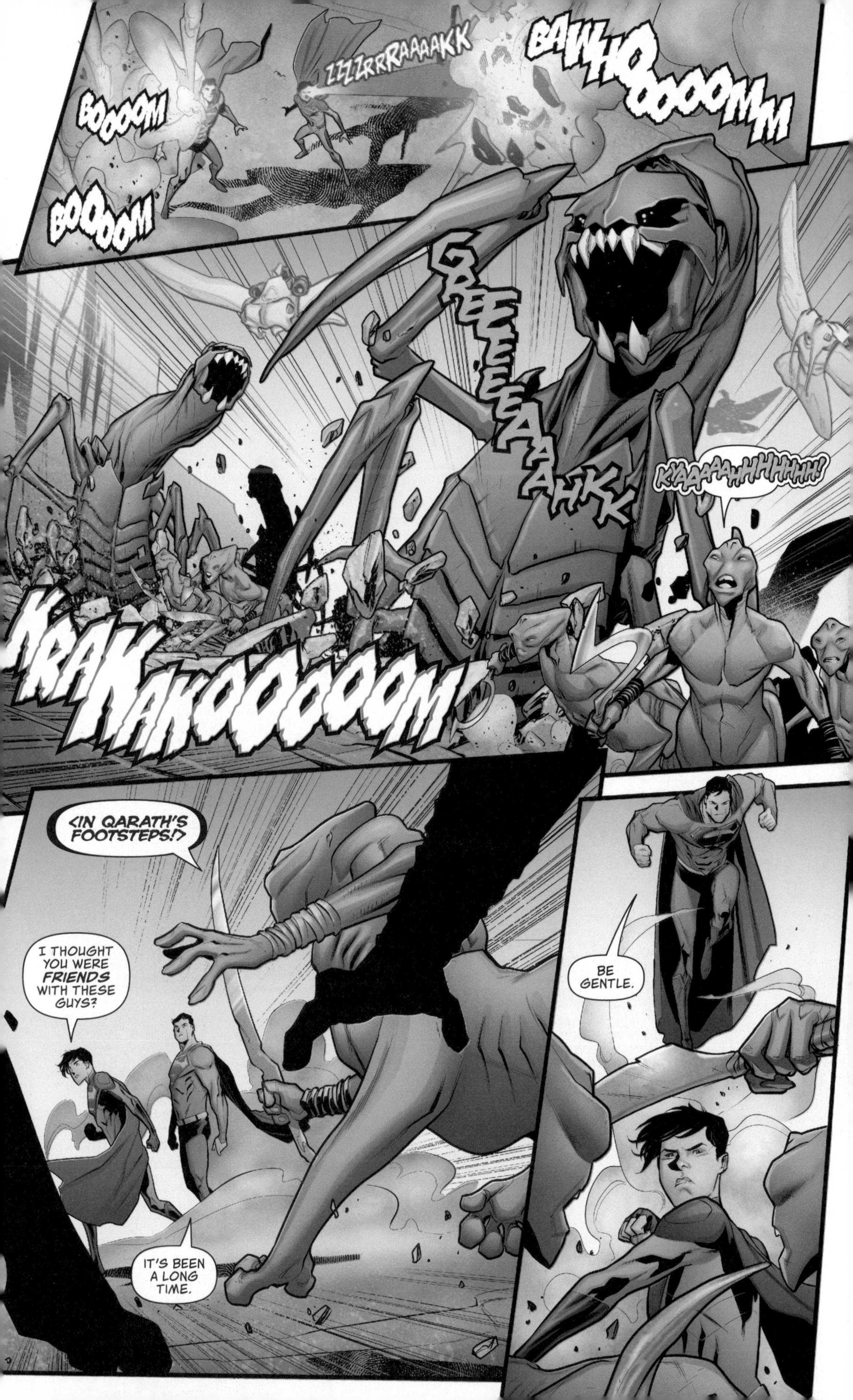
BOOOOM
BOOOOM
ZZZZrrrRAAAAKK
BAWHOOOOOOMM
GREEEEAAAHKK
KYAAAAAHHHHHH!
KRAKAKOOOOOOM
<IN QARATH'S FOOTSTEPS!>
I THOUGHT YOU WERE FRIENDS WITH THESE GUYS?
IT'S BEEN A LONG TIME.
BE GENTLE.

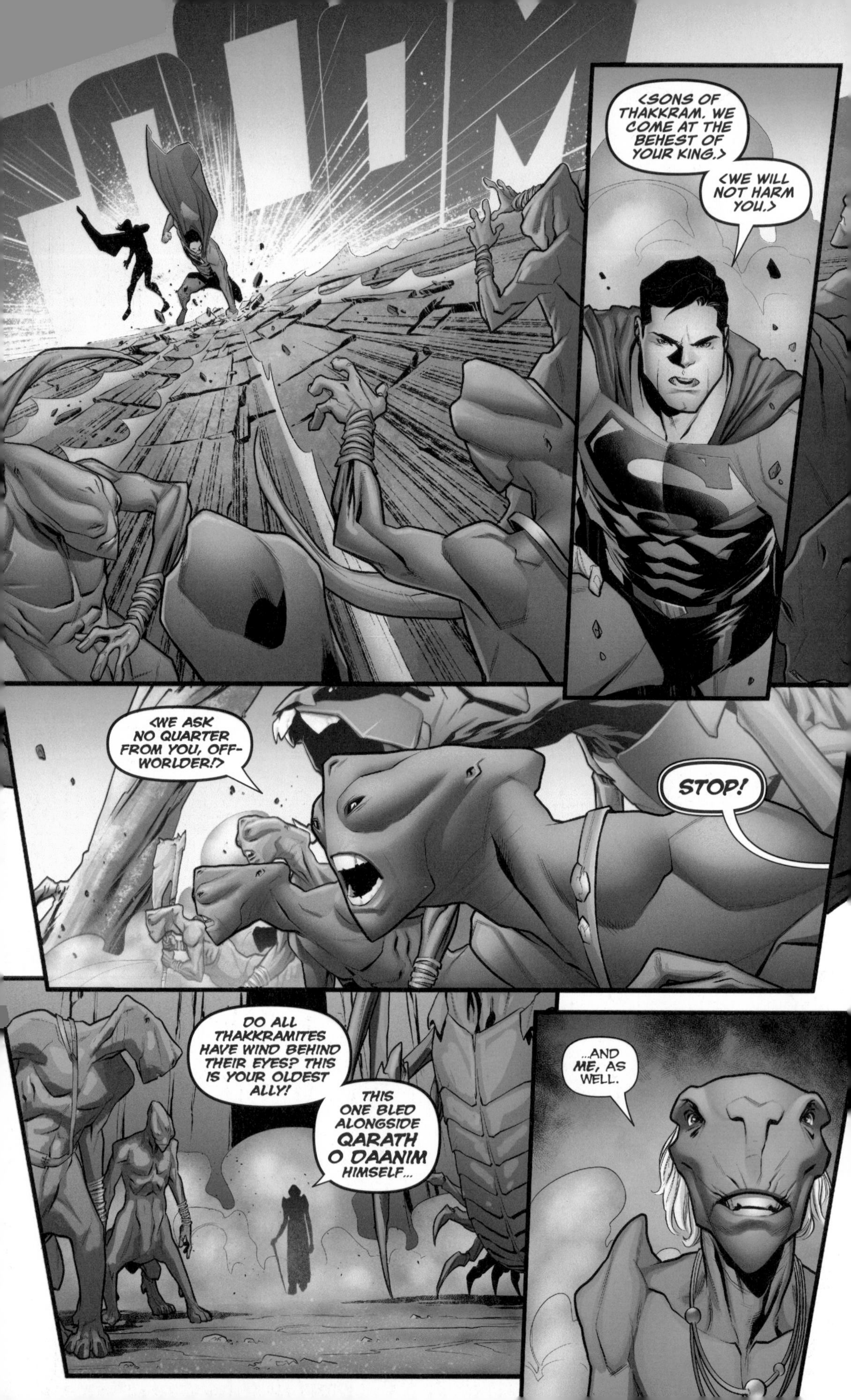
<SONS OF THAKKRAM. WE COME AT THE BEHEST OF YOUR KING.>
<WE WILL NOT HARM YOU.>
<WE ASK NO QUARTER FROM YOU, OFF-WORLDER!>
STOP!
DO ALL THAKKRAMITES HAVE WIND BEHIND THEIR EYES? THIS IS YOUR OLDEST ALLY!
THIS ONE BLED ALONGSIDE QARATH O DAANIM HIMSELF...
...AND ME, AS WELL.

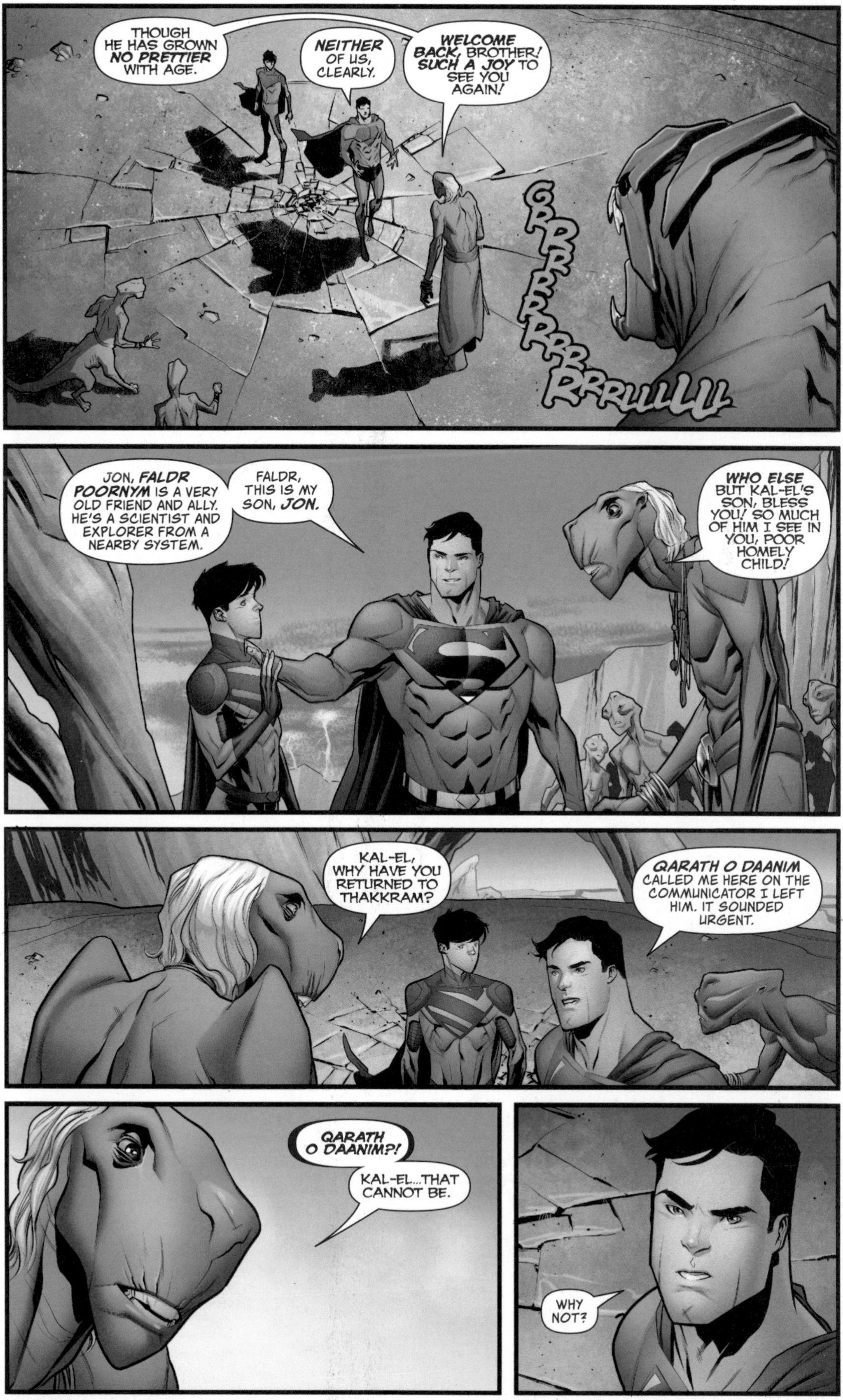

THOUGH HE HAS GROWN NO PRETTIER WITH AGE.
NEITHER OF US, CLEARLY.
WELCOME BACK, BROTHER! SUCH A JOY TO SEE YOU AGAIN!
GRRRRRRRRRRRRULLLLU
JON, FALDR POORNYM IS A VERY OLD FRIEND AND ALLY. HE'S A SCIENTIST AND EXPLORER FROM A NEARBY SYSTEM.
FALDR, THIS IS MY SON, JON.
WHO ELSE BUT KAL-EL'S SON, BLESS YOU! SO MUCH OF HIM I SEE IN YOU, POOR HOMELY CHILD!
KAL-EL, WHY HAVE YOU RETURNED TO THAKKRAM?
QARATH O DAANIM CALLED ME HERE ON THE COMMUNICATOR I LEFT HIM. IT SOUNDED URGENT.
QARATH O DAANIM?!
KAL-EL...THAT CANNOT BE.
WHY NOT?

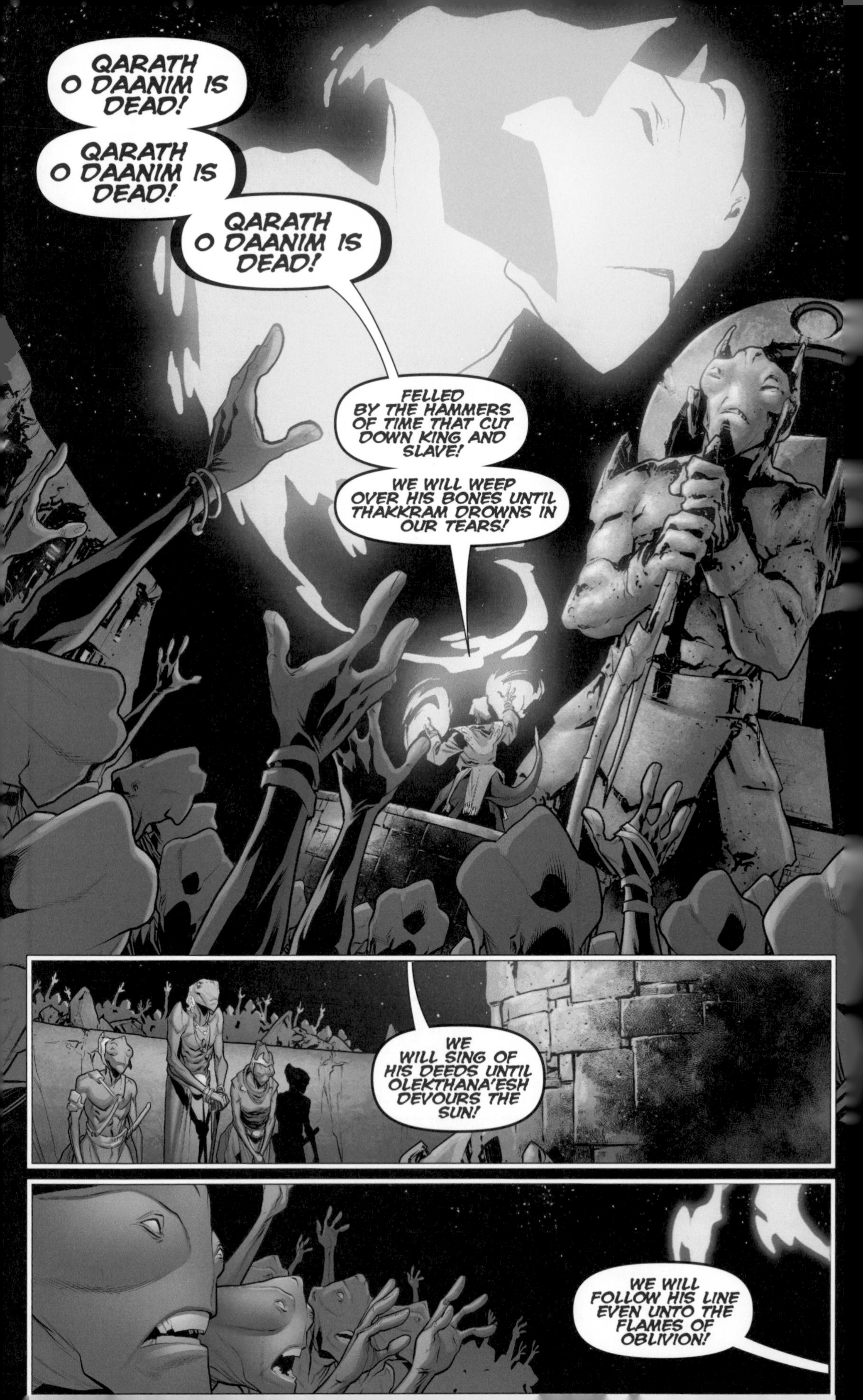

QARATH O DAANIM IS DEAD!
QARATH O DAANIM IS DEAD!
QARATH O DAANIM IS DEAD!
FELLED BY THE HAMMERS OF TIME THAT CUT DOWN KING AND SLAVE!
WE WILL WEEP OVER HIS BONES UNTIL THAKKRAM DROWNS IN OUR TEARS!
WE WILL SING OF HIS DEEDS UNTIL OLEKTHANA'ESH DEVOURS THE SUN!
WE WILL FOLLOW HIS LINE EVEN UNTO THE FLAMES OF OBLIVION!

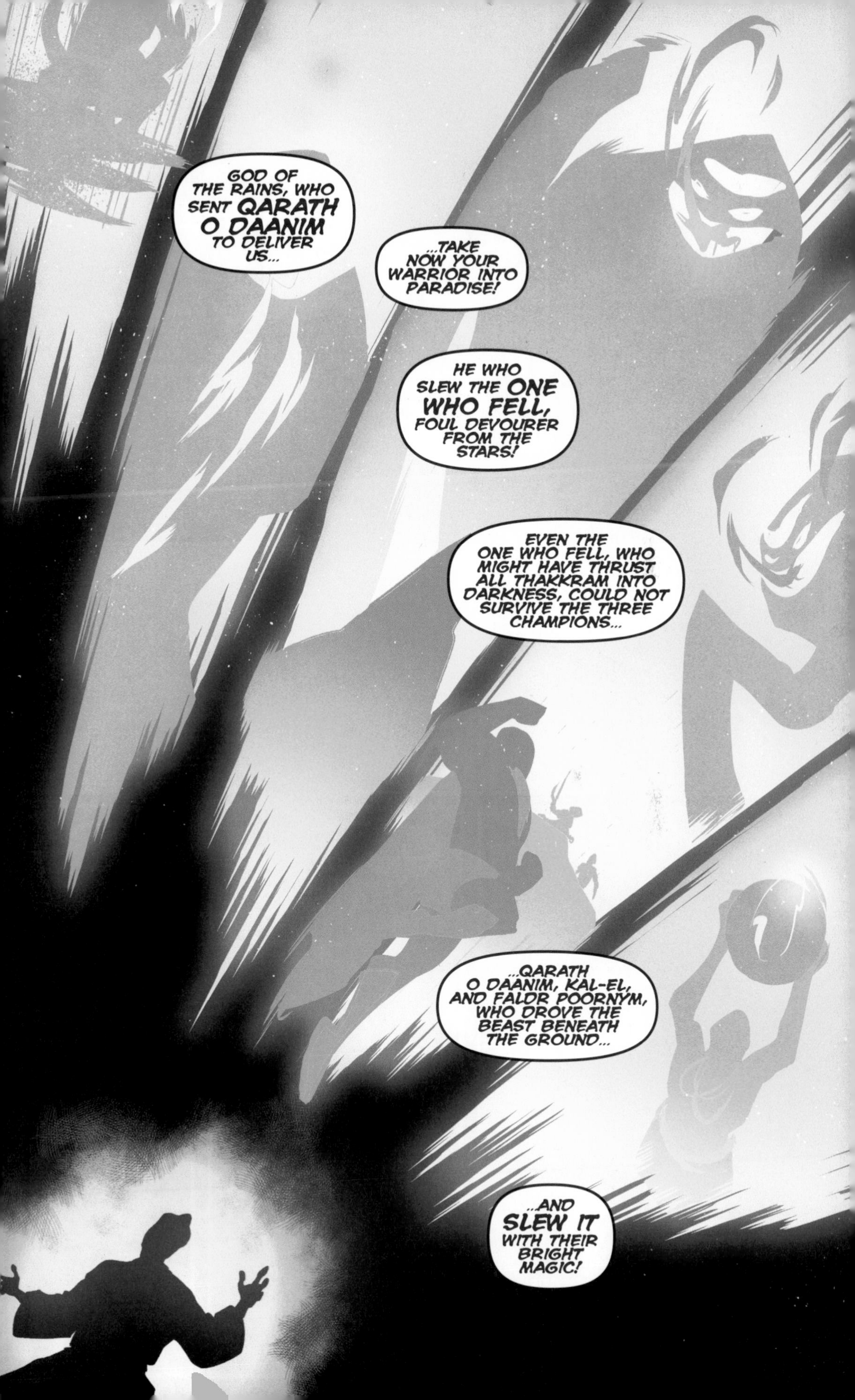
GOD OF THE RAINS, WHO SENT QARATH O DAANIM TO DELIVER US...
...TAKE NOW YOUR WARRIOR INTO PARADISE!
HE WHO SLEW THE ONE WHO FELL, FOUL DEVOURER FROM THE STARS!
EVEN THE ONE WHO FELL, WHO MIGHT HAVE THRUST ALL THAKKRAM INTO DARKNESS, COULD NOT SURVIVE THE THREE CHAMPIONS...
...QARATH O DAANIM, KAL-EL, AND FALDOR POORNYM, WHO DROVE THE BEAST BENEATH THE GROUND...
...AND SLEW IT WITH THEIR BRIGHT MAGIC!

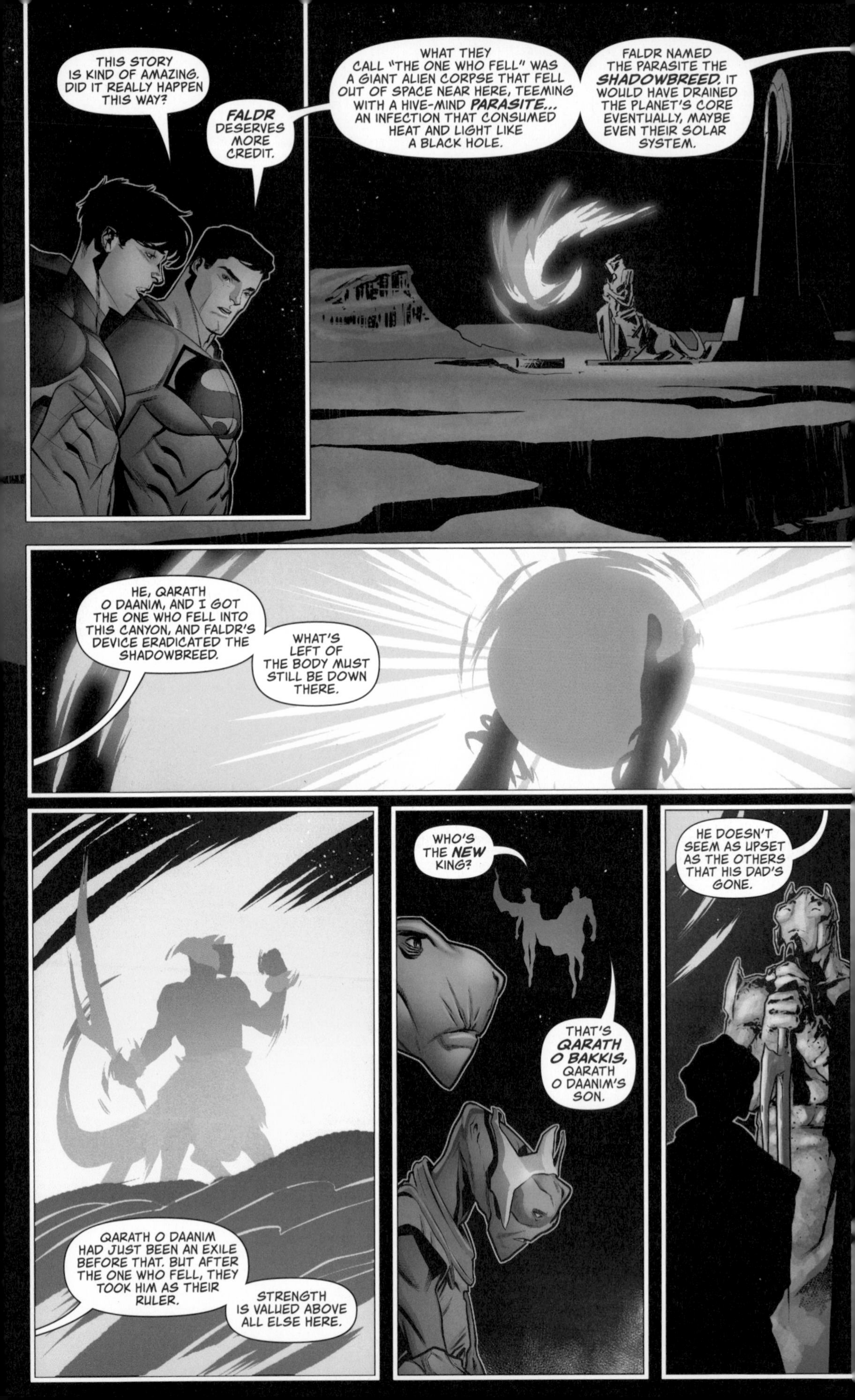

THIS STORY IS KIND OF AMAZING. DID IT REALLY HAPPEN THIS WAY?
FALDR DESERVES MORE CREDIT.
WHAT THEY CALL "THE ONE WHO FELL" WAS A GIANT ALIEN CORPSE THAT FELL OUT OF SPACE NEAR HERE, TEEMING WITH A HIVE-MIND PARASITE... AN INFECTION THAT CONSUMED HEAT AND LIGHT LIKE A BLACK HOLE.
FALDR NAMED THE PARASITE THE SHADOWBREED. IT WOULD HAVE DRAINED THE PLANET'S CORE EVENTUALLY, MAYBE EVEN THEIR SOLAR SYSTEM.
HE, QARATH O DAANIM, AND I GOT THE ONE WHO FELL INTO THIS CANYON, AND FALDR'S DEVICE ERADICATED THE SHADOWBREED.
WHAT'S LEFT OF THE BODY MUST STILL BE DOWN THERE.
QARATH O DAANIM HAD JUST BEEN AN EXILE BEFORE THAT. BUT AFTER THE ONE WHO FELL, THEY TOOK HIM AS THEIR RULER.
STRENGTH IS VALUED ABOVE ALL ELSE HERE.
WHO'S THE NEW KING?
THAT'S QARATH O BAKKIS, QARATH O DAANIM'S SON.
HE DOESN'T SEEM AS UPSET AS THE OTHERS THAT HIS DAD'S GONE.

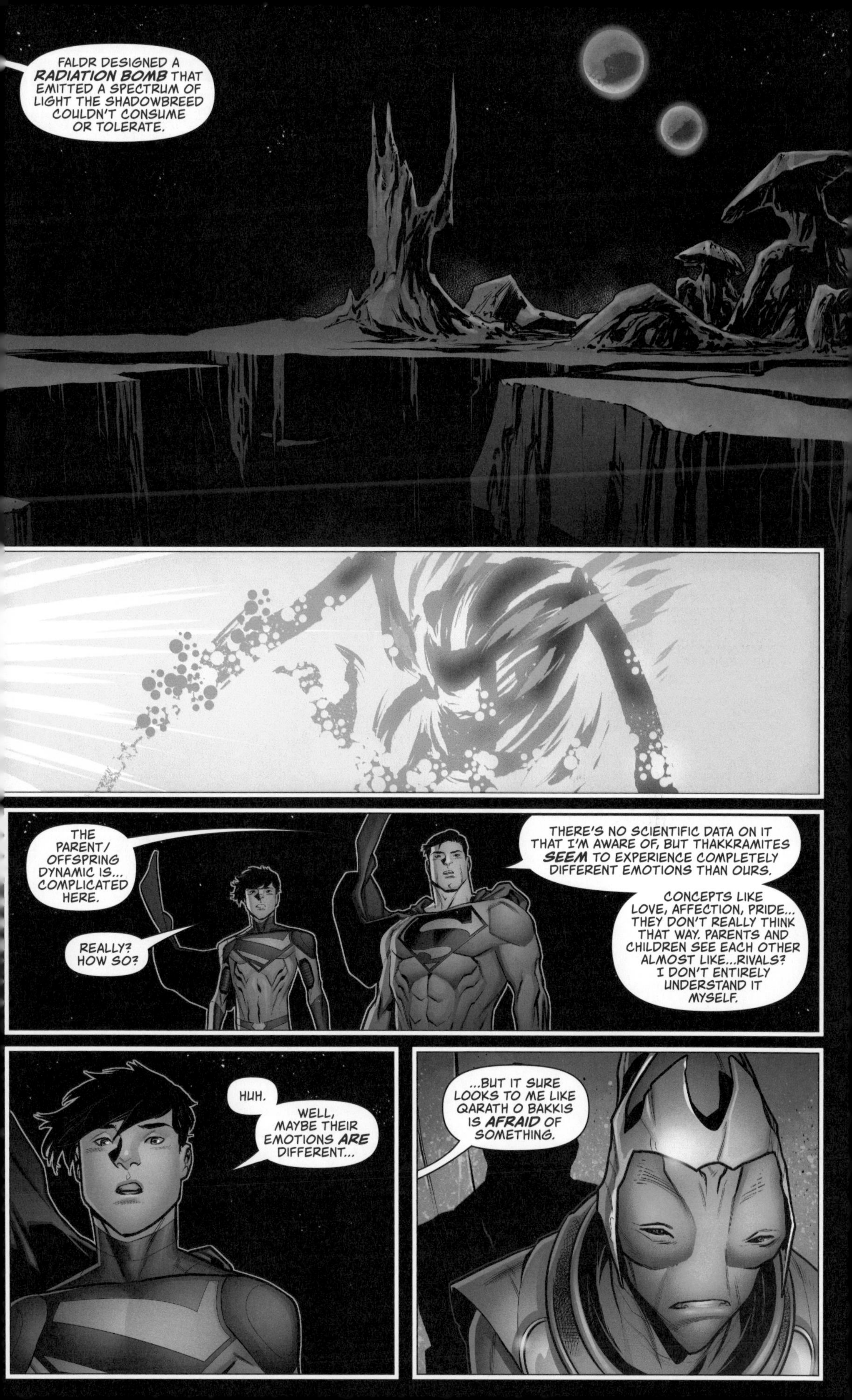
FALDR DESIGNED A ***RADIATION BOMB*** THAT EMITTED A SPECTRUM OF LIGHT THE SHADOWBREED COULDN'T CONSUME OR TOLERATE.
THE PARENT/ OFFSPRING DYNAMIC IS... COMPLICATED HERE.
REALLY? HOW SO?
THERE'S NO SCIENTIFIC DATA ON IT THAT I'M AWARE OF, BUT THAKKRAMITES ***SEEM*** TO EXPERIENCE COMPLETELY DIFFERENT EMOTIONS THAN OURS.
CONCEPTS LIKE LOVE, AFFECTION, PRIDE... THEY DON'T REALLY THINK THAT WAY. PARENTS AND CHILDREN SEE EACH OTHER ALMOST LIKE...RIVALS? I DON'T ENTIRELY UNDERSTAND IT MYSELF.
HUH.
WELL, MAYBE THEIR EMOTIONS ***ARE*** DIFFERENT...
...BUT IT SURE LOOKS TO ME LIKE QARATH O BAKKIS IS ***AFRAID*** OF SOMETHING.

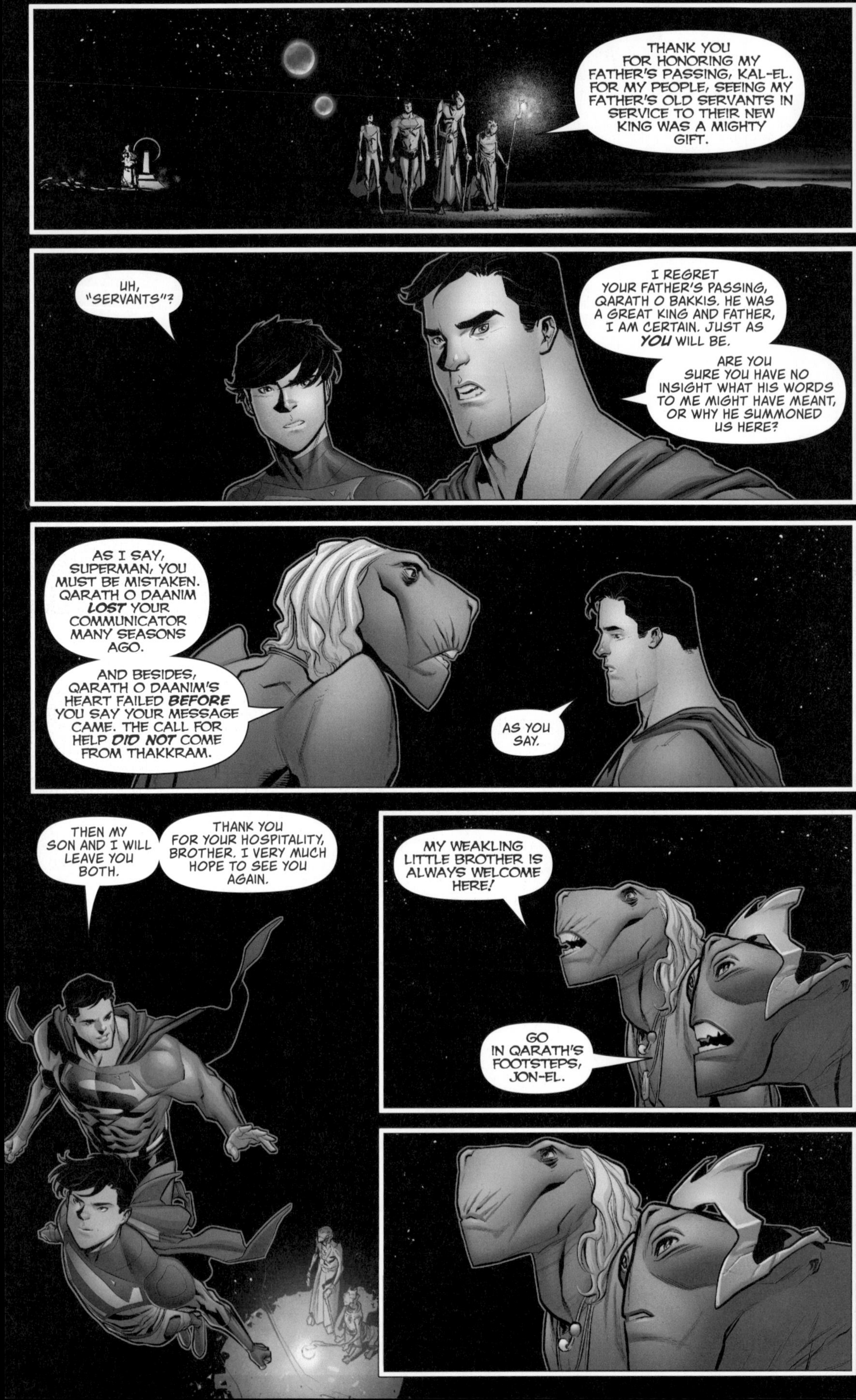
THANK YOU FOR HONORING MY FATHER'S PASSING, KAL-EL. FOR MY PEOPLE, SEEING MY FATHER'S OLD SERVANTS IN SERVICE TO THEIR NEW KING WAS A MIGHTY GIFT.
UH, "SERVANTS"?
I REGRET YOUR FATHER'S PASSING, QARATH O BAKKIS. HE WAS A GREAT KING AND FATHER, I AM CERTAIN. JUST AS ***YOU*** WILL BE.
ARE YOU SURE YOU HAVE NO INSIGHT WHAT HIS WORDS TO ME MIGHT HAVE MEANT, OR WHY HE SUMMONED US HERE?
AS I SAY, SUPERMAN, YOU MUST BE MISTAKEN. QARATH O DAANIM ***LOST*** YOUR COMMUNICATOR MANY SEASONS AGO.
AND BESIDES, QARATH O DAANIM'S HEART FAILED ***BEFORE*** YOU SAY YOUR MESSAGE CAME. THE CALL FOR HELP ***DID NOT*** COME FROM THAKKRAM.
AS YOU SAY.
THEN MY SON AND I WILL LEAVE YOU BOTH.
THANK YOU FOR YOUR HOSPITALITY, BROTHER. I VERY MUCH HOPE TO SEE YOU AGAIN.
MY WEAKLING LITTLE BROTHER IS ALWAYS WELCOME HERE!
GO IN QARATH'S FOOTSTEPS, JON-EL.

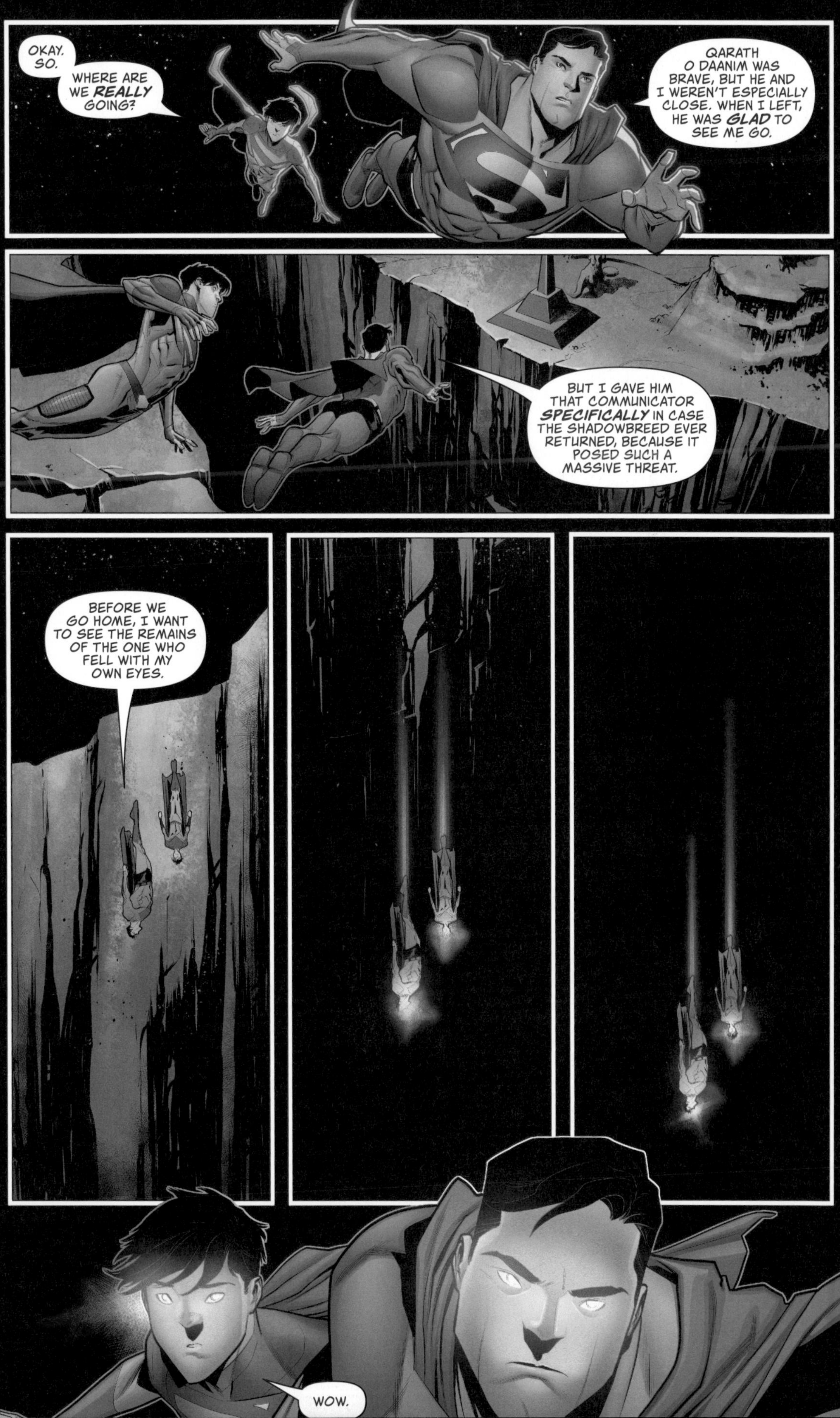

OKAY. SO.
WHERE ARE WE REALLY GOING?
QARATH O DAANIM WAS BRAVE, BUT HE AND I WEREN'T ESPECIALLY CLOSE. WHEN I LEFT, HE WAS GLAD TO SEE ME GO.
BUT I GAVE HIM THAT COMMUNICATOR SPECIFICALLY IN CASE THE SHADOWBREED EVER RETURNED, BECAUSE IT POSED SUCH A MASSIVE THREAT.
BEFORE WE GO HOME, I WANT TO SEE THE REMAINS OF THE ONE WHO FELL WITH MY OWN EYES.
WOW.

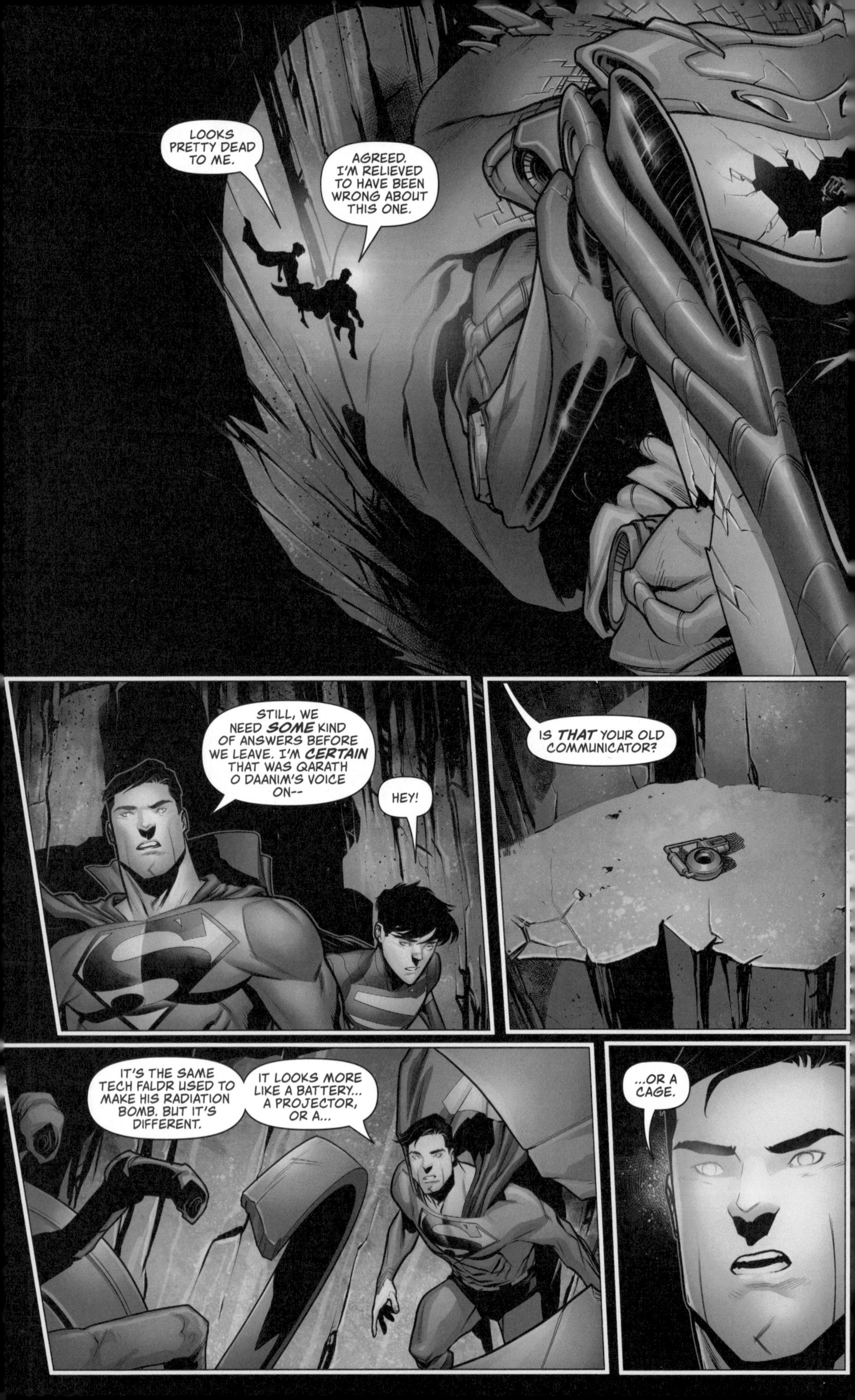
LOOKS PRETTY DEAD TO ME.
AGREED. I'M RELIEVED TO HAVE BEEN WRONG ABOUT THIS ONE.
STILL, WE NEED SOME KIND OF ANSWERS BEFORE WE LEAVE. I'M CERTAIN THAT WAS QARATH O DAANIM'S VOICE ON--
HEY!
IS THAT YOUR OLD COMMUNICATOR?
IT'S THE SAME TECH FALDR USED TO MAKE HIS RADIATION BOMB. BUT IT'S DIFFERENT.
IT LOOKS MORE LIKE A BATTERY... A PROJECTOR, OR A...
...OR A CAGE.

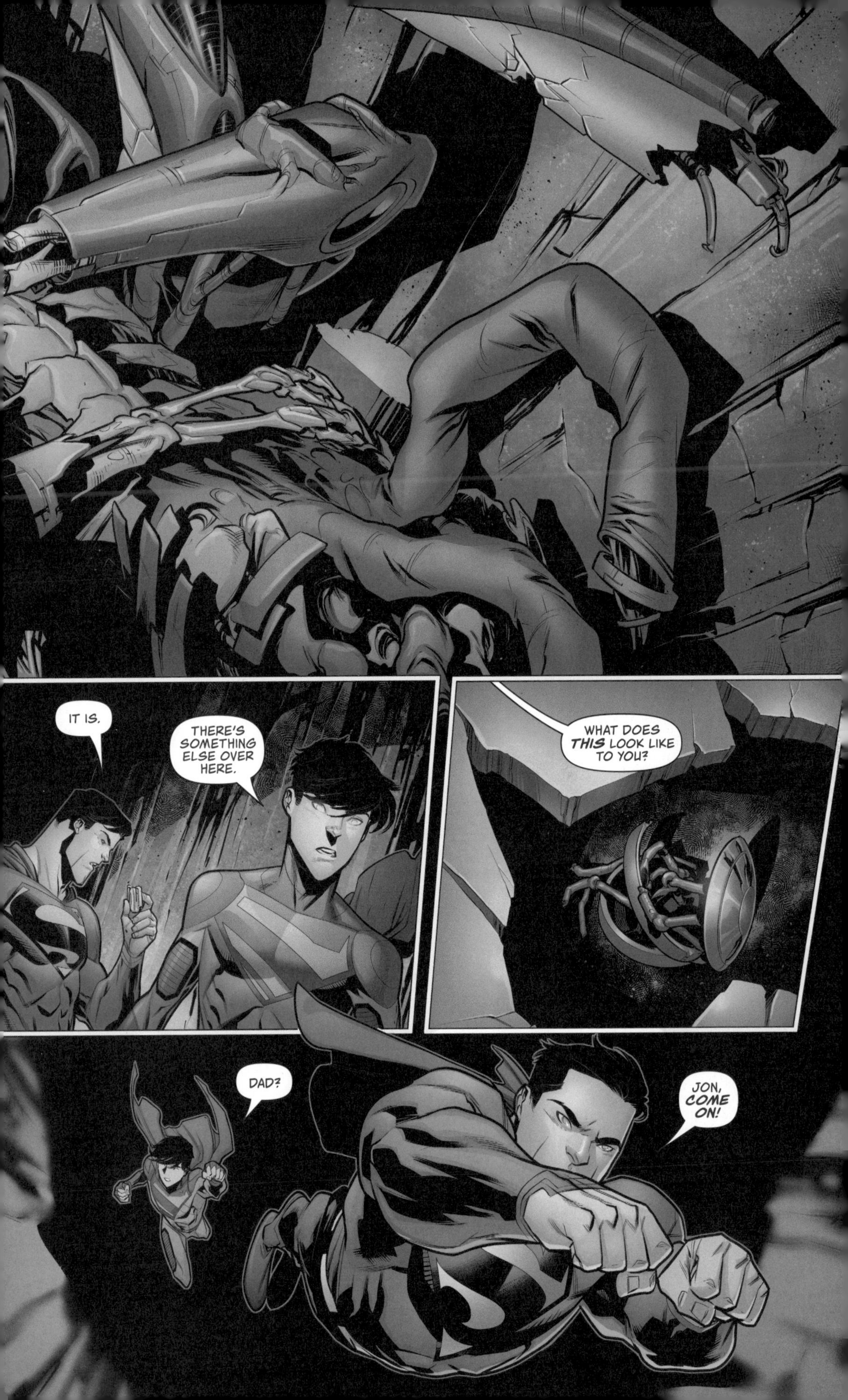
IT IS.
THERE'S SOMETHING ELSE OVER HERE.
WHAT DOES THIS LOOK LIKE TO YOU?
DAD?
JON, COME ON!

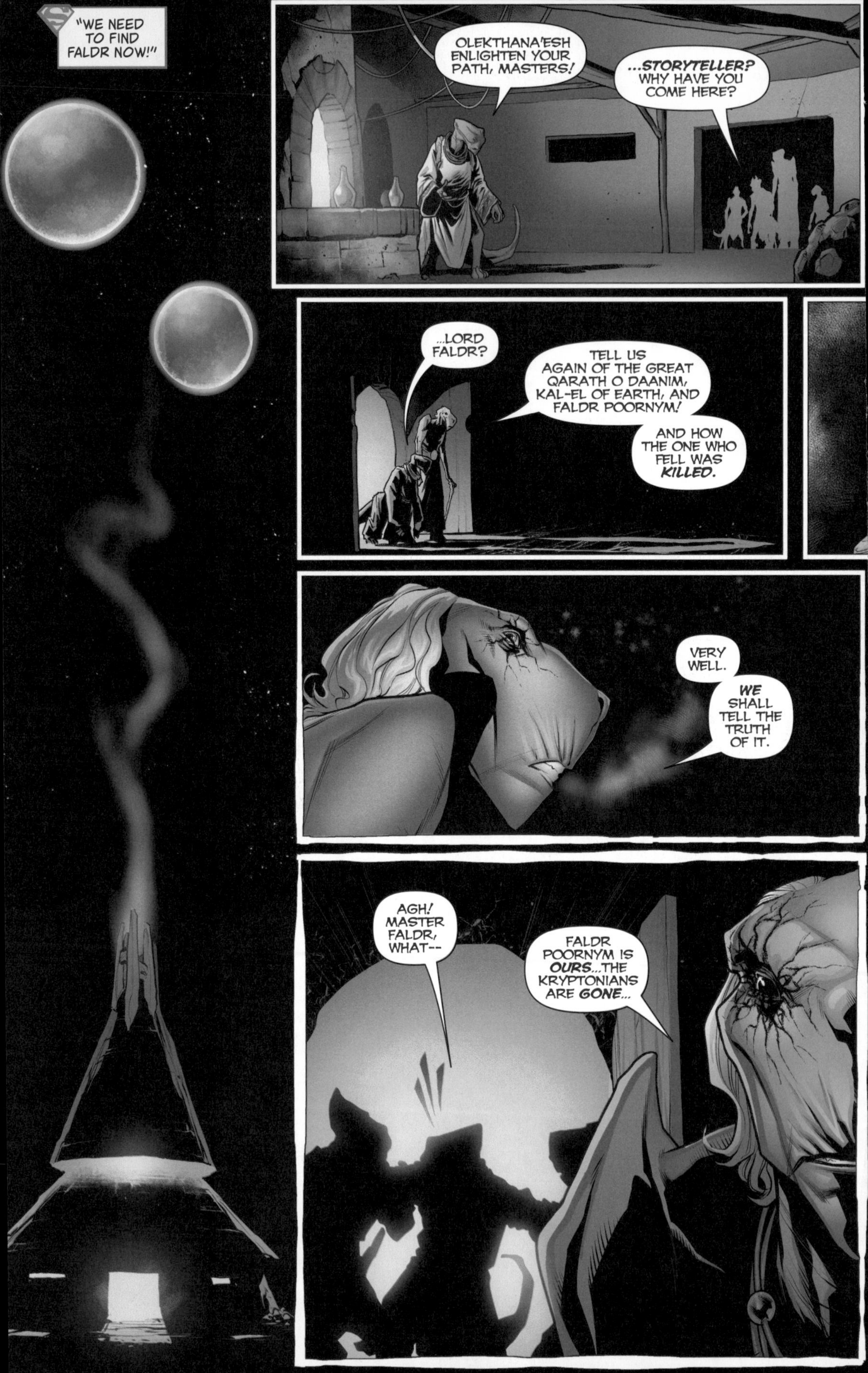
"WE NEED TO FIND FALDR NOW!"
OLEKTHANA'ESH ENLIGHTEN YOUR PATH, MASTERS!
...STORYTELLER? WHY HAVE YOU COME HERE?
...LORD FALDR?
TELL US AGAIN OF THE GREAT QARATH O DAANIM, KAL-EL OF EARTH, AND FALDR POORNYM!
AND HOW THE ONE WHO FELL WAS KILLED.
VERY WELL.
WE SHALL TELL THE TRUTH OF IT.
AGH! MASTER FALDR, WHAT--
FALDR POORNYM IS OURS...THE KRYPTONIANS ARE GONE...

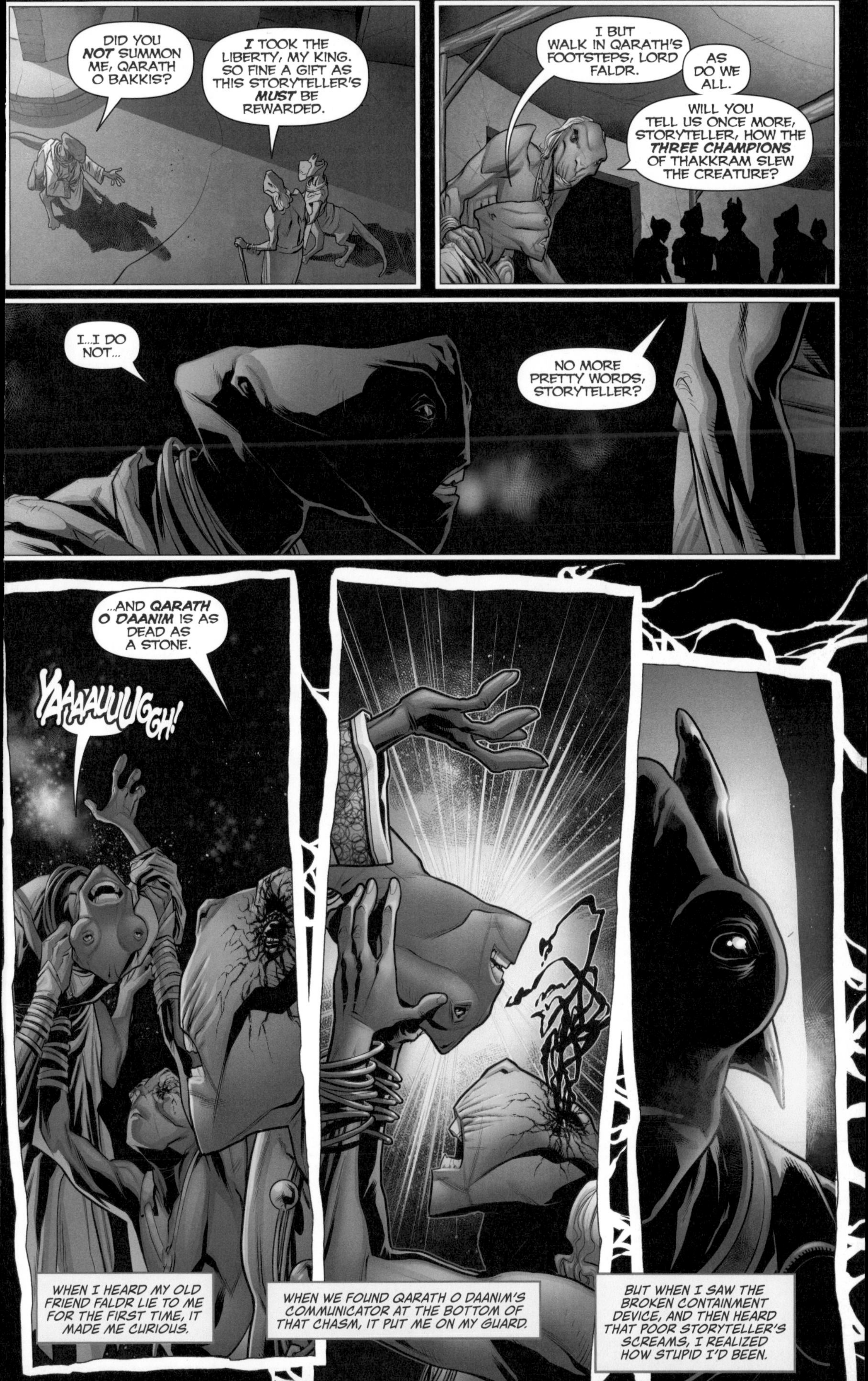

DID YOU NOT SUMMON ME, QARATH O BAKKIS?
I TOOK THE LIBERTY, MY KING. SO FINE A GIFT AS THIS STORYTELLER'S MUST BE REWARDED.
I BUT WALK IN QARATH'S FOOTSTEPS, LORD FALDR.
AS DO WE ALL.
WILL YOU TELL US ONCE MORE, STORYTELLER, HOW THE THREE CHAMPIONS OF THAKKRAM SLEW THE CREATURE?
I...I DO NOT...
NO MORE PRETTY WORDS, STORYTELLER?
...AND QARATH O DAANIM IS AS DEAD AS A STONE.
YAAAAUUUUGGH!
WHEN I HEARD MY OLD FRIEND FALDR LIE TO ME FOR THE FIRST TIME, IT MADE ME CURIOUS.
WHEN WE FOUND QARATH O DAANIM'S COMMUNICATOR AT THE BOTTOM OF THAT CHASM, IT PUT ME ON MY GUARD.
BUT WHEN I SAW THE BROKEN CONTAINMENT DEVICE, AND THEN HEARD THAT POOR STORYTELLER'S SCREAMS, I REALIZED HOW STUPID I'D BEEN.

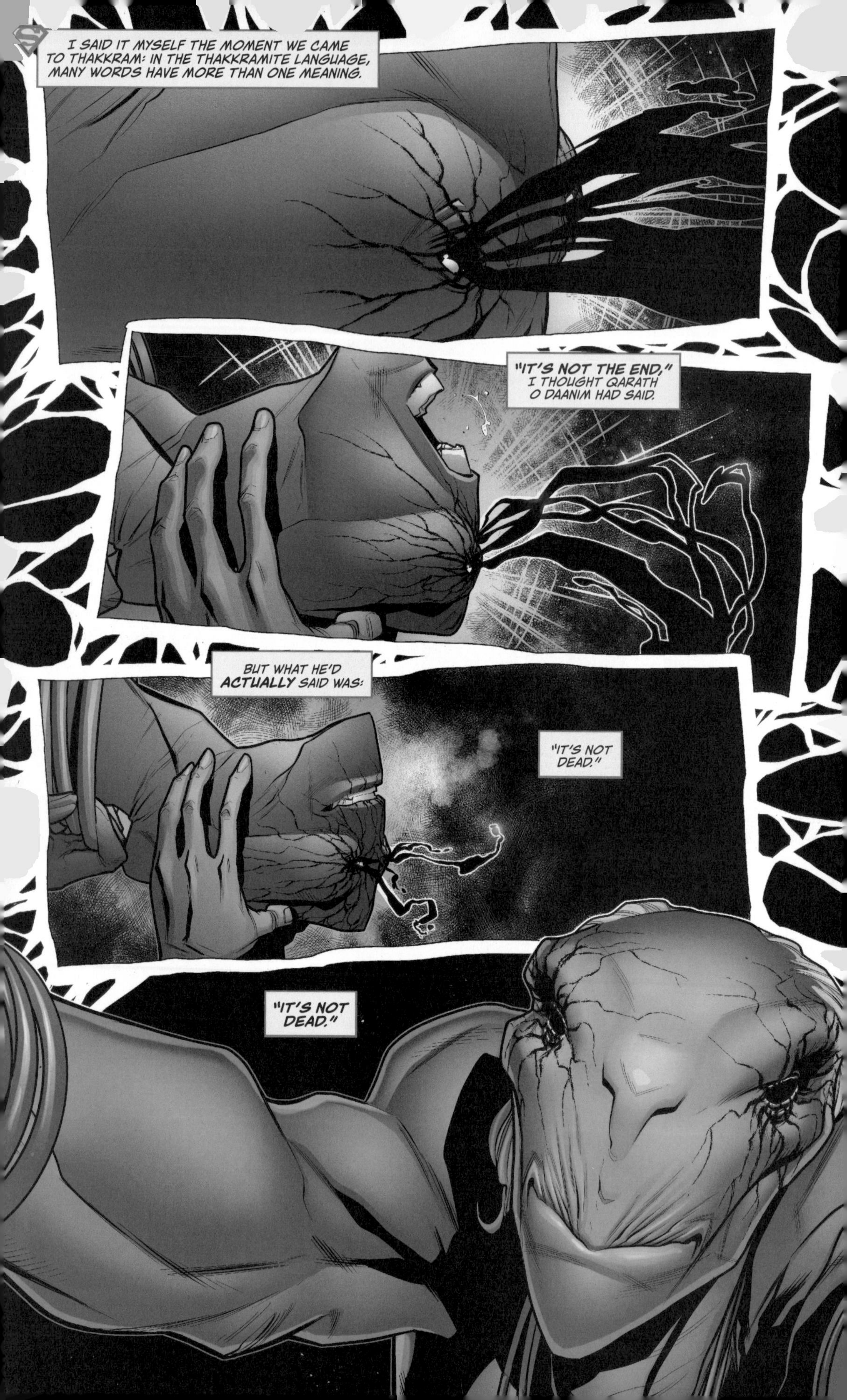
I SAID IT MYSELF THE MOMENT WE CAME TO THAKKRAM: IN THE THAKKRAMITE LANGUAGE, MANY WORDS HAVE MORE THAN ONE MEANING.
"IT'S NOT THE END," I THOUGHT QARATH O DAANIM HAD SAID.
BUT WHAT HE'D **ACTUALLY** SAID WAS:
"IT'S NOT DEAD."
"IT'S NOT DEAD."

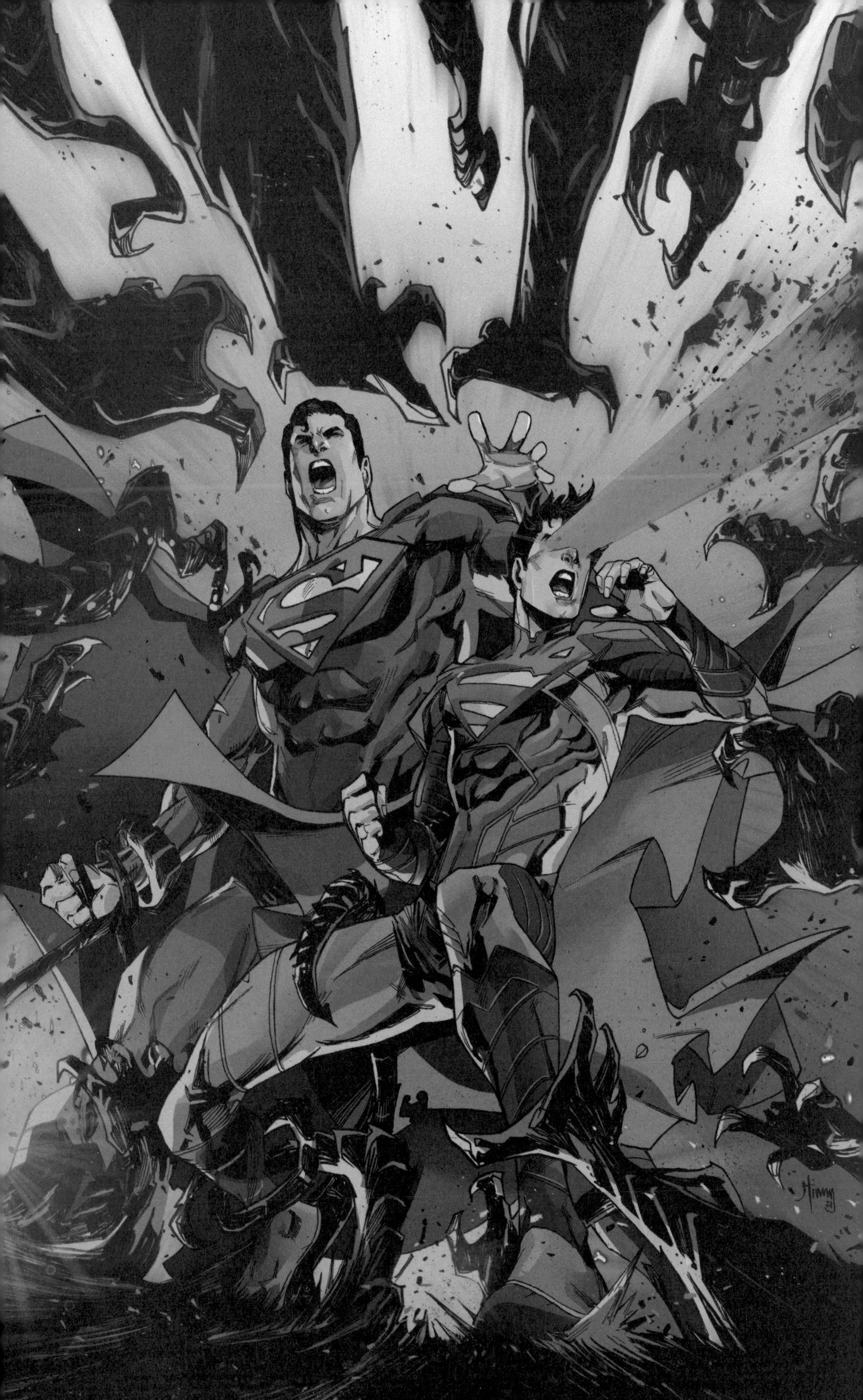

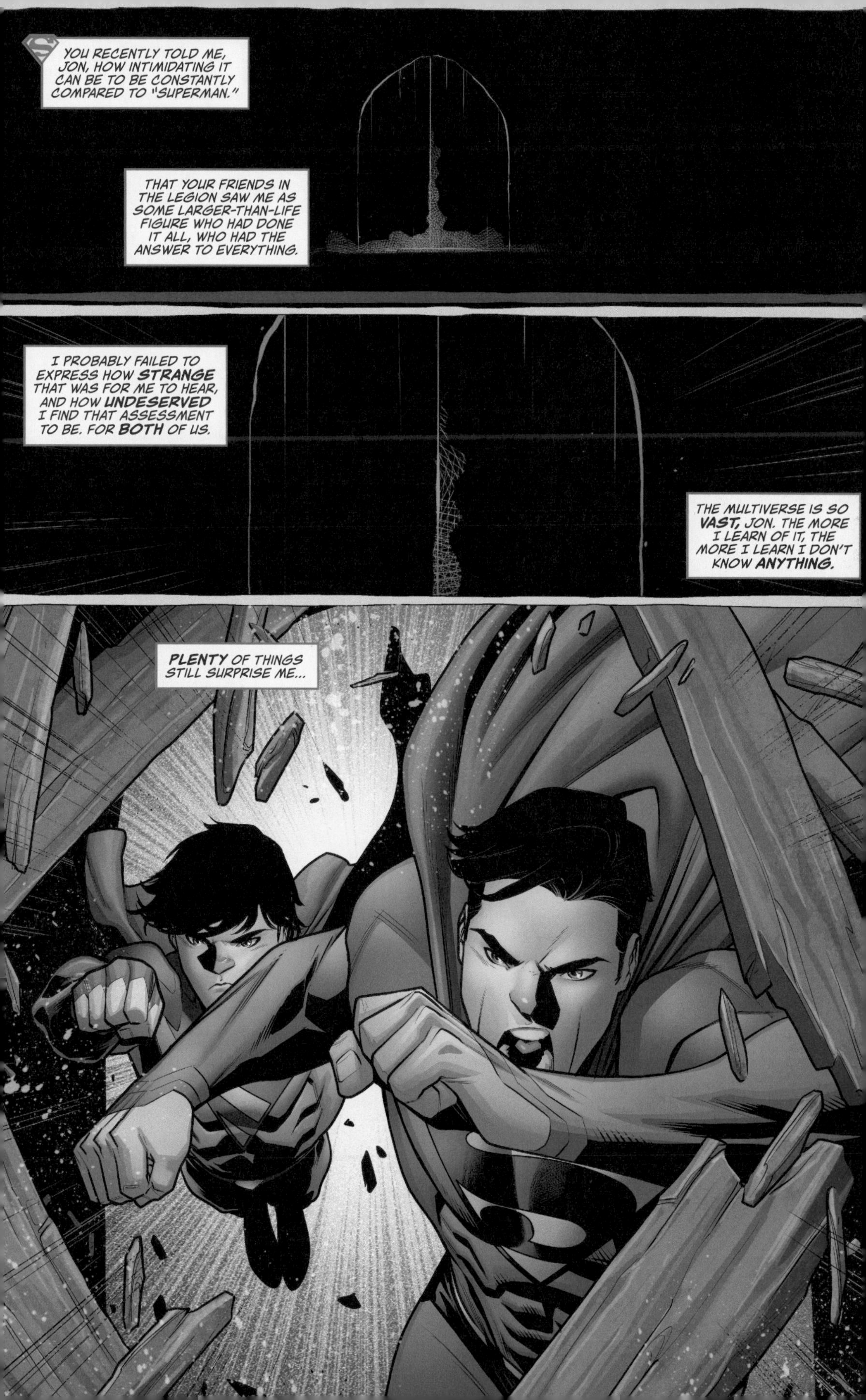
YOU RECENTLY TOLD ME, JON, HOW INTIMIDATING IT CAN BE TO BE CONSTANTLY COMPARED TO "SUPERMAN."
THAT YOUR FRIENDS IN THE LEGION SAW ME AS SOME LARGER-THAN-LIFE FIGURE WHO HAD DONE IT ALL, WHO HAD THE ANSWER TO EVERYTHING.
I PROBABLY FAILED TO EXPRESS HOW STRANGE THAT WAS FOR ME TO HEAR, AND HOW UNDESERVED I FIND THAT ASSESSMENT TO BE. FOR BOTH OF US.
THE MULTIVERSE IS SO VAST, JON. THE MORE I LEARN OF IT, THE MORE I LEARN I DON'T KNOW ANYTHING.
PLENTY OF THINGS STILL SURPRISE ME...

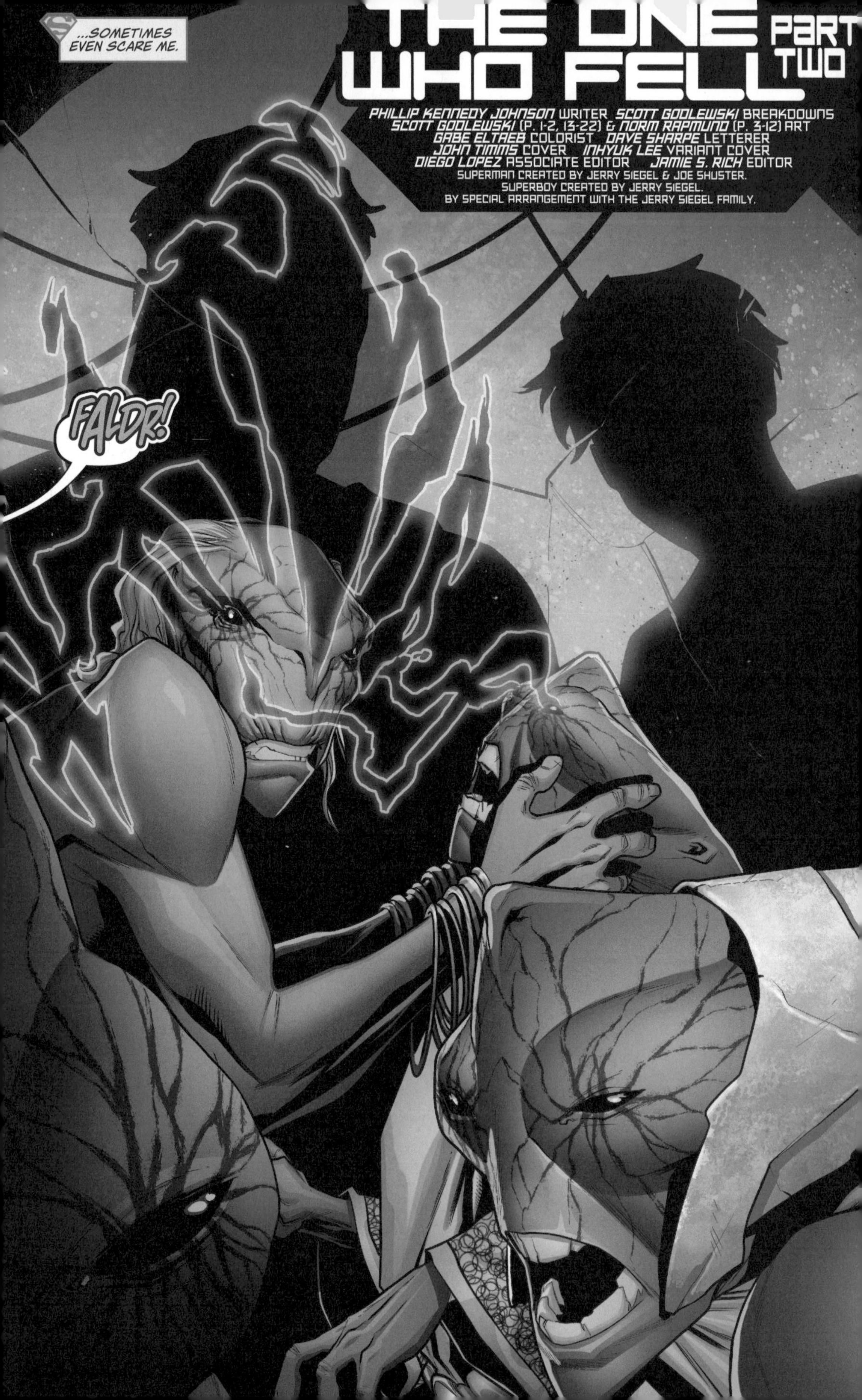

...SOMETIMES EVEN SCARE ME.
THE ONE WHO FELL PART TWO
PHILLIP KENNEDY JOHNSON WRITER SCOTT GODLEWSKI BREAKDOWNS
SCOTT GODLEWSKI (P. 1-2, 13-22) & NORM RAPMUND (P. 3-12) ART
GABE ELTAEB COLORIST DAVE SHARPE LETTERER
JOHN TIMMS COVER INHYUK LEE VARIANT COVER
DIEGO LOPEZ ASSOCIATE EDITOR JAMIE S. RICH EDITOR
SUPERMAN CREATED BY JERRY SIEGEL & JOE SHUSTER.
SUPERBOY CREATED BY JERRY SIEGEL.
BY SPECIAL ARRANGEMENT WITH THE JERRY SIEGEL FAMILY.
FALDR!

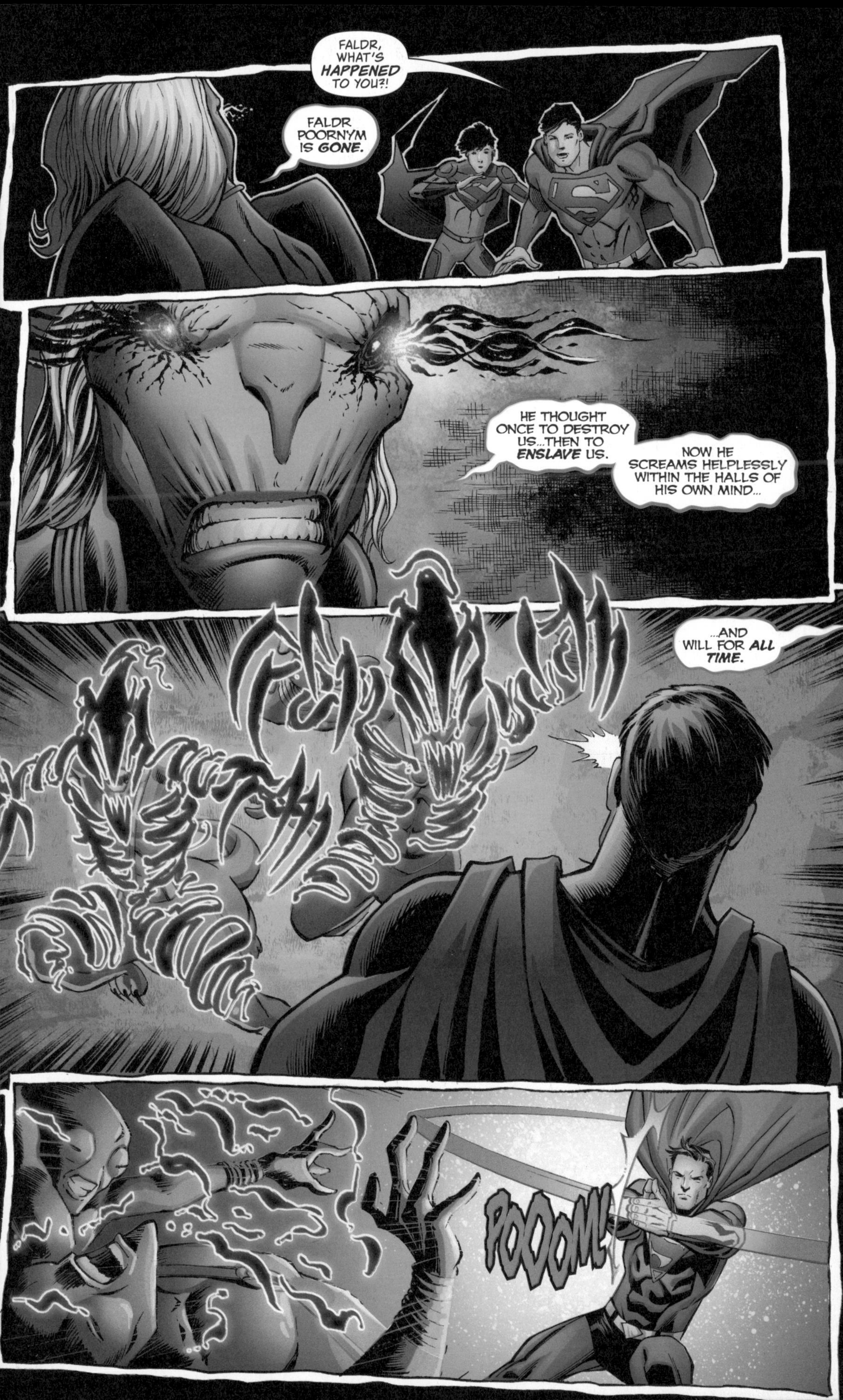
FALDR, WHAT'S HAPPENED TO YOU?!
FALDR POORNYM IS GONE.
HE THOUGHT ONCE TO DESTROY US...THEN TO ENSLAVE US.
NOW HE SCREAMS HELPLESSLY WITHIN THE HALLS OF HIS OWN MIND...
...AND WILL FOR ALL TIME.
POOOM!

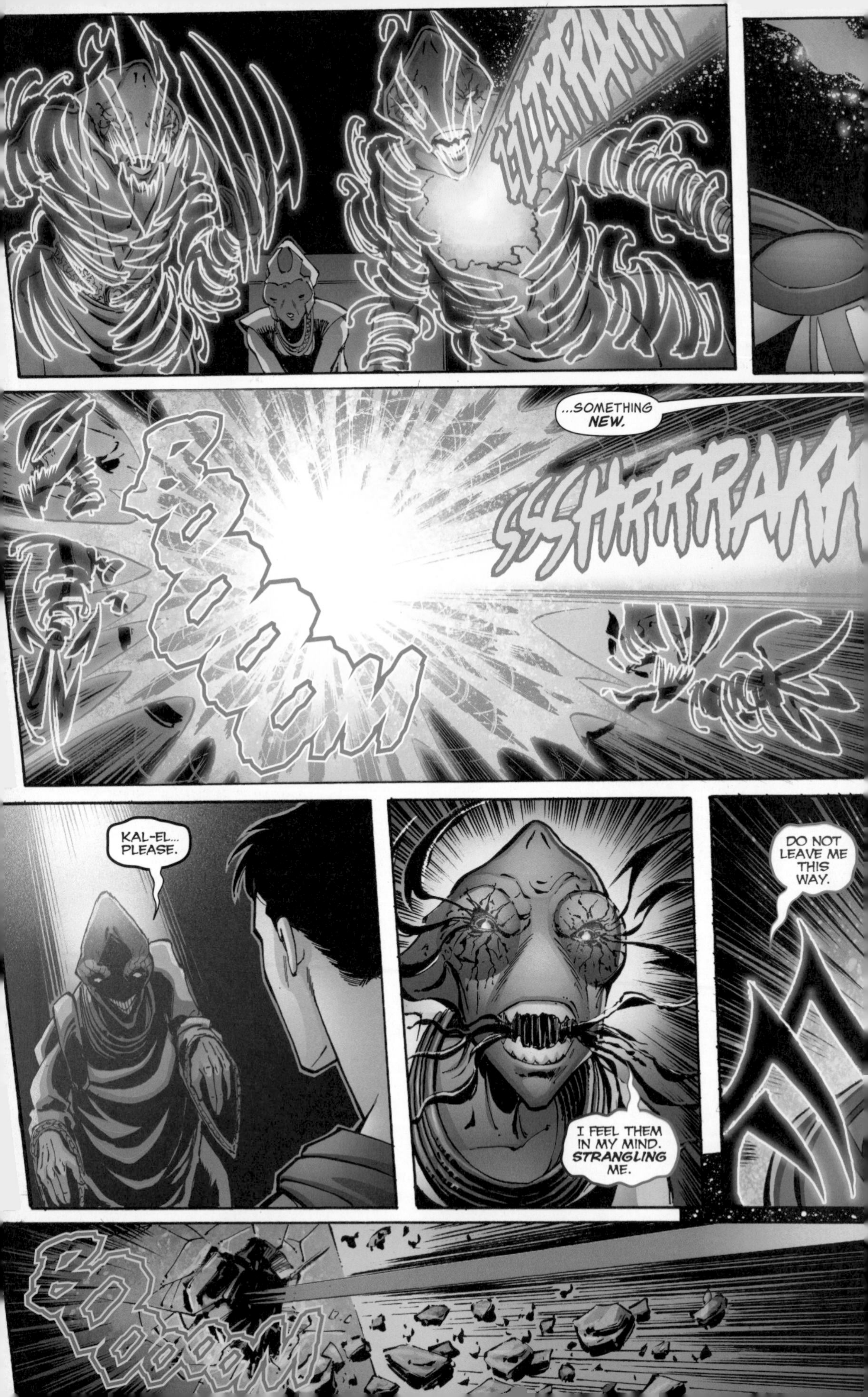
SZZERRAOOM
...SOMETHING NEW.
BOOOM
SSSHRRRAKK
KAL-EL... PLEASE.
I FEEL THEM IN MY MIND. STRANGLING ME.
DO NOT LEAVE ME THIS WAY.
BOOOOOM

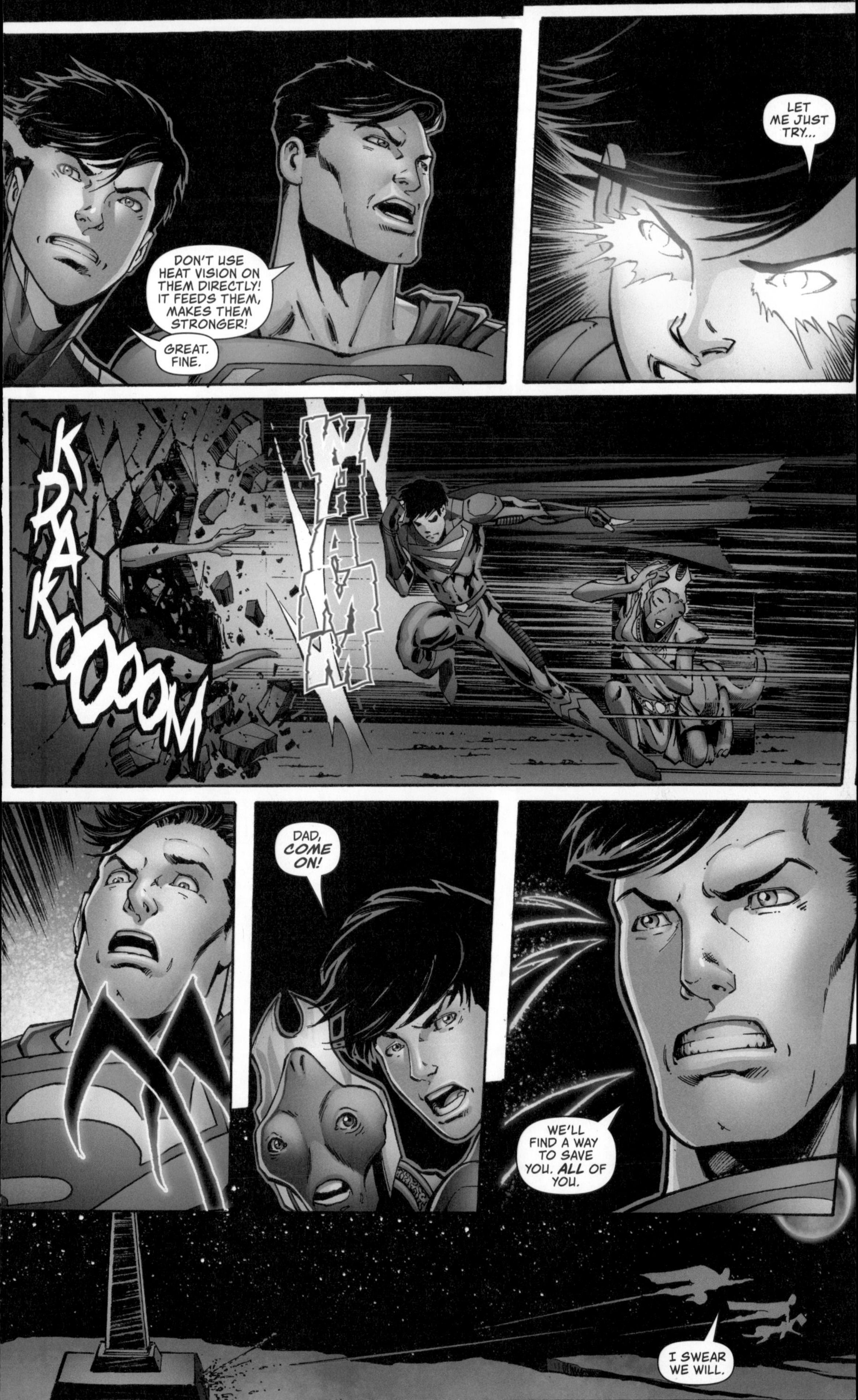
DON'T USE HEAT VISION ON THEM DIRECTLY! IT FEEDS THEM, MAKES THEM STRONGER!
GREAT. FINE.
LET ME JUST TRY...
KRAKOOOOM
DAD, COME ON!
WE'LL FIND A WAY TO SAVE YOU. ALL OF YOU.
I SWEAR WE WILL.

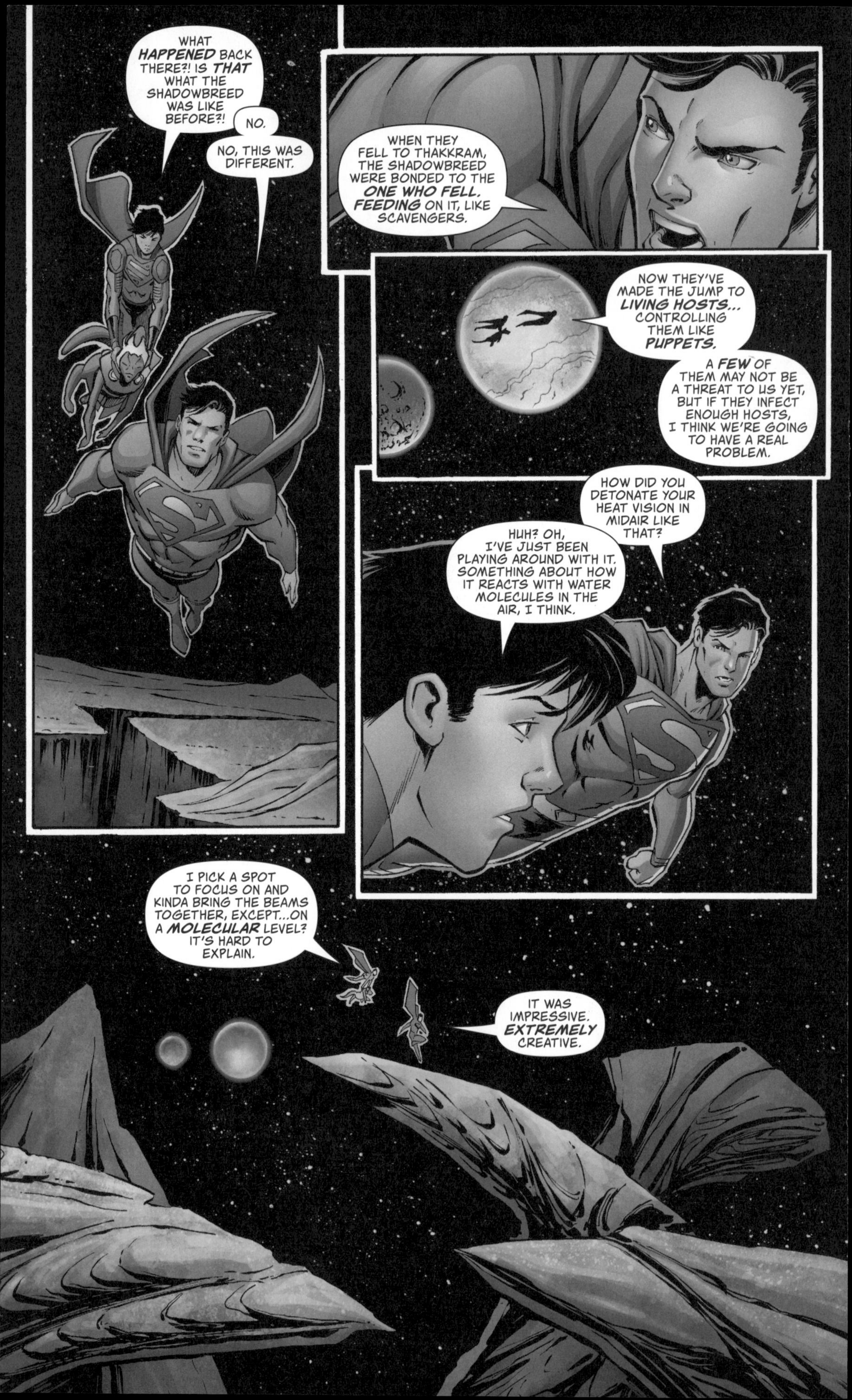
WHAT HAPPENED BACK THERE?! IS THAT WHAT THE SHADOWBREED WAS LIKE BEFORE?!
NO.
NO, THIS WAS DIFFERENT.
WHEN THEY FELL TO THAKKRAM, THE SHADOWBREED WERE BONDED TO THE ONE WHO FELL, FEEDING ON IT, LIKE SCAVENGERS.
NOW THEY'VE MADE THE JUMP TO LIVING HOSTS... CONTROLLING THEM LIKE PUPPETS.
A FEW OF THEM MAY NOT BE A THREAT TO US YET, BUT IF THEY INFECT ENOUGH HOSTS, I THINK WE'RE GOING TO HAVE A REAL PROBLEM.
HOW DID YOU DETONATE YOUR HEAT VISION IN MIDAIR LIKE THAT?
HUH? OH, I'VE JUST BEEN PLAYING AROUND WITH IT. SOMETHING ABOUT HOW IT REACTS WITH WATER MOLECULES IN THE AIR, I THINK.
I PICK A SPOT TO FOCUS ON AND KINDA BRING THE BEAMS TOGETHER, EXCEPT...ON A MOLECULAR LEVEL? IT'S HARD TO EXPLAIN.
IT WAS IMPRESSIVE. EXTREMELY CREATIVE.

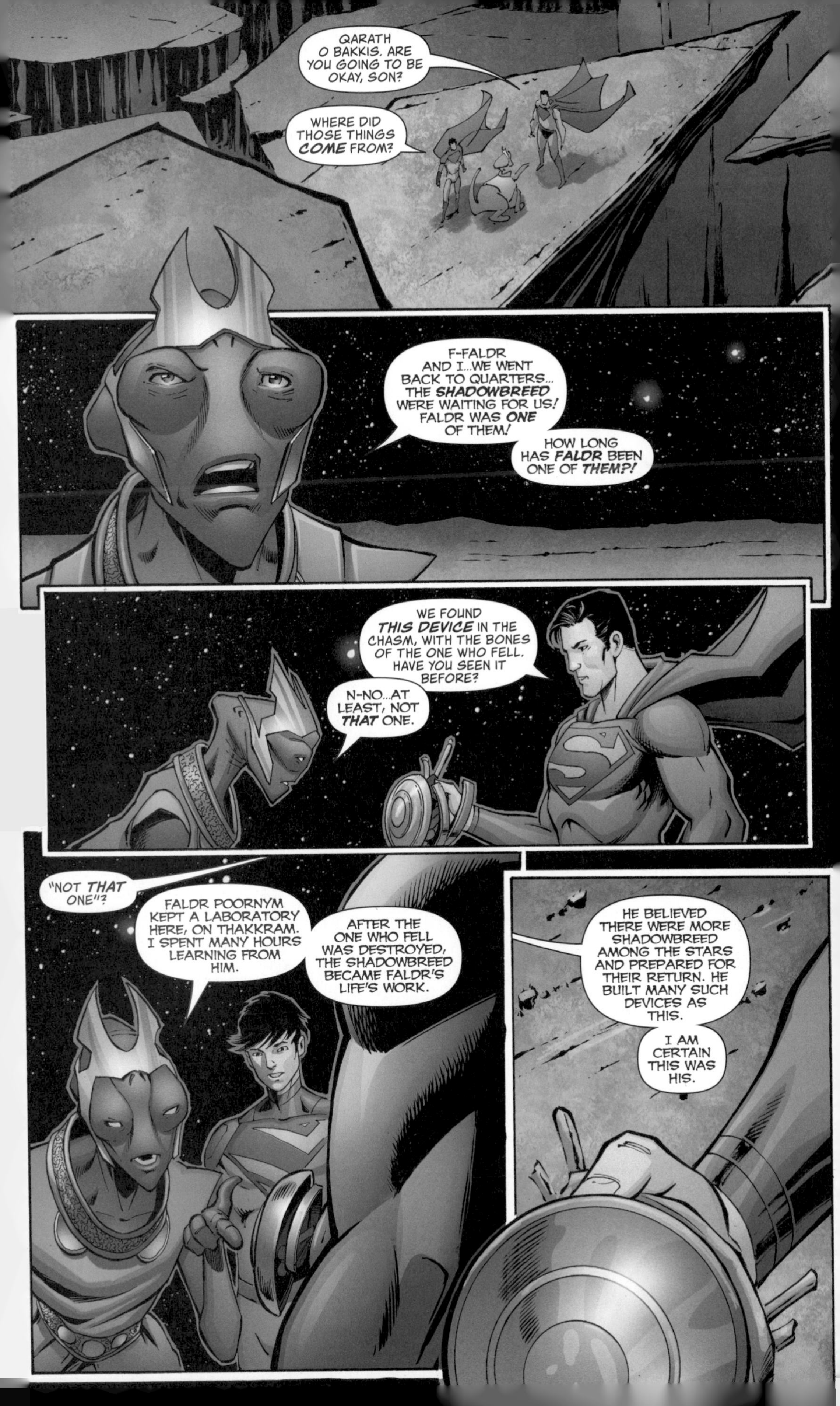

QARATH O BAKKIS. ARE YOU GOING TO BE OKAY, SON?
WHERE DID THOSE THINGS COME FROM?
F-FALDR AND I...WE WENT BACK TO QUARTERS... THE SHADOWBREED WERE WAITING FOR US! FALDR WAS ONE OF THEM!
HOW LONG HAS FALDR BEEN ONE OF THEM?!
WE FOUND THIS DEVICE IN THE CHASM, WITH THE BONES OF THE ONE WHO FELL. HAVE YOU SEEN IT BEFORE?
N-NO...AT LEAST, NOT THAT ONE.
"NOT THAT ONE"?
FALDR POORNYM KEPT A LABORATORY HERE, ON THAKKRAM. I SPENT MANY HOURS LEARNING FROM HIM.
AFTER THE ONE WHO FELL WAS DESTROYED, THE SHADOWBREED BECAME FALDR'S LIFE'S WORK.
HE BELIEVED THERE WERE MORE SHADOWBREED AMONG THE STARS AND PREPARED FOR THEIR RETURN. HE BUILT MANY SUCH DEVICES AS THIS.
I AM CERTAIN THIS WAS HIS.

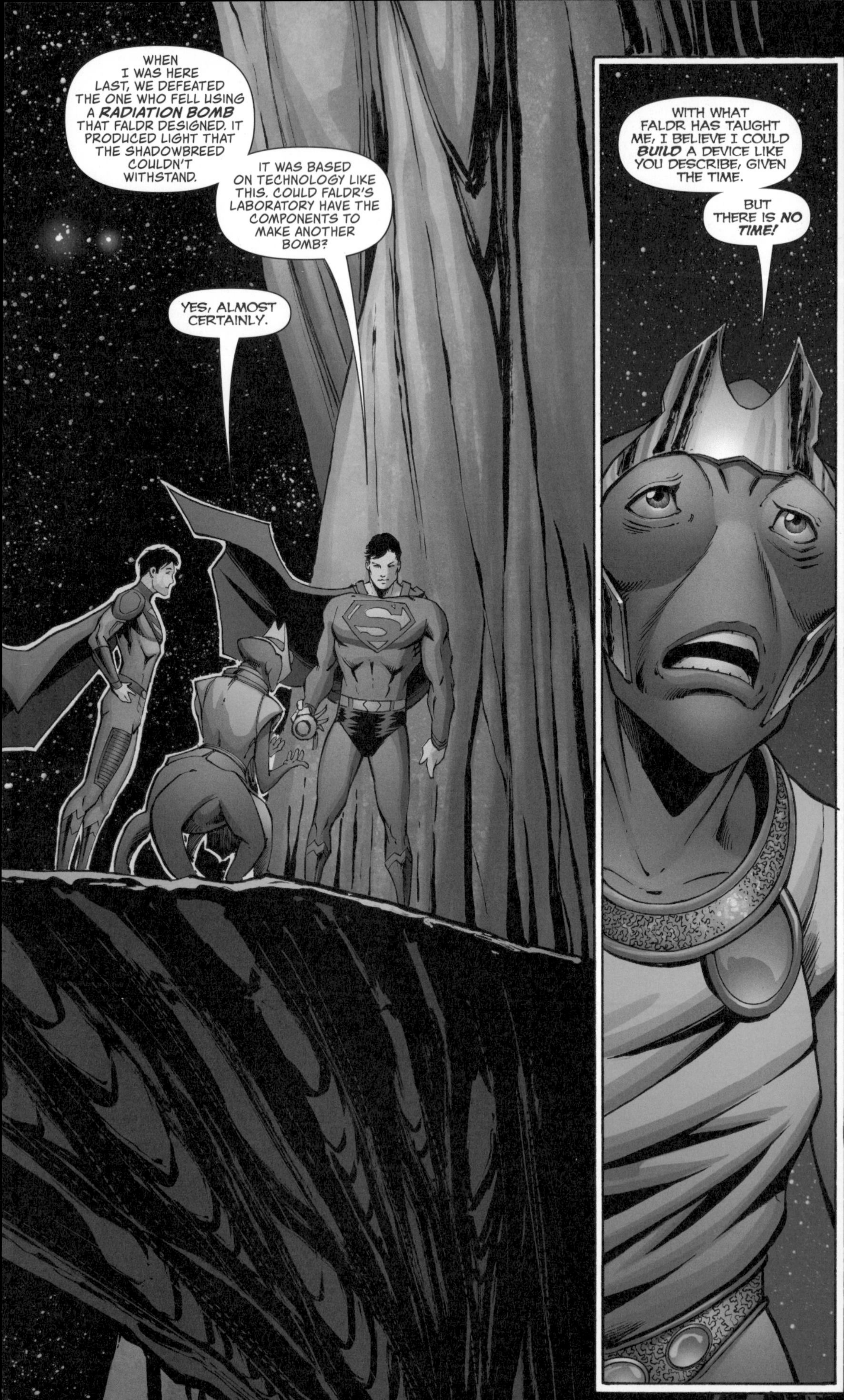
WHEN I WAS HERE LAST, WE DEFEATED THE ONE WHO FELL USING A RADIATION BOMB THAT FALDR DESIGNED. IT PRODUCED LIGHT THAT THE SHADOWBREED COULDN'T WITHSTAND.
IT WAS BASED ON TECHNOLOGY LIKE THIS. COULD FALDR'S LABORATORY HAVE THE COMPONENTS TO MAKE ANOTHER BOMB?
YES, ALMOST CERTAINLY.
WITH WHAT FALDR HAS TAUGHT ME, I BELIEVE I COULD BUILD A DEVICE LIKE YOU DESCRIBE, GIVEN THE TIME.
BUT THERE IS NO TIME!

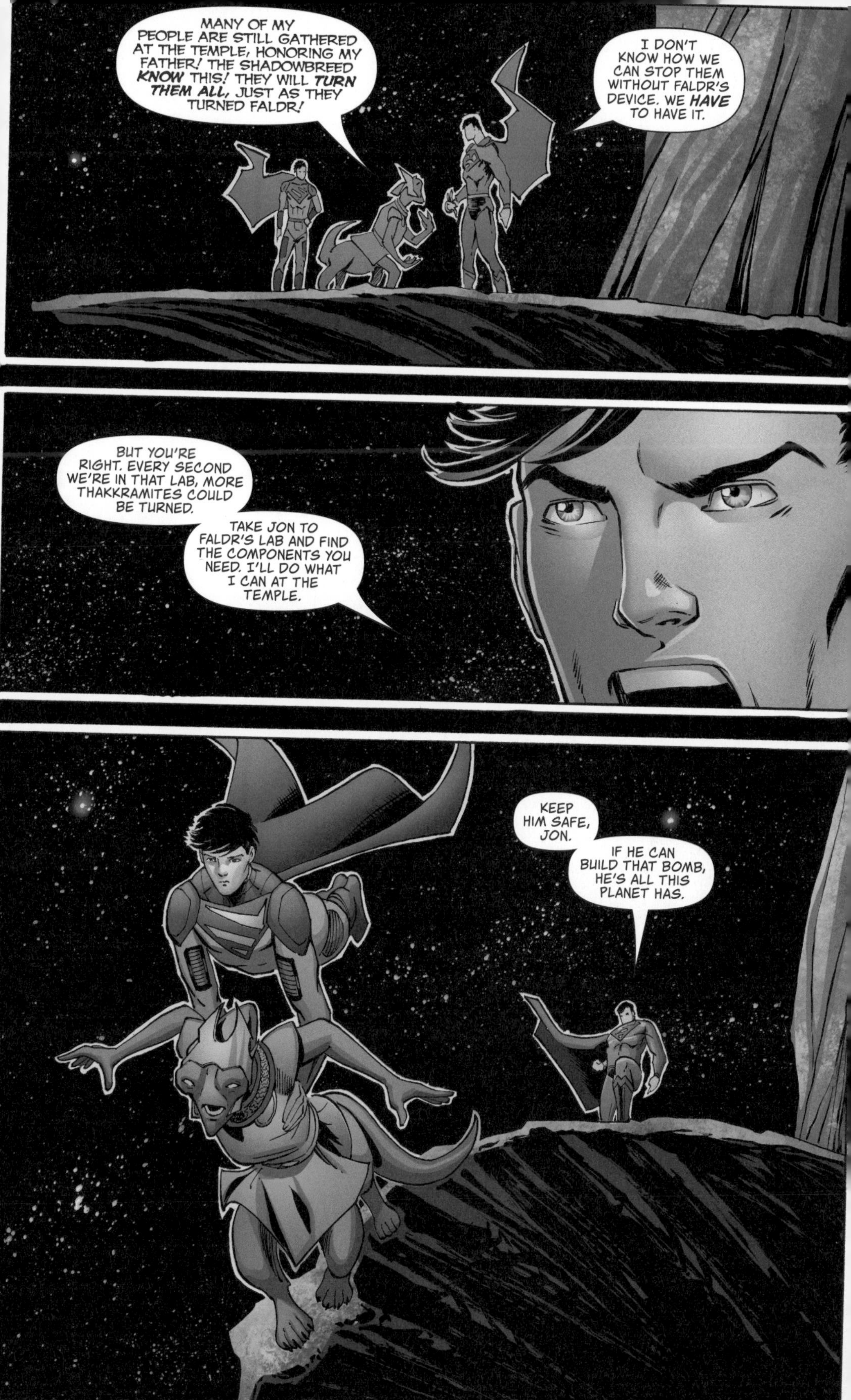
MANY OF MY PEOPLE ARE STILL GATHERED AT THE TEMPLE, HONORING MY FATHER! THE SHADOWBREED KNOW THIS! THEY WILL TURN THEM ALL, JUST AS THEY TURNED FALDR!
I DON'T KNOW HOW WE CAN STOP THEM WITHOUT FALDR'S DEVICE. WE HAVE TO HAVE IT.
BUT YOU'RE RIGHT. EVERY SECOND WE'RE IN THAT LAB, MORE THAKKRAMITES COULD BE TURNED.
TAKE JON TO FALDR'S LAB AND FIND THE COMPONENTS YOU NEED. I'LL DO WHAT I CAN AT THE TEMPLE.
KEEP HIM SAFE, JON.
IF HE CAN BUILD THAT BOMB, HE'S ALL THIS PLANET HAS.

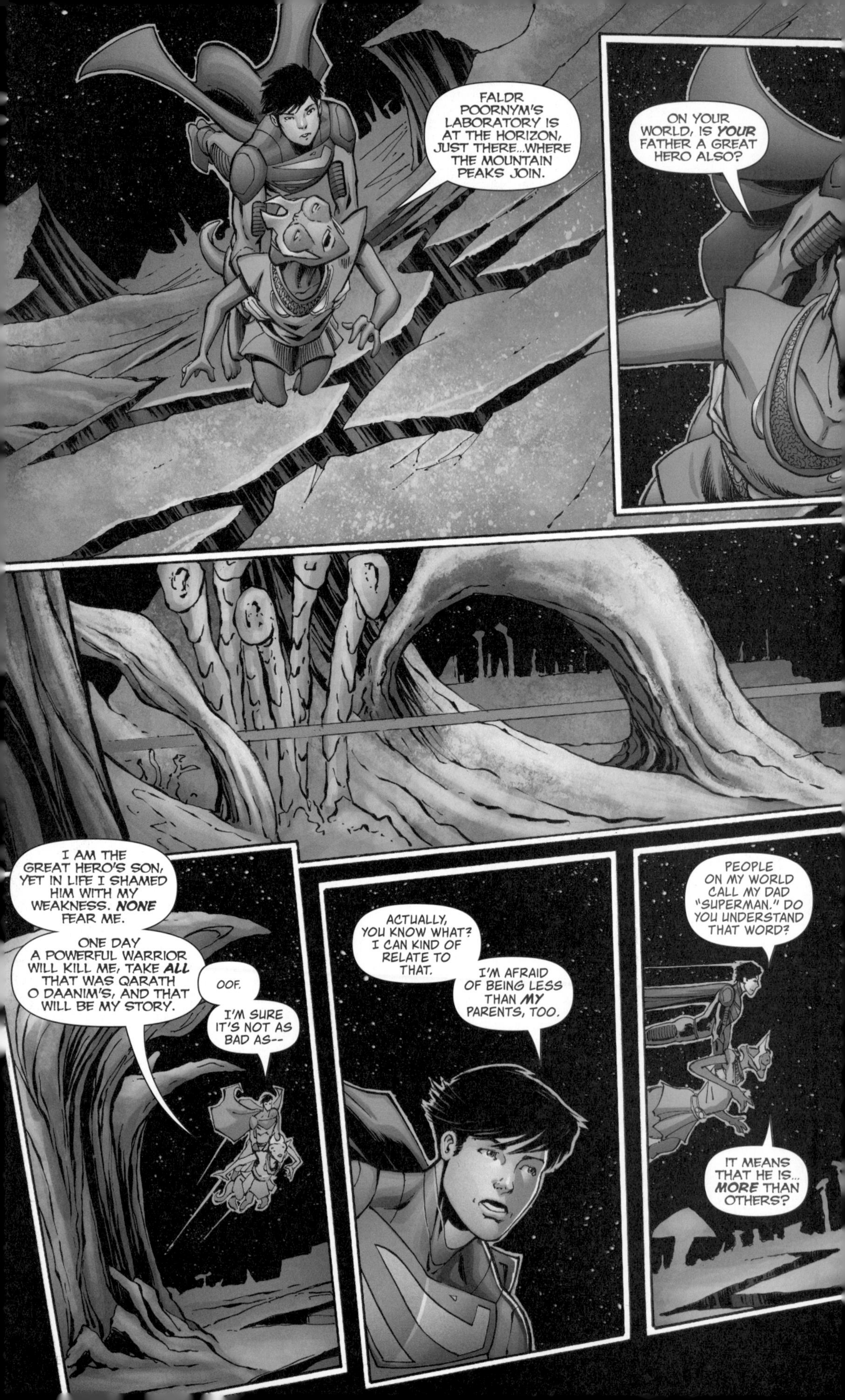
FALDR POORNYM'S LABORATORY IS AT THE HORIZON, JUST THERE...WHERE THE MOUNTAIN PEAKS JOIN.
ON YOUR WORLD, IS YOUR FATHER A GREAT HERO ALSO?
I AM THE GREAT HERO'S SON, YET IN LIFE I SHAMED HIM WITH MY WEAKNESS. NONE FEAR ME.
ONE DAY A POWERFUL WARRIOR WILL KILL ME, TAKE ALL THAT WAS QARATH O DAANIM'S, AND THAT WILL BE MY STORY.
OOF.
I'M SURE IT'S NOT AS BAD AS--
ACTUALLY, YOU KNOW WHAT? I CAN KIND OF RELATE TO THAT.
I'M AFRAID OF BEING LESS THAN MY PARENTS, TOO.
PEOPLE ON MY WORLD CALL MY DAD "SUPERMAN." DO YOU UNDERSTAND THAT WORD?
IT MEANS THAT HE IS... MORE THAN OTHERS?

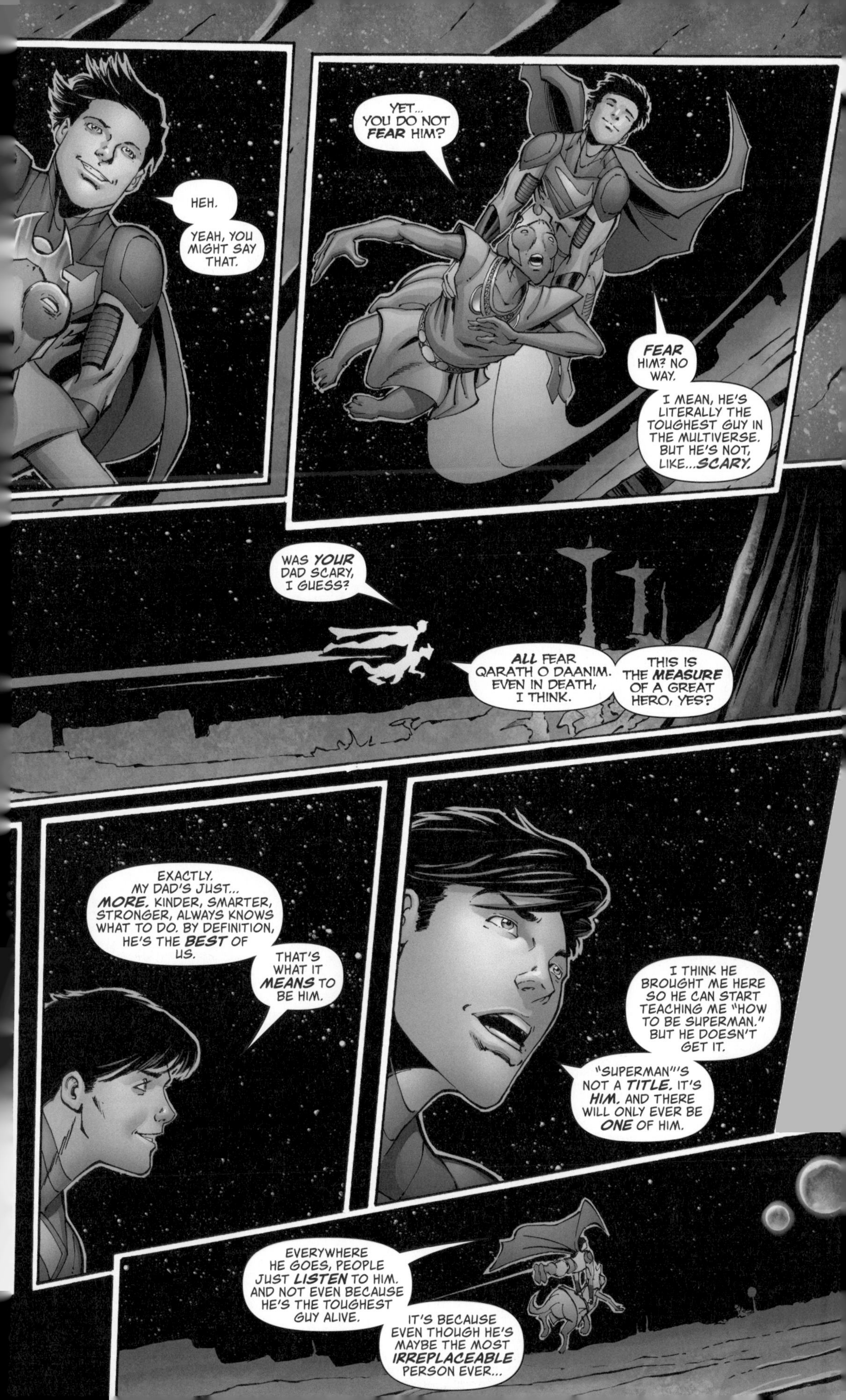
HEH.
YEAH, YOU MIGHT SAY THAT.
YET... YOU DO NOT FEAR HIM?
FEAR HIM? NO WAY.
I MEAN, HE'S LITERALLY THE TOUGHEST GUY IN THE MULTIVERSE. BUT HE'S NOT, LIKE...SCARY.
WAS YOUR DAD SCARY, I GUESS?
ALL FEAR QARATH O DAANIM. EVEN IN DEATH, I THINK.
THIS IS THE MEASURE OF A GREAT HERO, YES?
EXACTLY. MY DAD'S JUST... MORE. KINDER, SMARTER, STRONGER, ALWAYS KNOWS WHAT TO DO. BY DEFINITION, HE'S THE BEST OF US.
THAT'S WHAT IT MEANS TO BE HIM.
I THINK HE BROUGHT ME HERE SO HE CAN START TEACHING ME "HOW TO BE SUPERMAN." BUT HE DOESN'T GET IT.
"SUPERMAN"'S NOT A TITLE. IT'S HIM. AND THERE WILL ONLY EVER BE ONE OF HIM.
EVERYWHERE HE GOES, PEOPLE JUST LISTEN TO HIM. AND NOT EVEN BECAUSE HE'S THE TOUGHEST GUY ALIVE.
IT'S BECAUSE EVEN THOUGH HE'S MAYBE THE MOST IRREPLACEABLE PERSON EVER...

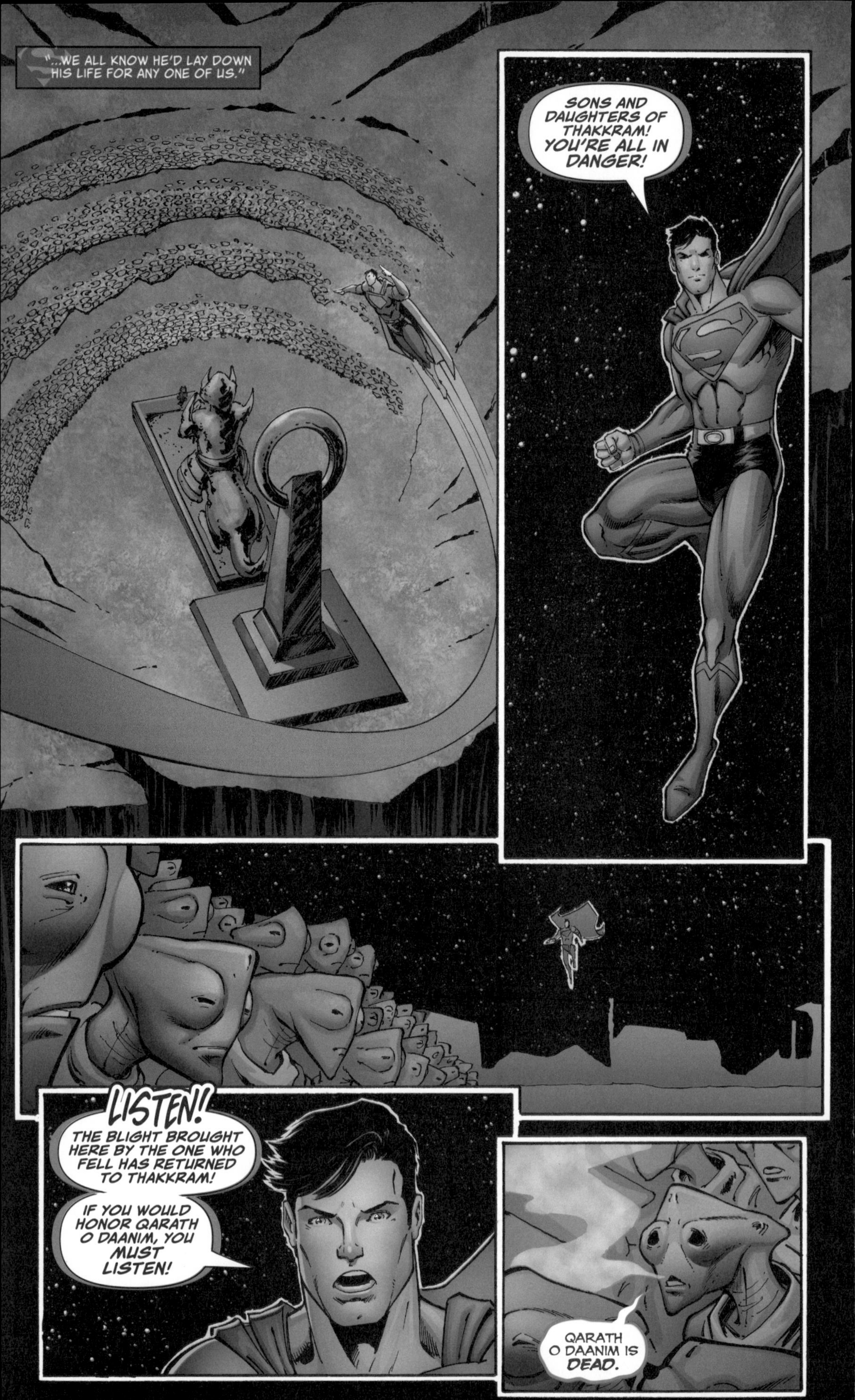
"...WE ALL KNOW HE'D LAY DOWN HIS LIFE FOR ANY ONE OF US."
SONS AND DAUGHTERS OF THAKKRAM! YOU'RE ALL IN DANGER!
LISTEN!
THE BLIGHT BROUGHT HERE BY THE ONE WHO FELL HAS RETURNED TO THAKKRAM!
IF YOU WOULD HONOR QARATH O DAANIM, YOU MUST LISTEN!
QARATH O DAANIM IS DEAD.

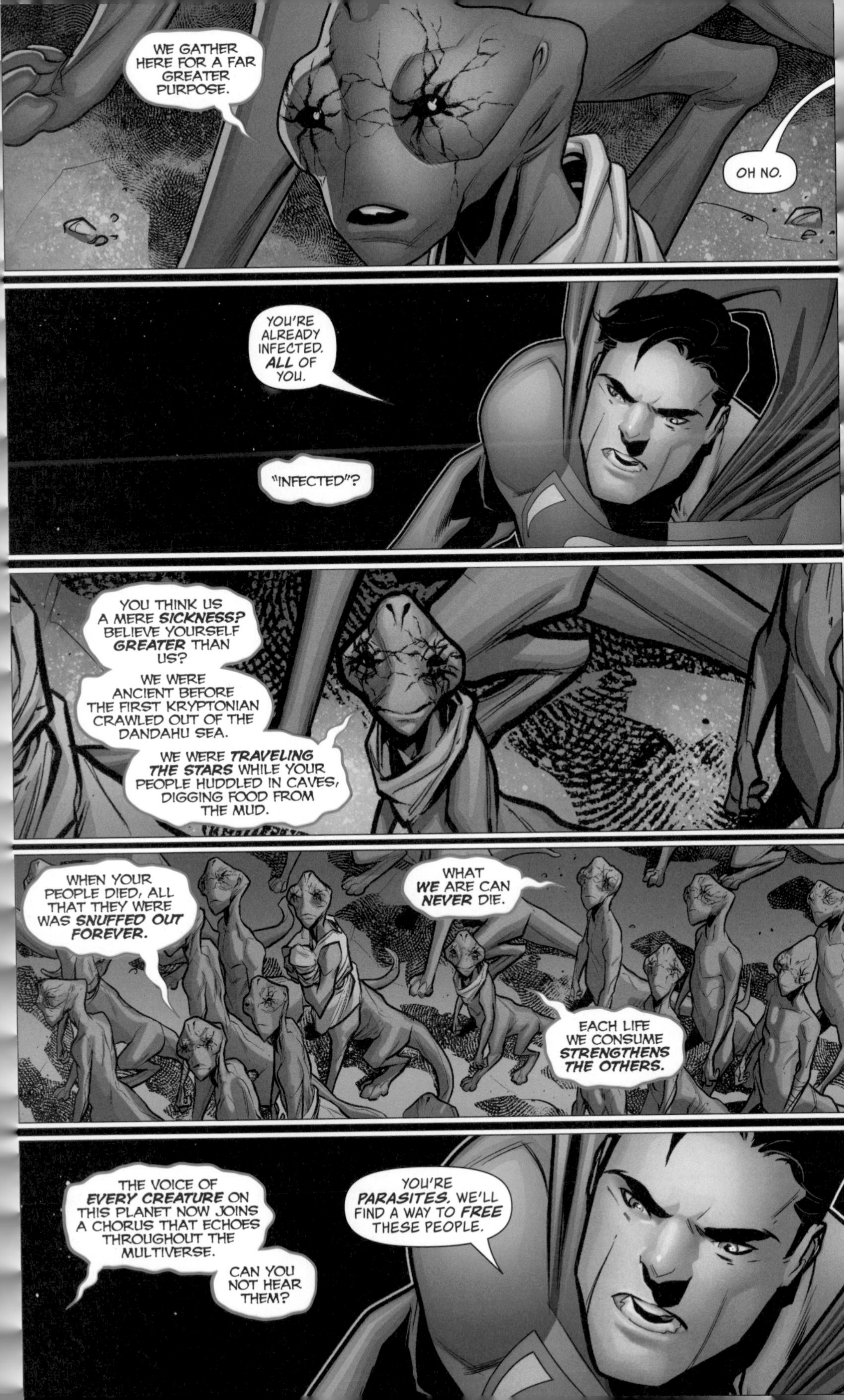
WE GATHER HERE FOR A FAR GREATER PURPOSE.
OH NO.
YOU'RE ALREADY INFECTED. ALL OF YOU.
"INFECTED"?
YOU THINK US A MERE SICKNESS? BELIEVE YOURSELF GREATER THAN US?
WE WERE ANCIENT BEFORE THE FIRST KRYPTONIAN CRAWLED OUT OF THE DANDAHU SEA.
WE WERE TRAVELING THE STARS WHILE YOUR PEOPLE HUDDLED IN CAVES, DIGGING FOOD FROM THE MUD.
WHEN YOUR PEOPLE DIED, ALL THAT THEY WERE WAS SNUFFED OUT FOREVER.
WHAT WE ARE CAN NEVER DIE.
EACH LIFE WE CONSUME STRENGTHENS THE OTHERS.
THE VOICE OF EVERY CREATURE ON THIS PLANET NOW JOINS A CHORUS THAT ECHOES THROUGHOUT THE MULTIVERSE.
CAN YOU NOT HEAR THEM?
YOU'RE PARASITES. WE'LL FIND A WAY TO FREE THESE PEOPLE.

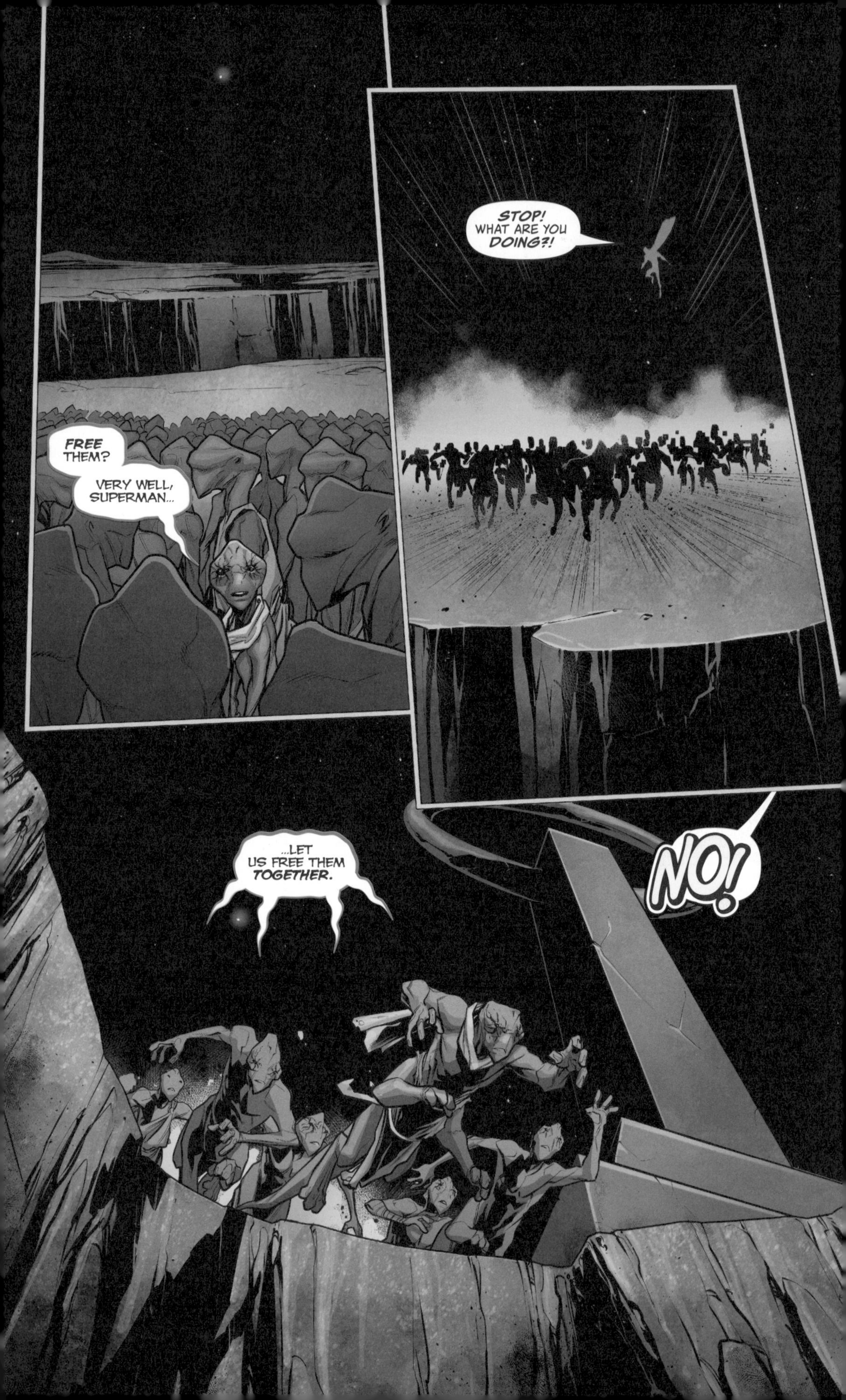

FREE THEM?
VERY WELL, SUPERMAN...
STOP! WHAT ARE YOU DOING?!
...LET US FREE THEM TOGETHER.
NO!

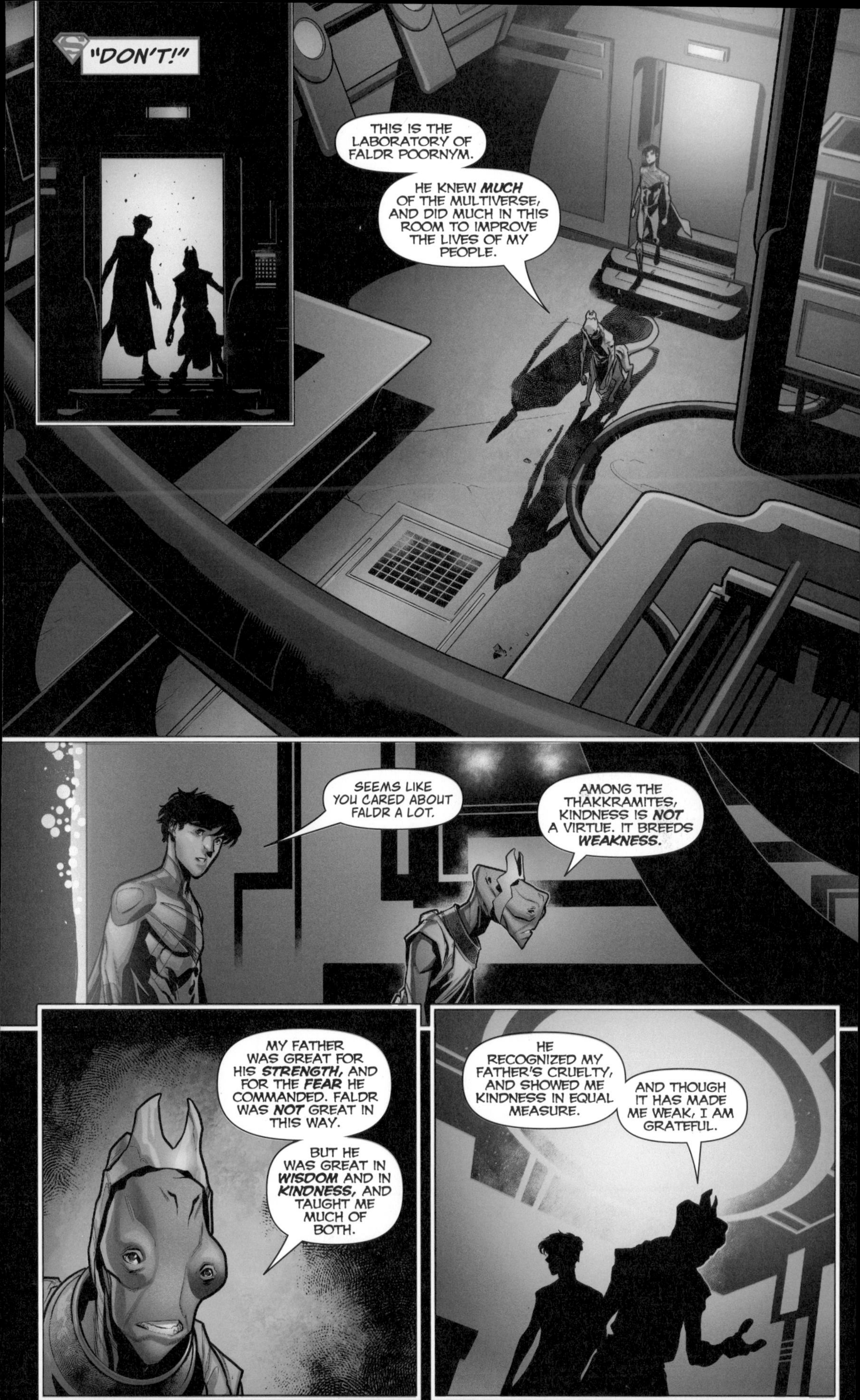
"DON'T!"
THIS IS THE LABORATORY OF FALDR POORNYM.
HE KNEW *MUCH* OF THE MULTIVERSE, AND DID MUCH IN THIS ROOM TO IMPROVE THE LIVES OF MY PEOPLE.
SEEMS LIKE YOU CARED ABOUT FALDR A LOT.
AMONG THE THAKKRAMITES, KINDNESS IS *NOT* A VIRTUE. IT BREEDS *WEAKNESS.*
MY FATHER WAS GREAT FOR HIS *STRENGTH,* AND FOR THE *FEAR* HE COMMANDED. FALDR WAS *NOT* GREAT IN THIS WAY.
BUT HE WAS GREAT IN *WISDOM* AND IN *KINDNESS,* AND TAUGHT ME MUCH OF BOTH.
HE RECOGNIZED MY FATHER'S CRUELTY, AND SHOWED ME KINDNESS IN EQUAL MEASURE.
AND THOUGH IT HAS MADE ME WEAK, I AM GRATEFUL.

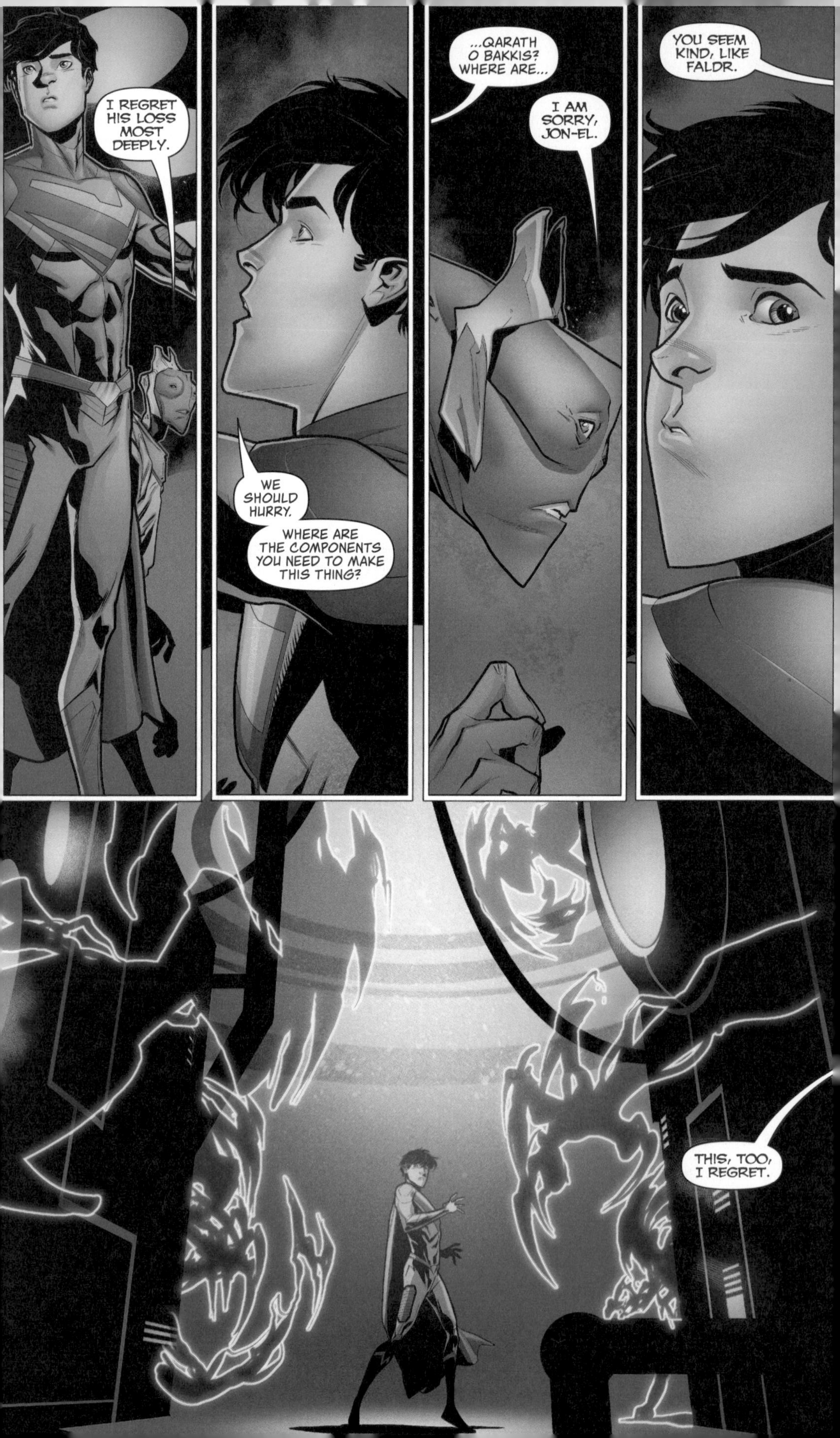
I REGRET HIS LOSS MOST DEEPLY.
WE SHOULD HURRY.
WHERE ARE THE COMPONENTS YOU NEED TO MAKE THIS THING?
...QARATH O BAKKIS? WHERE ARE...
I AM SORRY, JON-EL.
YOU SEEM KIND, LIKE FALDR.
THIS, TOO, I REGRET.

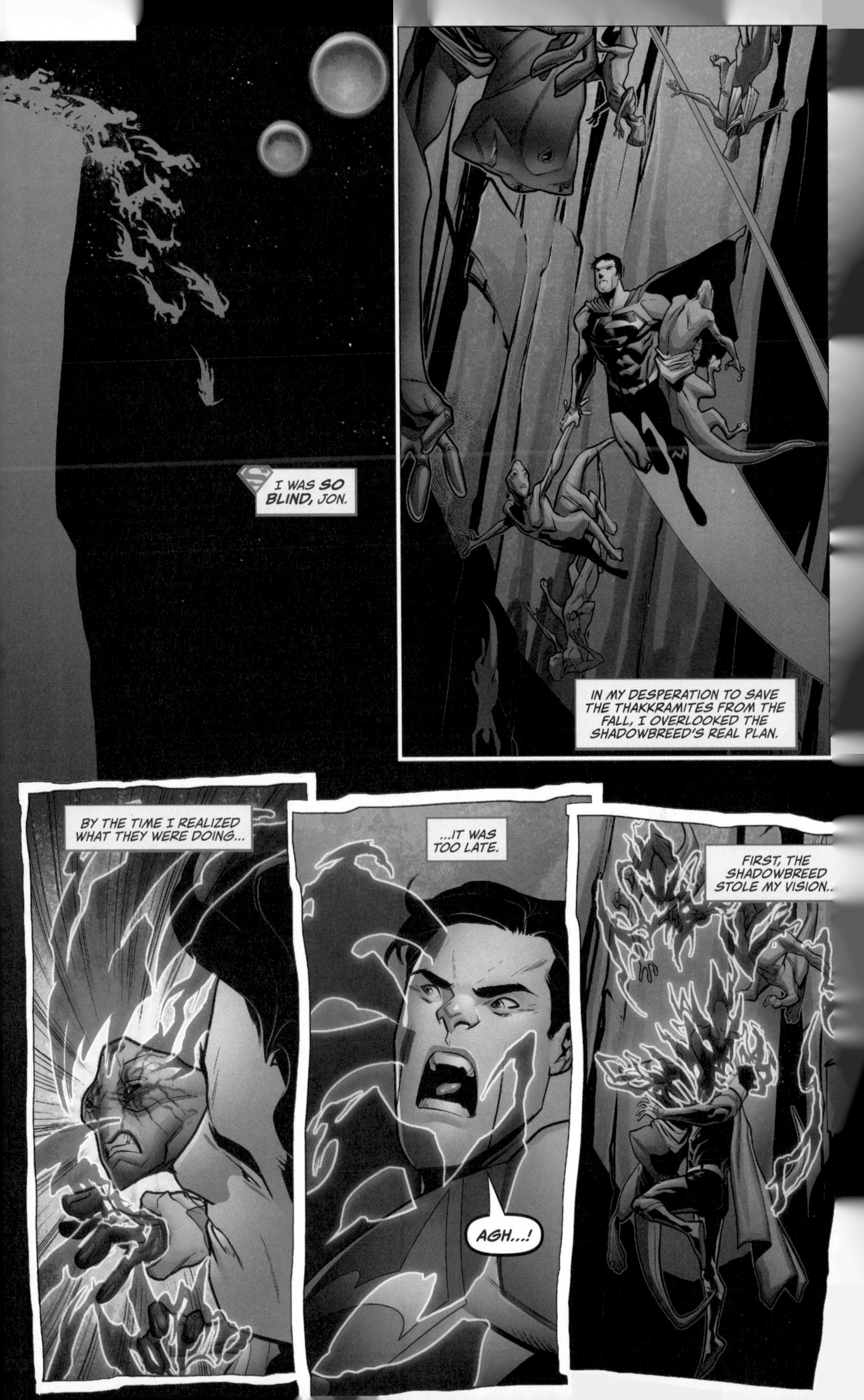

I WAS SO BLIND, JON.
IN MY DESPERATION TO SAVE THE THAKKRAMITES FROM THE FALL, I OVERLOOKED THE SHADOWBREED'S REAL PLAN.
BY THE TIME I REALIZED WHAT THEY WERE DOING...
...IT WAS TOO LATE.
AGH...!
FIRST, THE SHADOWBREED STOLE MY VISION...

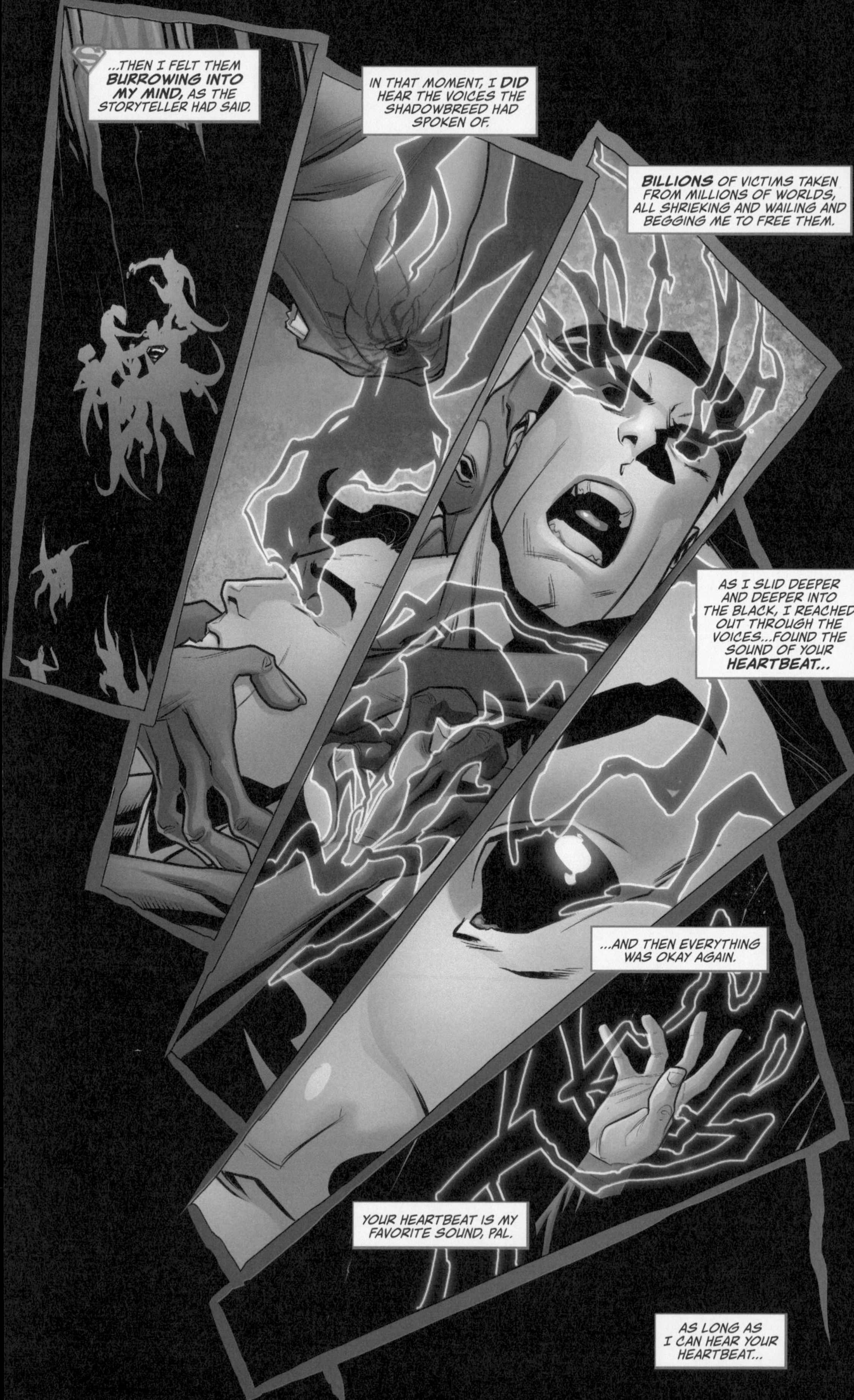
...THEN I FELT THEM BURROWING INTO MY MIND, AS THE STORYTELLER HAD SAID.
IN THAT MOMENT, I DID HEAR THE VOICES THE SHADOWBREED HAD SPOKEN OF.
BILLIONS OF VICTIMS TAKEN FROM MILLIONS OF WORLDS, ALL SHRIEKING AND WAILING AND BEGGING ME TO FREE THEM.
AS I SLID DEEPER AND DEEPER INTO THE BLACK, I REACHED OUT THROUGH THE VOICES...FOUND THE SOUND OF YOUR HEARTBEAT...
...AND THEN EVERYTHING WAS OKAY AGAIN.
YOUR HEARTBEAT IS MY FAVORITE SOUND, PAL.
AS LONG AS I CAN HEAR YOUR HEARTBEAT...

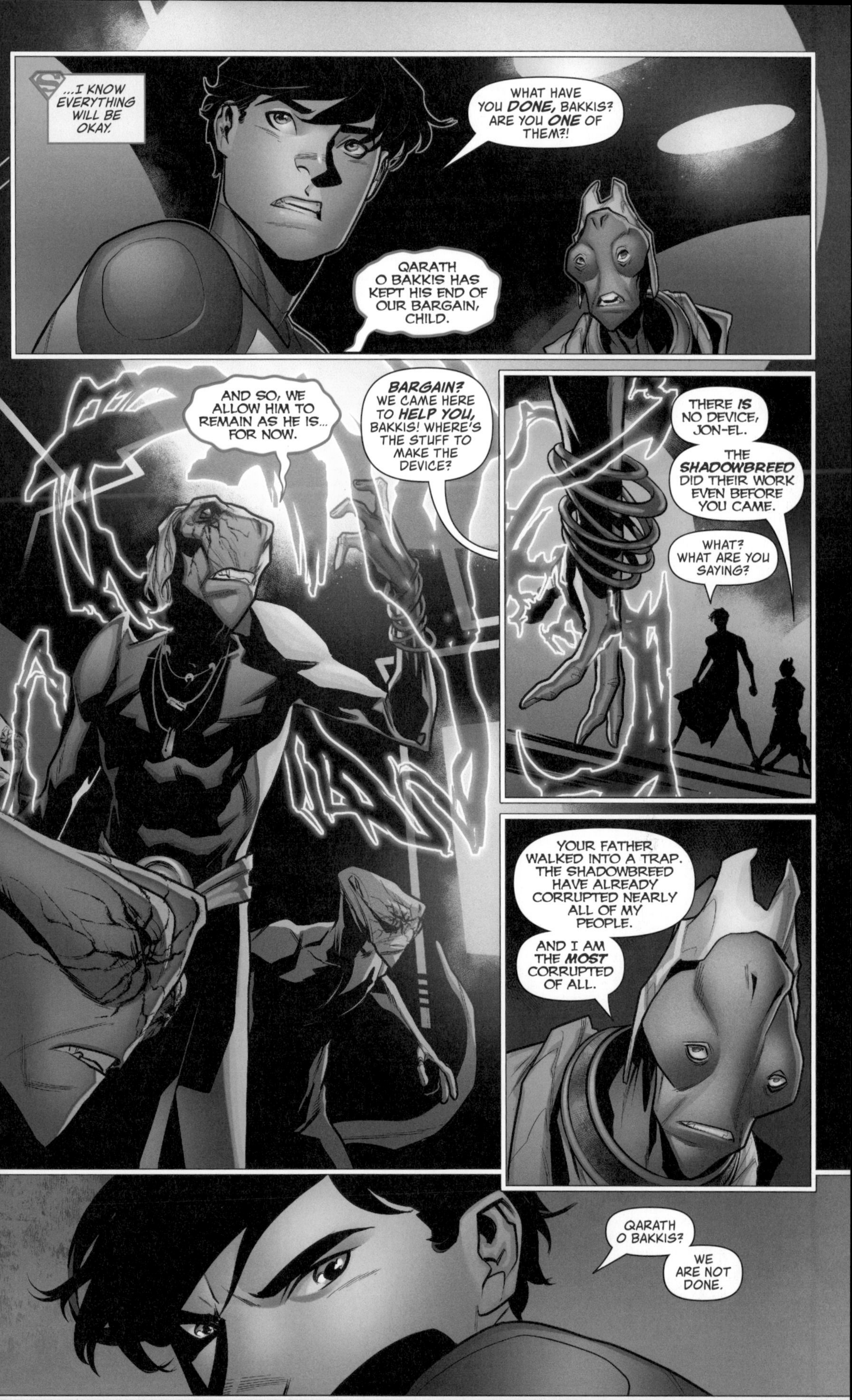

...I KNOW EVERYTHING WILL BE OKAY.
WHAT HAVE YOU **DONE,** BAKKIS? ARE YOU **ONE** OF THEM?!
QARATH O BAKKIS HAS KEPT HIS END OF OUR BARGAIN, CHILD.
AND SO, WE ALLOW HIM TO REMAIN AS HE IS... FOR NOW.
BARGAIN? WE CAME HERE TO **HELP YOU,** BAKKIS! WHERE'S THE STUFF TO MAKE THE DEVICE?
THERE **IS** NO DEVICE, JON-EL.
THE **SHADOWBREED** DID THEIR WORK EVEN BEFORE YOU CAME.
WHAT? WHAT ARE YOU SAYING?
YOUR FATHER WALKED INTO A TRAP. THE SHADOWBREED HAVE ALREADY CORRUPTED NEARLY ALL OF MY PEOPLE.
AND I AM THE **MOST** CORRUPTED OF ALL.
QARATH O BAKKIS?
WE ARE NOT DONE.

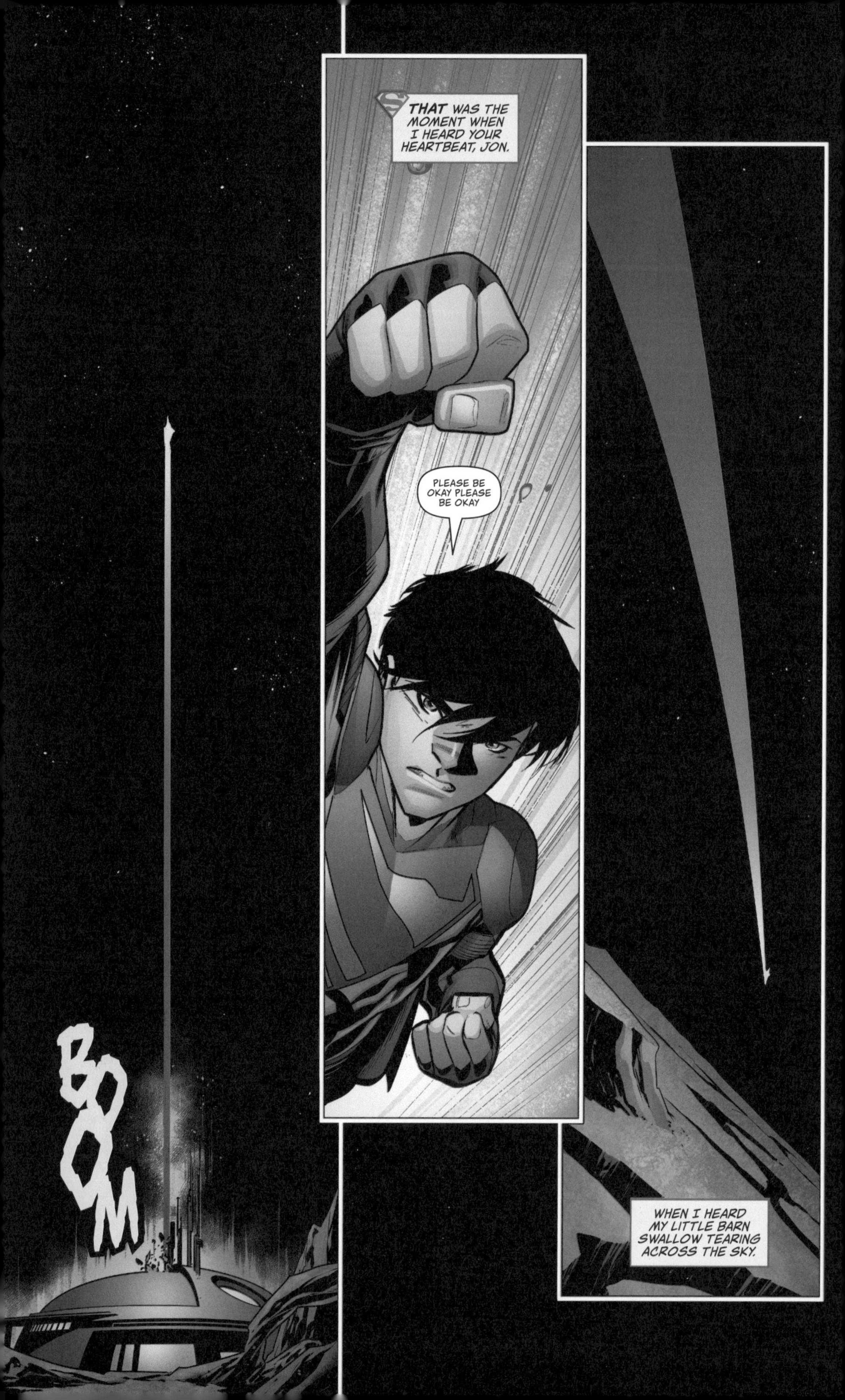
BOOM
THAT WAS THE MOMENT WHEN I HEARD YOUR HEARTBEAT, JON.
PLEASE BE OKAY PLEASE BE OKAY
WHEN I HEARD MY LITTLE BARN SWALLOW TEARING ACROSS THE SKY.

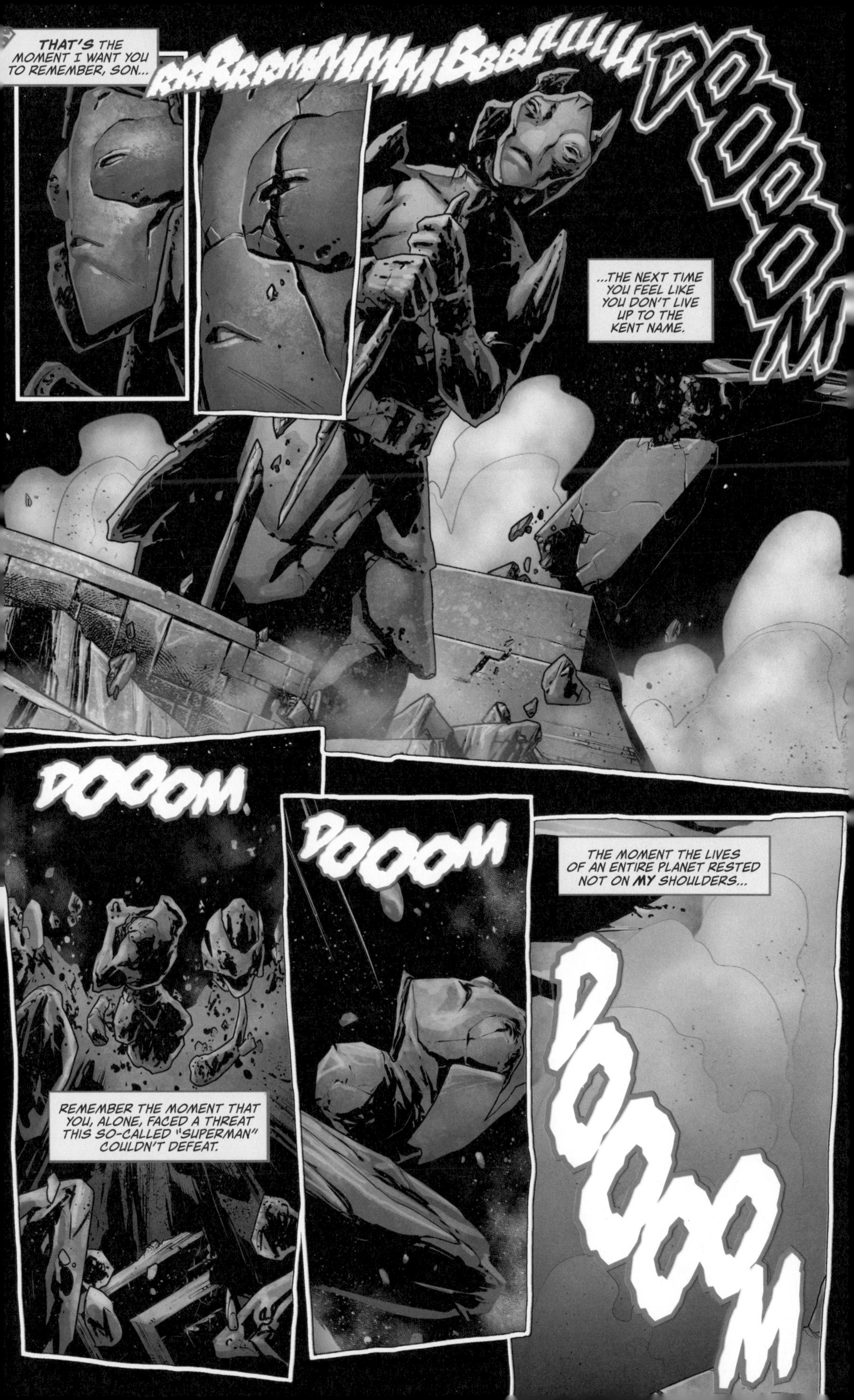
THAT'S THE MOMENT I WANT YOU TO REMEMBER, SON...
RRRRRRMMMMMBBBLLLLL
DOOOOOM
...THE NEXT TIME YOU FEEL LIKE YOU DON'T LIVE UP TO THE KENT NAME.
DOOOM.
REMEMBER THE MOMENT THAT YOU, ALONE, FACED A THREAT THIS SO-CALLED "SUPERMAN" COULDN'T DEFEAT.
DOOOM
THE MOMENT THE LIVES OF AN ENTIRE PLANET RESTED NOT ON MY SHOULDERS...
DOOOOOM

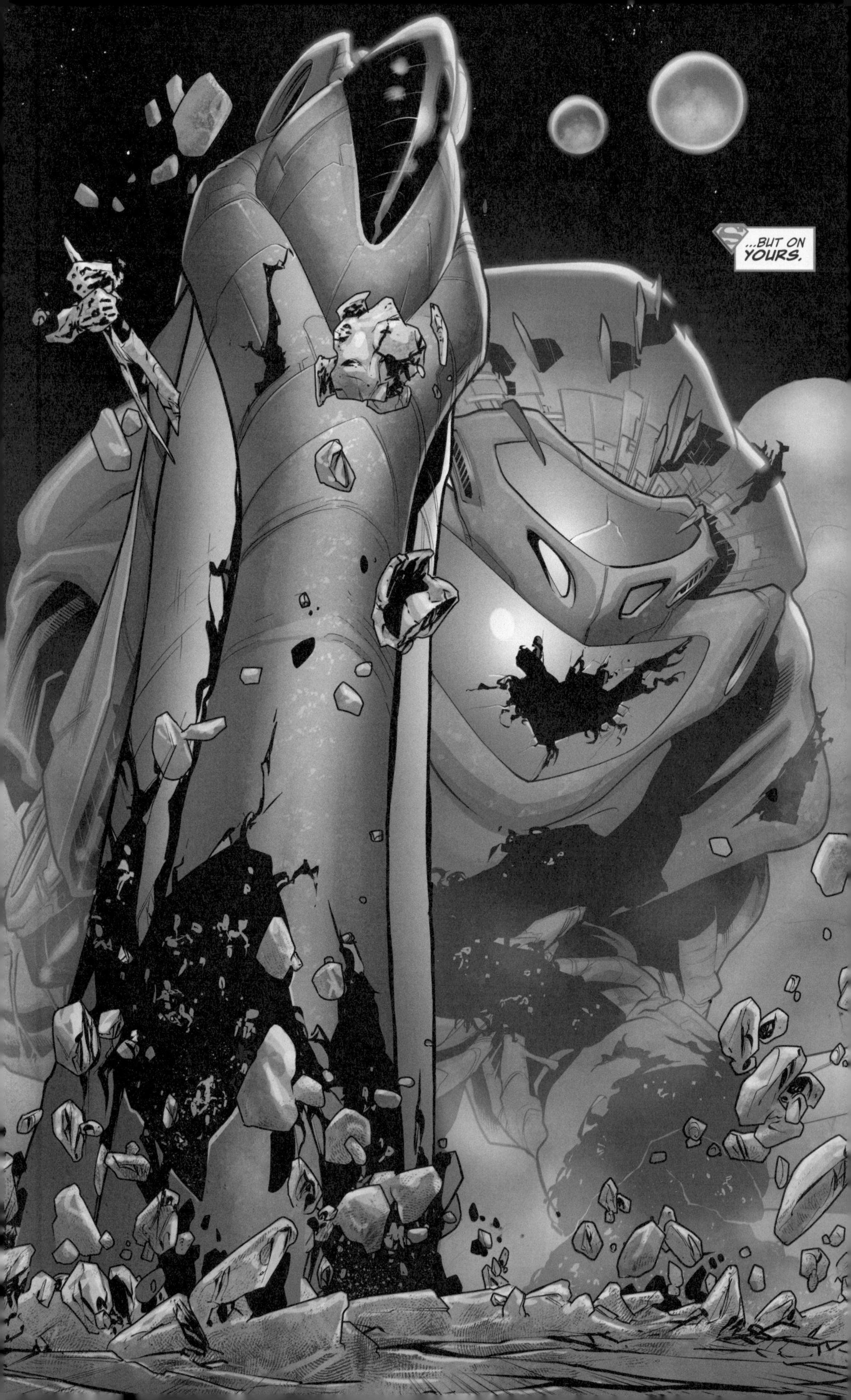
...BUT ON
YOURS.

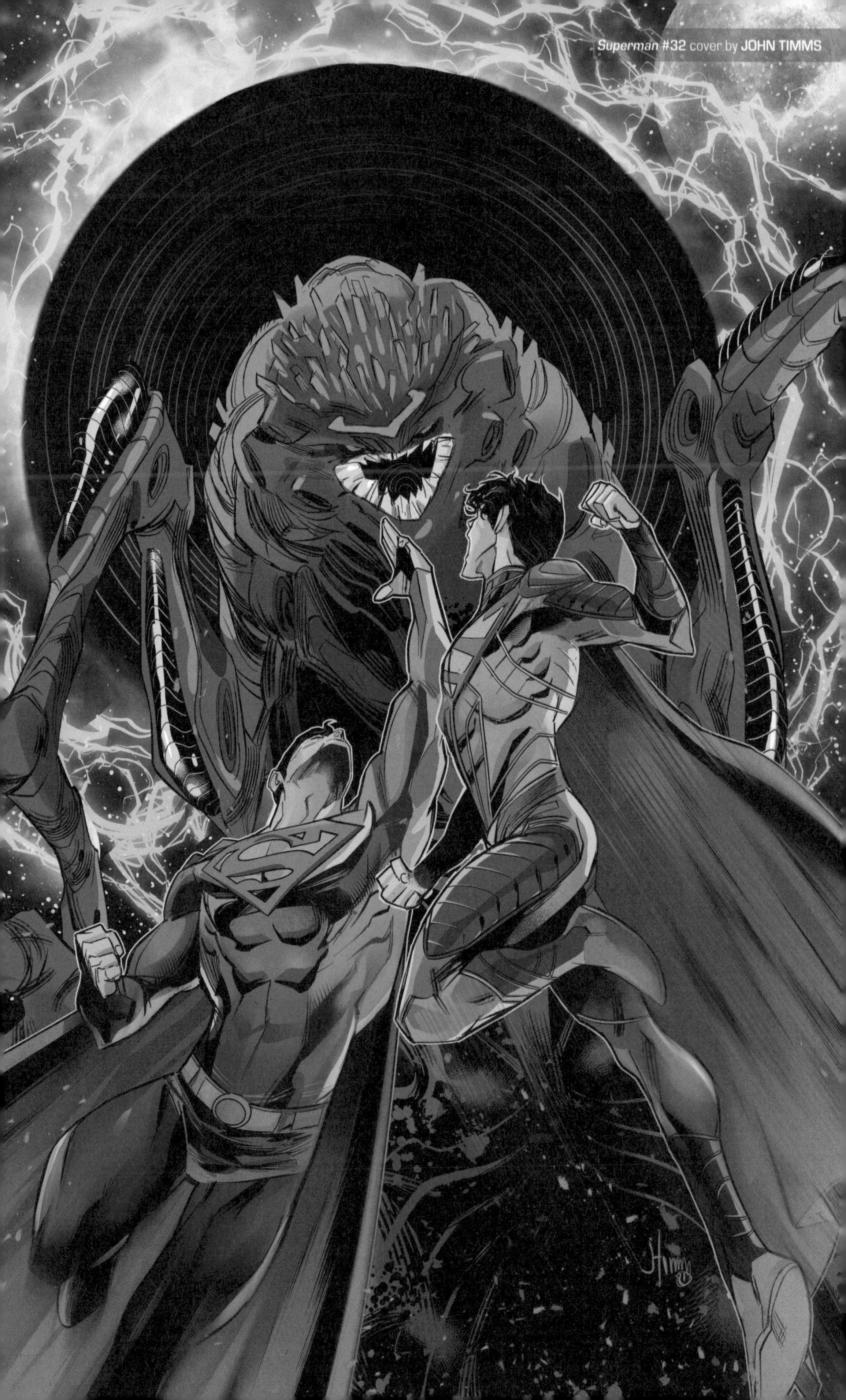

Superman #32 cover by **JOHN TIMMS**

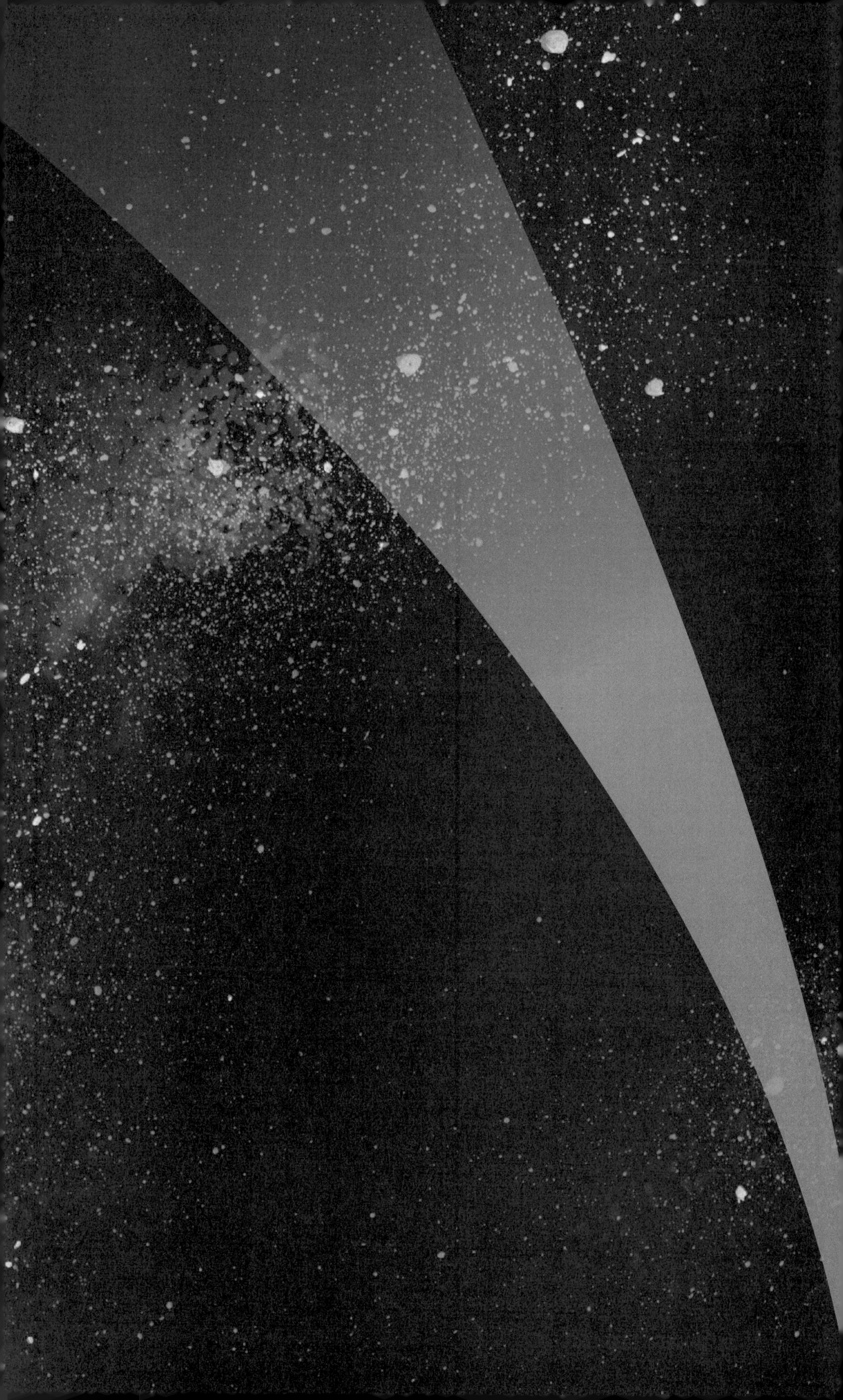

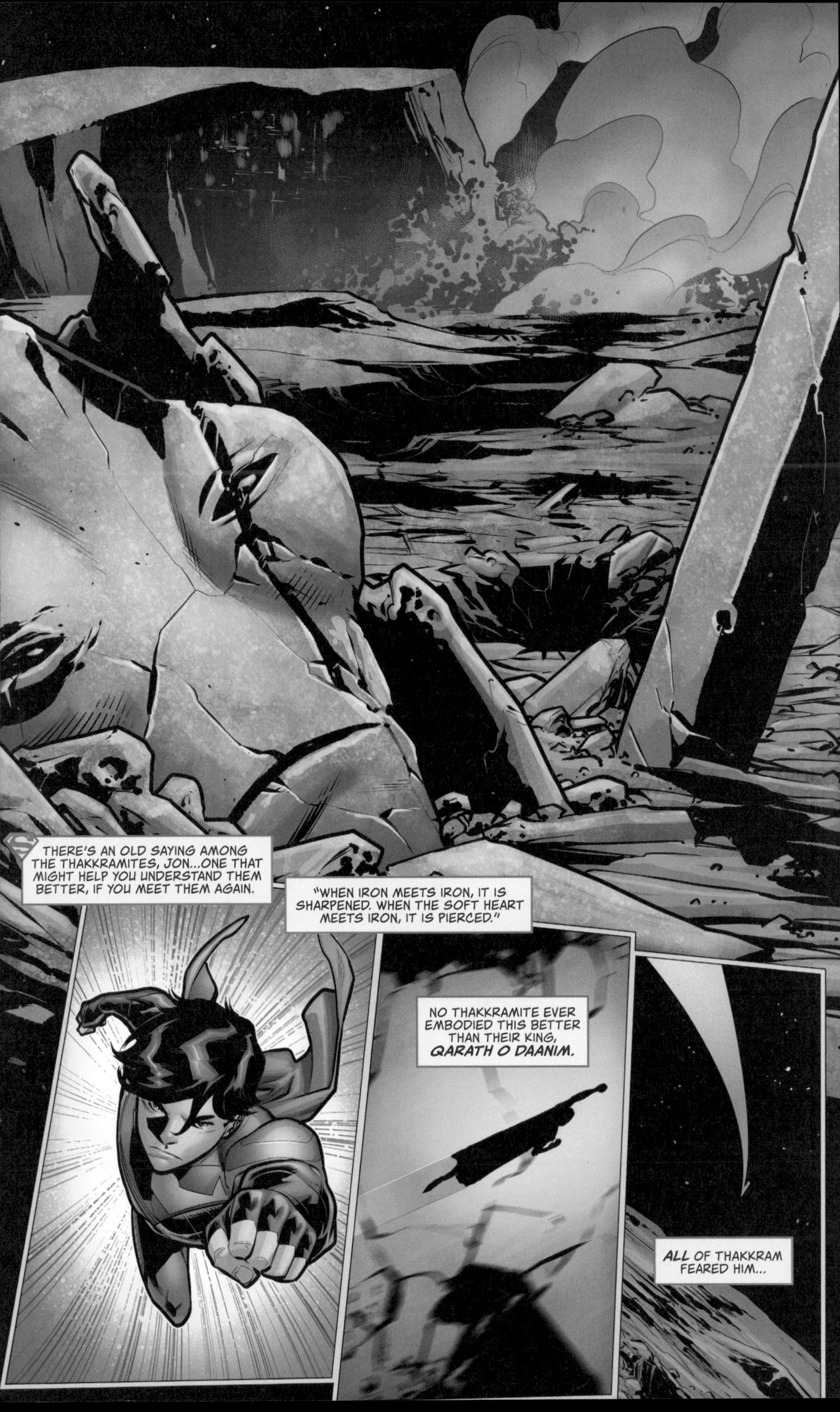
THERE'S AN OLD SAYING AMONG THE THAKKRAMITES, JON...ONE THAT MIGHT HELP YOU UNDERSTAND THEM BETTER, IF YOU MEET THEM AGAIN.
"WHEN IRON MEETS IRON, IT IS SHARPENED. WHEN THE SOFT HEART MEETS IRON, IT IS PIERCED."
NO THAKKRAMITE EVER EMBODIED THIS BETTER THAN THEIR KING, ***QARATH O DAANIM.***
ALL OF THAKKRAM FEARED HIM...

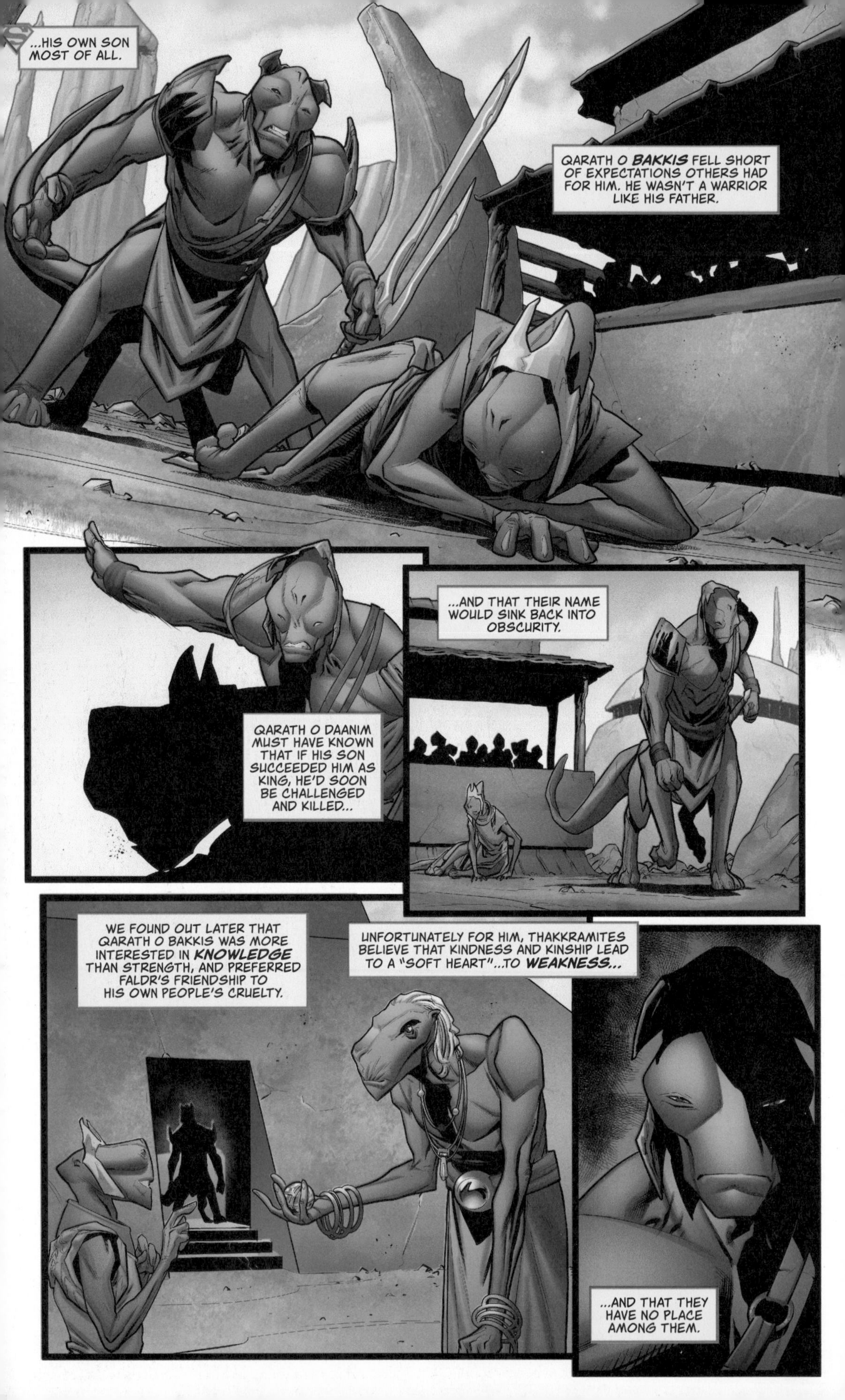
...HIS OWN SON MOST OF ALL.
QARATH O BAKKIS FELL SHORT OF EXPECTATIONS OTHERS HAD FOR HIM. HE WASN'T A WARRIOR LIKE HIS FATHER.
QARATH O DAANIM MUST HAVE KNOWN THAT IF HIS SON SUCCEEDED HIM AS KING, HE'D SOON BE CHALLENGED AND KILLED...
...AND THAT THEIR NAME WOULD SINK BACK INTO OBSCURITY.
WE FOUND OUT LATER THAT QARATH O BAKKIS WAS MORE INTERESTED IN KNOWLEDGE THAN STRENGTH, AND PREFERRED FALDR'S FRIENDSHIP TO HIS OWN PEOPLE'S CRUELTY.
UNFORTUNATELY FOR HIM, THAKKRAMITES BELIEVE THAT KINDNESS AND KINSHIP LEAD TO A "SOFT HEART"...TO WEAKNESS...
...AND THAT THEY HAVE NO PLACE AMONG THEM.

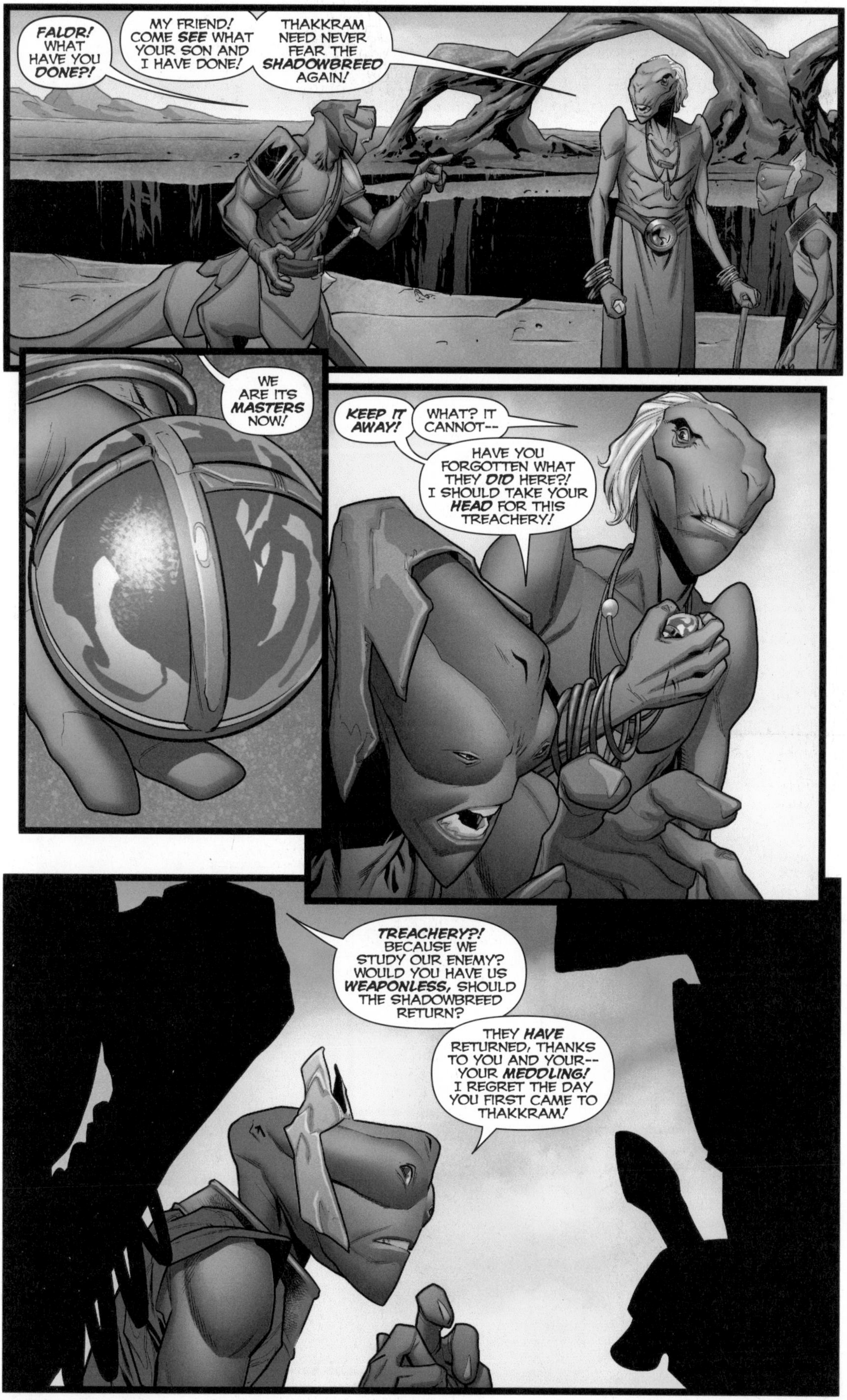
FALDR! WHAT HAVE YOU DONE?!
MY FRIEND! COME SEE WHAT YOUR SON AND I HAVE DONE!
THAKKRAM NEED NEVER FEAR THE SHADOWBREED AGAIN!
WE ARE ITS MASTERS NOW!
KEEP IT AWAY!
WHAT? IT CANNOT--
HAVE YOU FORGOTTEN WHAT THEY DID HERE?! I SHOULD TAKE YOUR HEAD FOR THIS TREACHERY!
TREACHERY?! BECAUSE WE STUDY OUR ENEMY? WOULD YOU HAVE US WEAPONLESS, SHOULD THE SHADOWBREED RETURN?
THEY HAVE RETURNED, THANKS TO YOU AND YOUR-- YOUR MEDDLING! I REGRET THE DAY YOU FIRST CAME TO THAKKRAM!

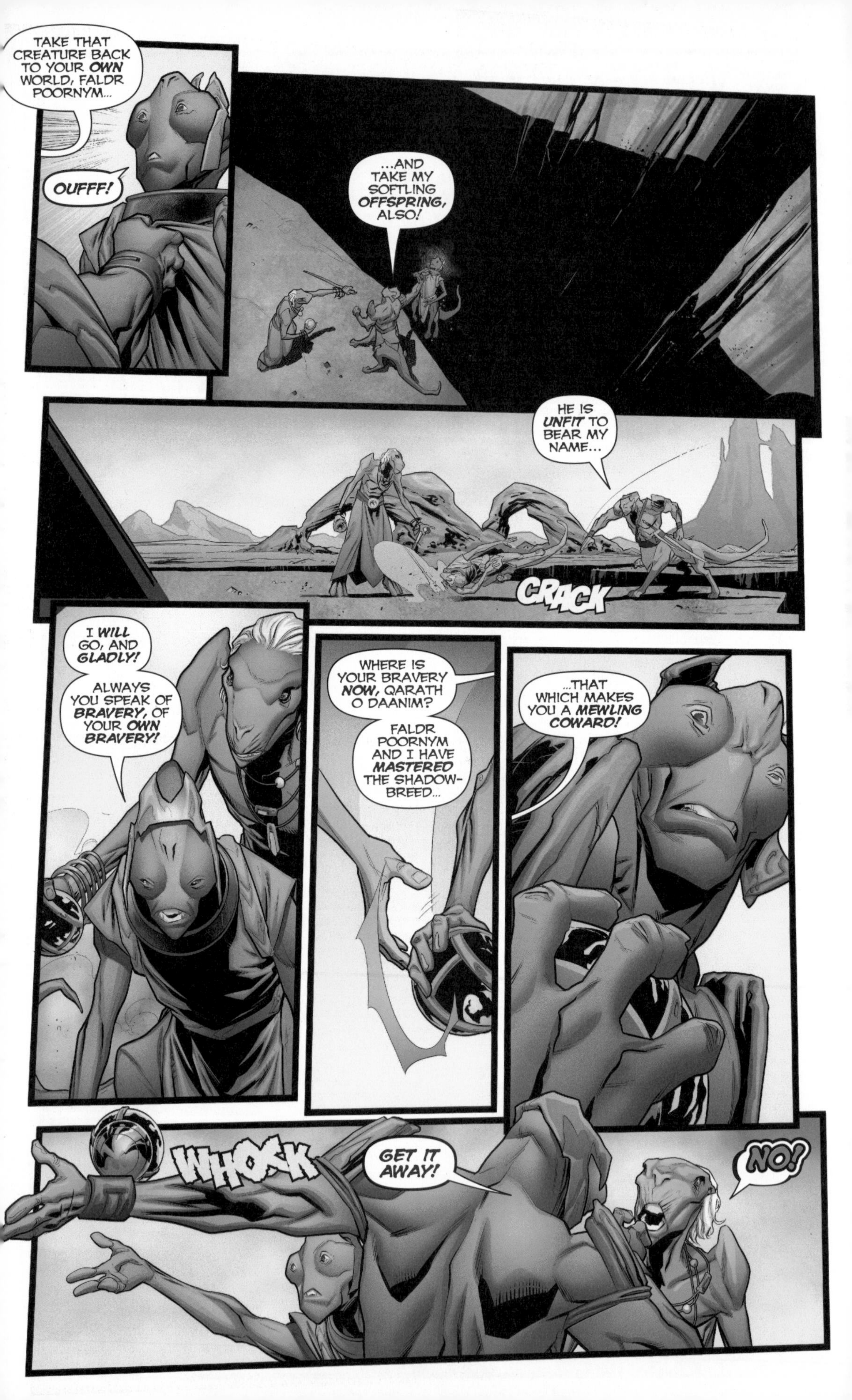

TAKE THAT CREATURE BACK TO YOUR OWN WORLD, FALDR POORNYM...
OUFFF!
...AND TAKE MY SOFTLING OFFSPRING, ALSO!
HE IS UNFIT TO BEAR MY NAME...
CRACK
I WILL GO, AND GLADLY!
ALWAYS YOU SPEAK OF BRAVERY, OF YOUR OWN BRAVERY!
WHERE IS YOUR BRAVERY NOW, QARATH O DAANIM?
FALDR POORNYM AND I HAVE MASTERED THE SHADOW-BREED...
...THAT WHICH MAKES YOU A MEWLING COWARD!
WHOCK
GET IT AWAY!
NO!

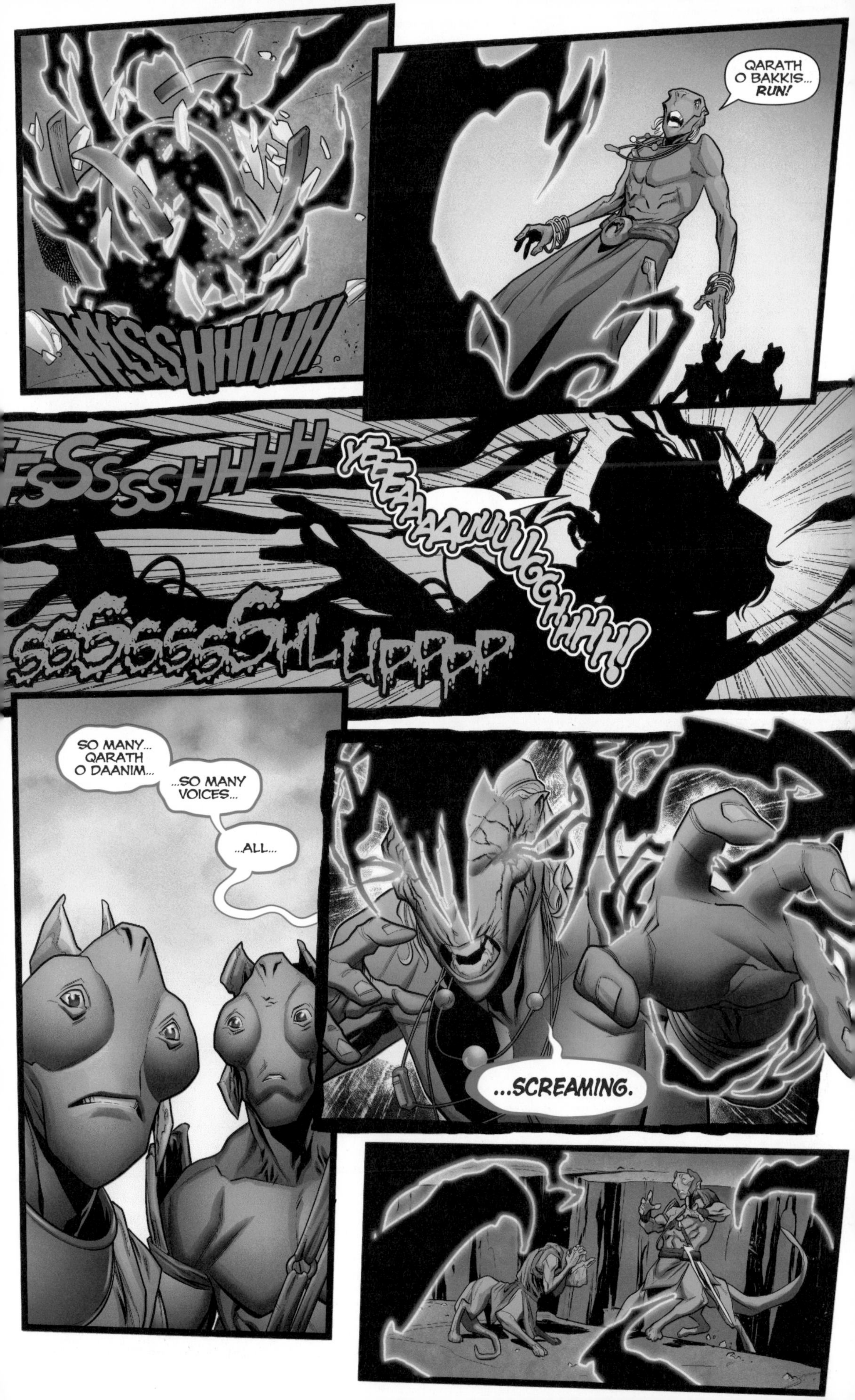
KKSSHHHHH
QARATH O BAKKIS... RUN!
FSSSSSHHHH
YEEEAAAAUUUUGGHHHH!
SSSSSSSSHLLIPPPPP
SO MANY... QARATH O DAANIM...
...SO MANY VOICES...
...ALL...
...SCREAMING.

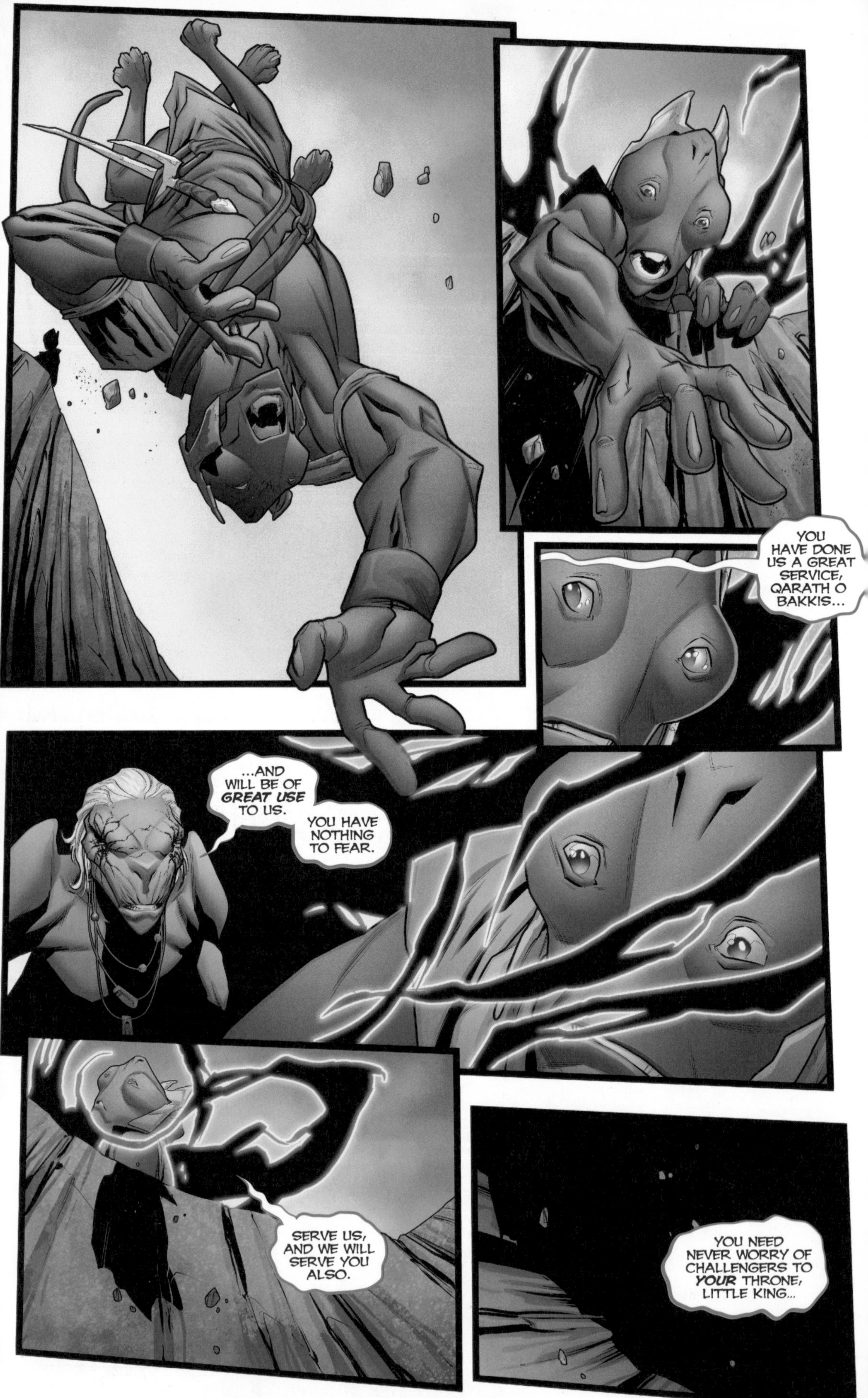
YOU HAVE DONE US A GREAT SERVICE, QARATH O BAKKIS...
...AND WILL BE OF GREAT USE TO US.
YOU HAVE NOTHING TO FEAR.
SERVE US, AND WE WILL SERVE YOU ALSO.
YOU NEED NEVER WORRY OF CHALLENGERS TO YOUR THRONE, LITTLE KING...

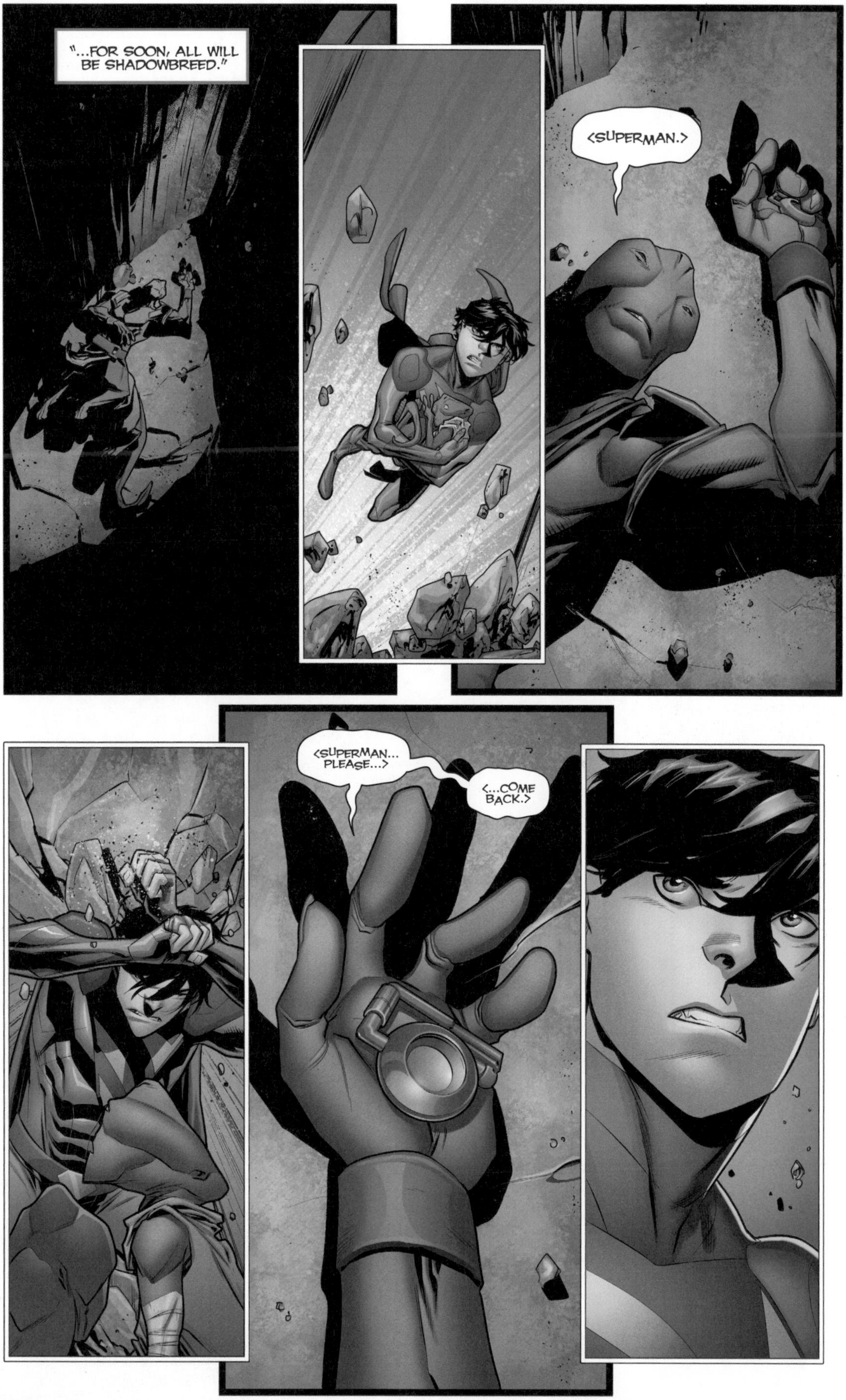
"...FOR SOON, ALL WILL BE SHADOWBREED."
<SUPERMAN.>
<SUPERMAN... PLEASE...>
<...COME BACK.>

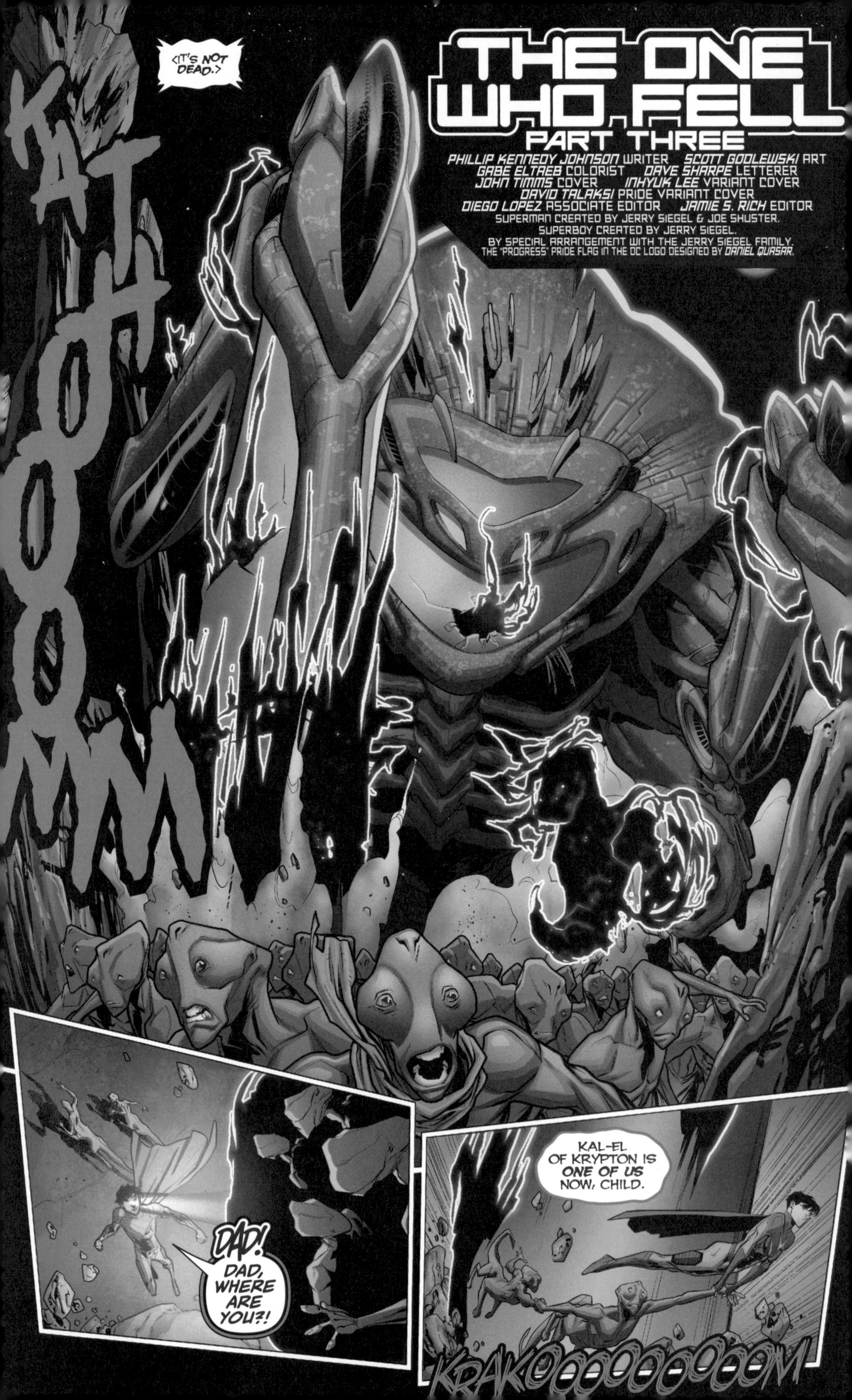

KATHOOOOM
<IT'S NOT DEAD.>
THE ONE WHO FELL
PART THREE
PHILLIP KENNEDY JOHNSON WRITER SCOTT GODLEWSKI ART
GABE ELTAEB COLORIST DAVE SHARPE LETTERER
JOHN TIMMS COVER INHYUK LEE VARIANT COVER
DAVID TALAKSI PRIDE VARIANT COVER
DIEGO LOPEZ ASSOCIATE EDITOR JAMIE S. RICH EDITOR
SUPERMAN CREATED BY JERRY SIEGEL & JOE SHUSTER.
SUPERBOY CREATED BY JERRY SIEGEL.
BY SPECIAL ARRANGEMENT WITH THE JERRY SIEGEL FAMILY.
THE "PROGRESS" PRIDE FLAG IN THE DC LOGO DESIGNED BY DANIEL QUASAR.
DAD! DAD, WHERE ARE YOU?!
KAL-EL OF KRYPTON IS ONE OF US NOW, CHILD.
KRAKOOOOOOOOOOM

ZZZRRRAKKKK

KAFHOOOOOM

AS IS ALL OF *THAKKRAM*, SAVE THESE FEW.

AS *ALL* WILL BE, IN TIME.

YEAH, WELL... I GUESS WE'LL SEE.

SZZRRRIPP

BUT ONLY AN *IDIOT* BETS AGAINST MY DAD.

KOOOOOM

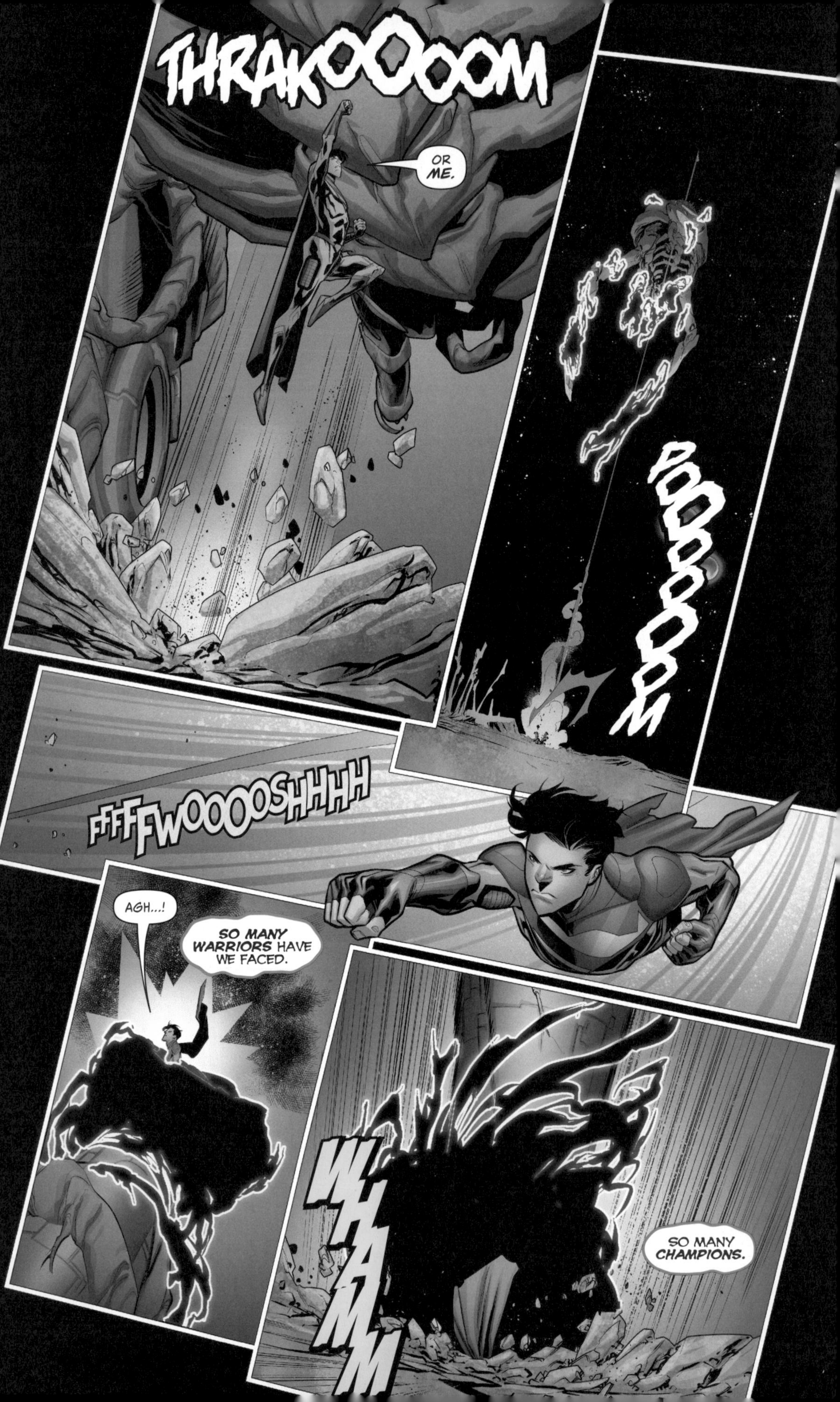
THRAKOOOOOM
OR ME.
DOOOOOOOOM
FFFFWOOOOSHHHH
AGH...!
SO MANY WARRIORS HAVE WE FACED.
WHAMM
SO MANY CHAMPIONS.

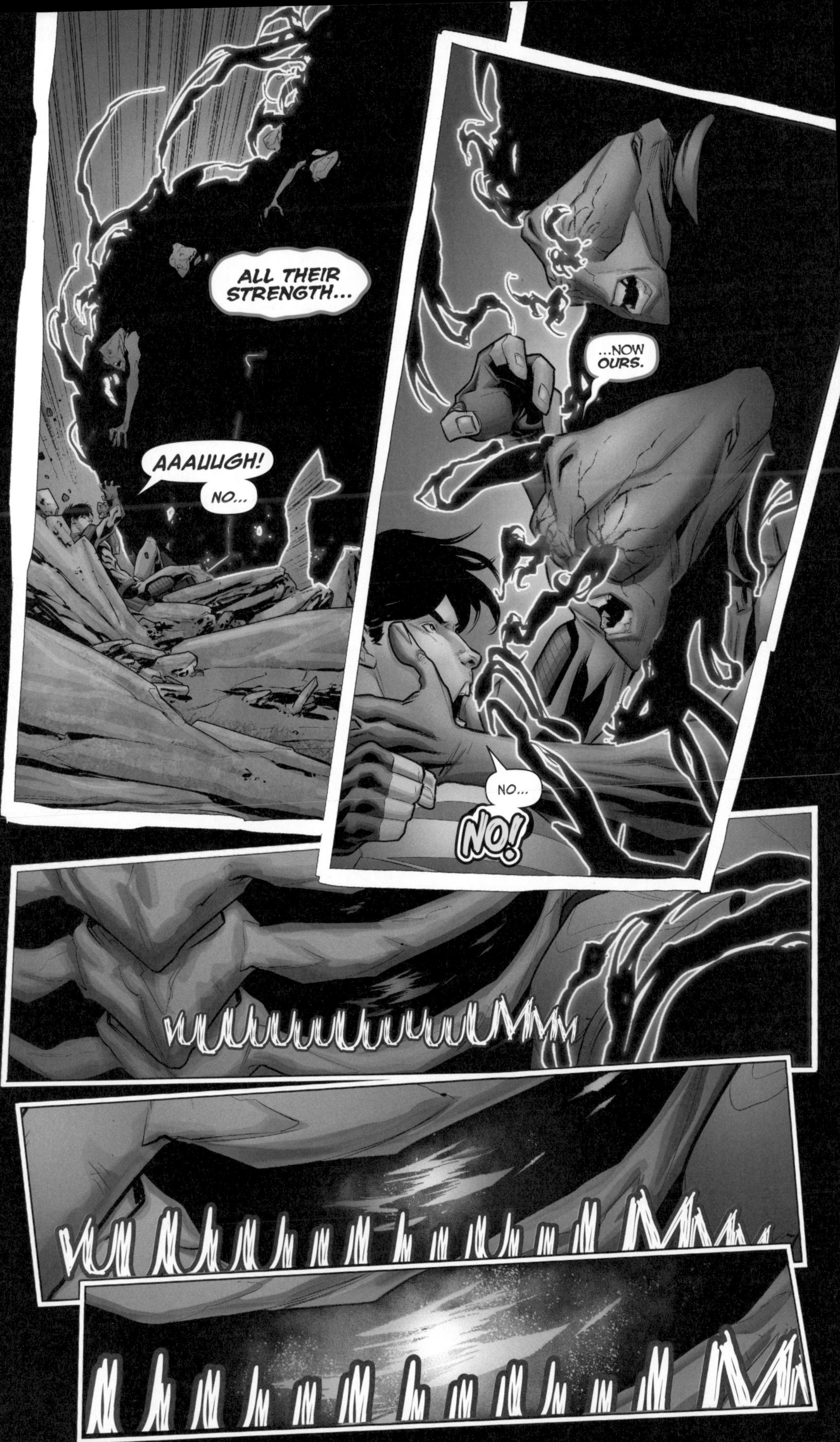
ALL THEIR STRENGTH...
...NOW OURS.
AAAUUGH!
NO...
NO...
NO!

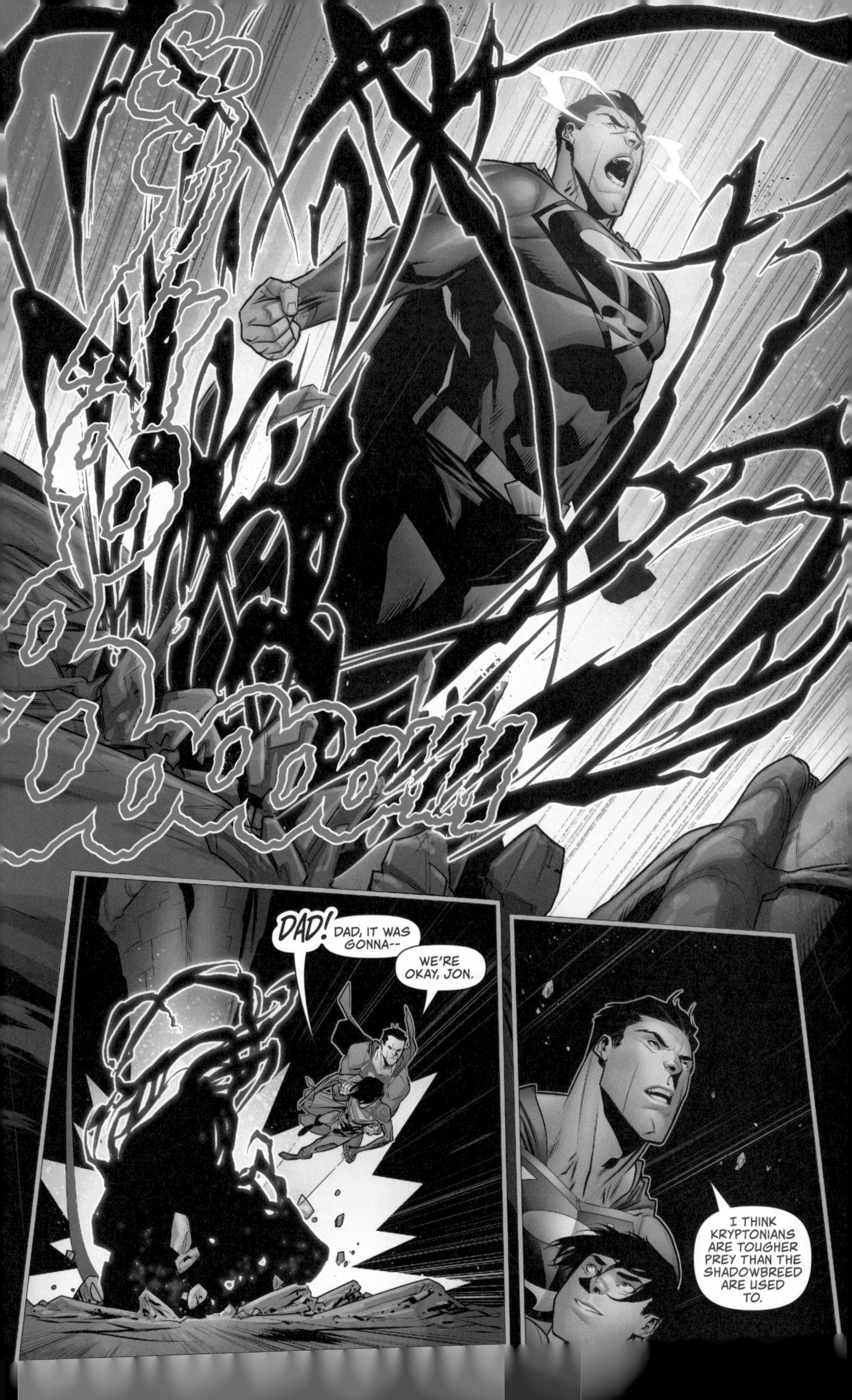

DAD! DAD, IT WAS GONNA--
WE'RE OKAY, JON.
I THINK KRYPTONIANS ARE TOUGHER PREY THAN THE SHADOWBREED ARE USED TO.

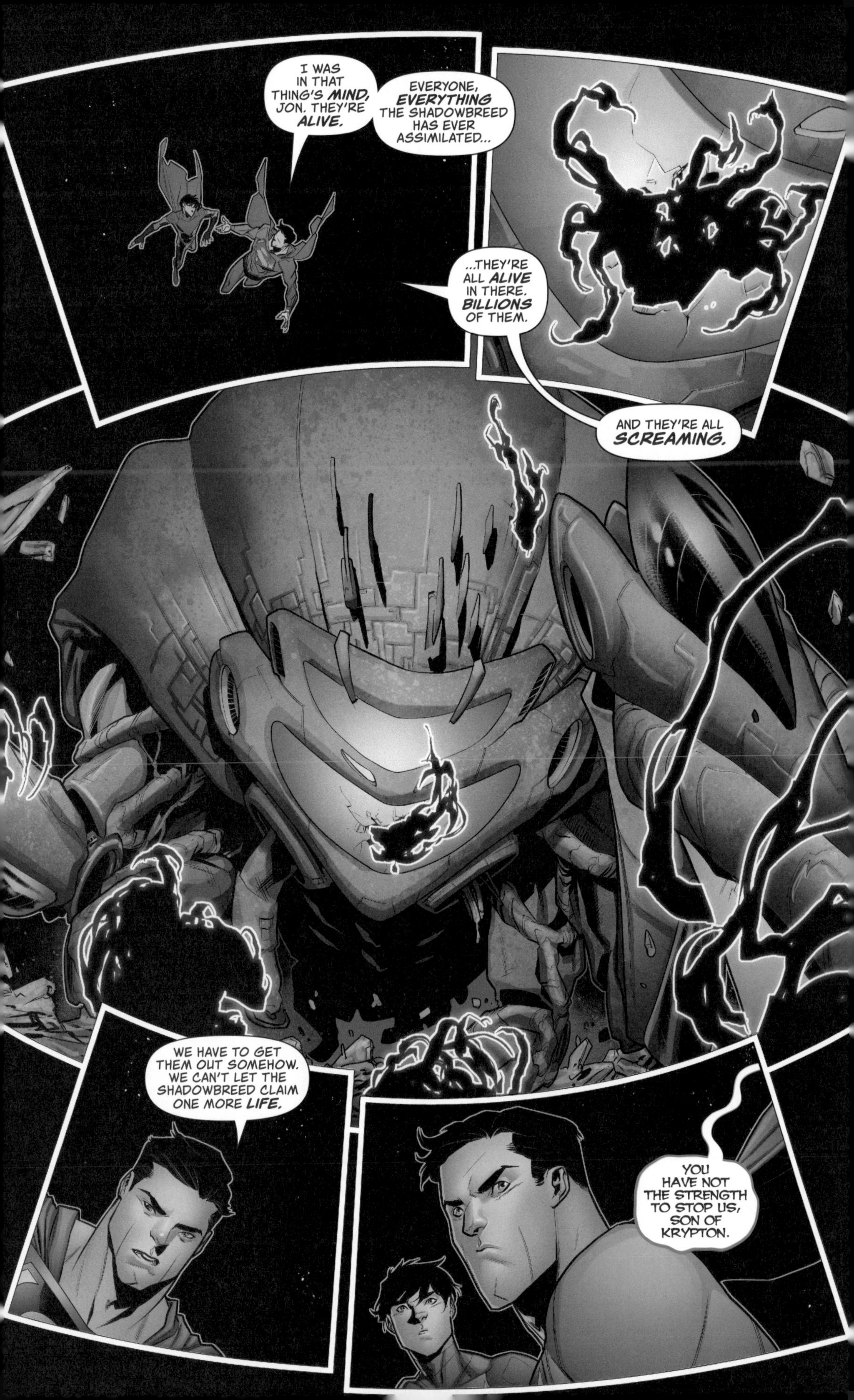
I WAS IN THAT THING'S *MIND,* JON. THEY'RE *ALIVE.*
EVERYONE, *EVERYTHING* THE SHADOWBREED HAS EVER ASSIMILATED...
...THEY'RE ALL *ALIVE* IN THERE. *BILLIONS* OF THEM.
AND THEY'RE ALL *SCREAMING.*
WE HAVE TO GET THEM OUT SOMEHOW. WE CAN'T LET THE SHADOWBREED CLAIM ONE MORE *LIFE.*
YOU HAVE NOT THE STRENGTH TO STOP US, SON OF KRYPTON.

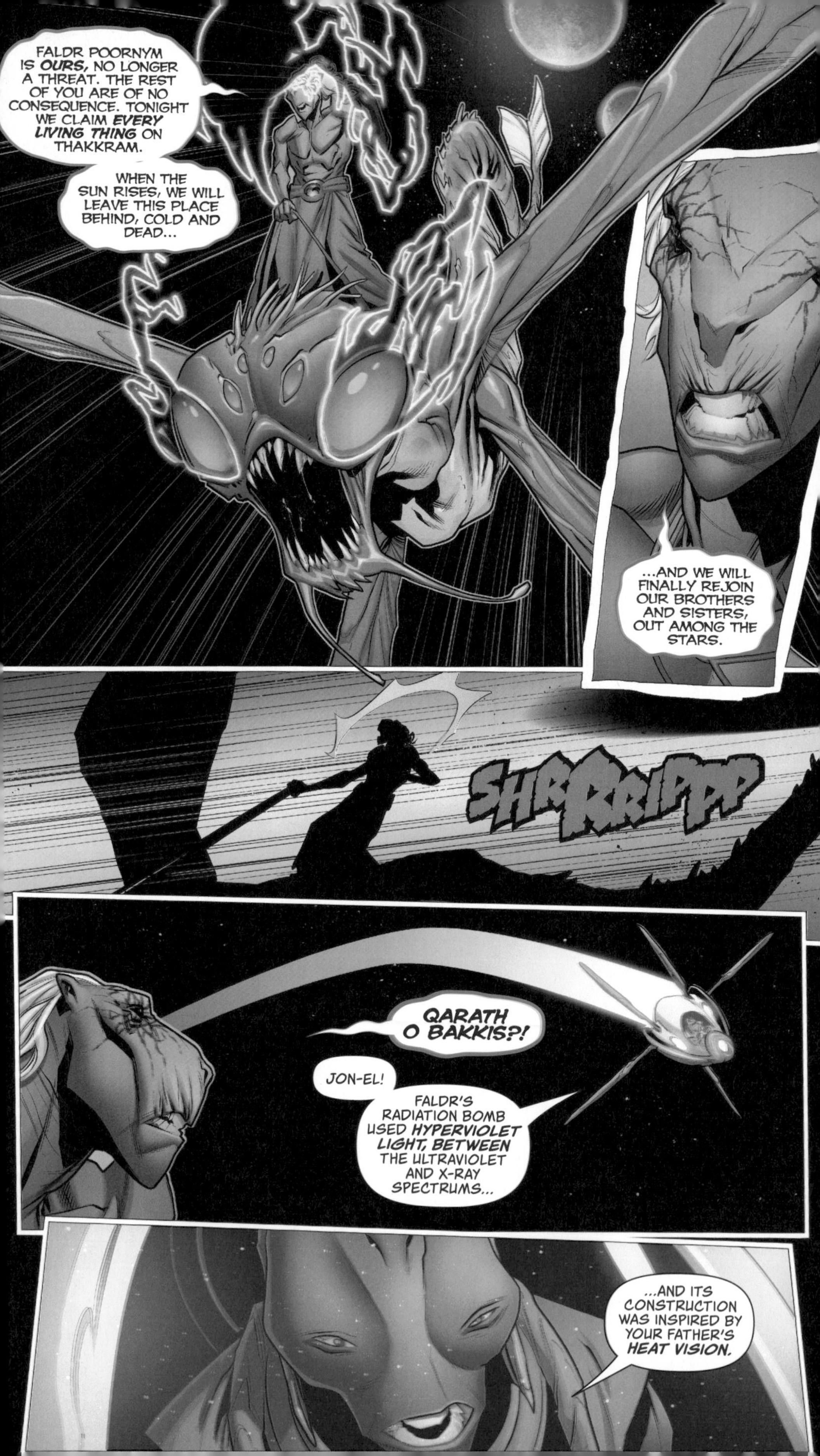
FALDR POORNYM IS OURS, NO LONGER A THREAT. THE REST OF YOU ARE OF NO CONSEQUENCE. TONIGHT WE CLAIM EVERY LIVING THING ON THAKKRAM.
WHEN THE SUN RISES, WE WILL LEAVE THIS PLACE BEHIND, COLD AND DEAD...
...AND WE WILL FINALLY REJOIN OUR BROTHERS AND SISTERS, OUT AMONG THE STARS.
SHRRRIPPP
QARATH O BAKKIS?!
JON-EL!
FALDR'S RADIATION BOMB USED HYPERVIOLET LIGHT, BETWEEN THE ULTRAVIOLET AND X-RAY SPECTRUMS...
...AND ITS CONSTRUCTION WAS INSPIRED BY YOUR FATHER'S HEAT VISION.

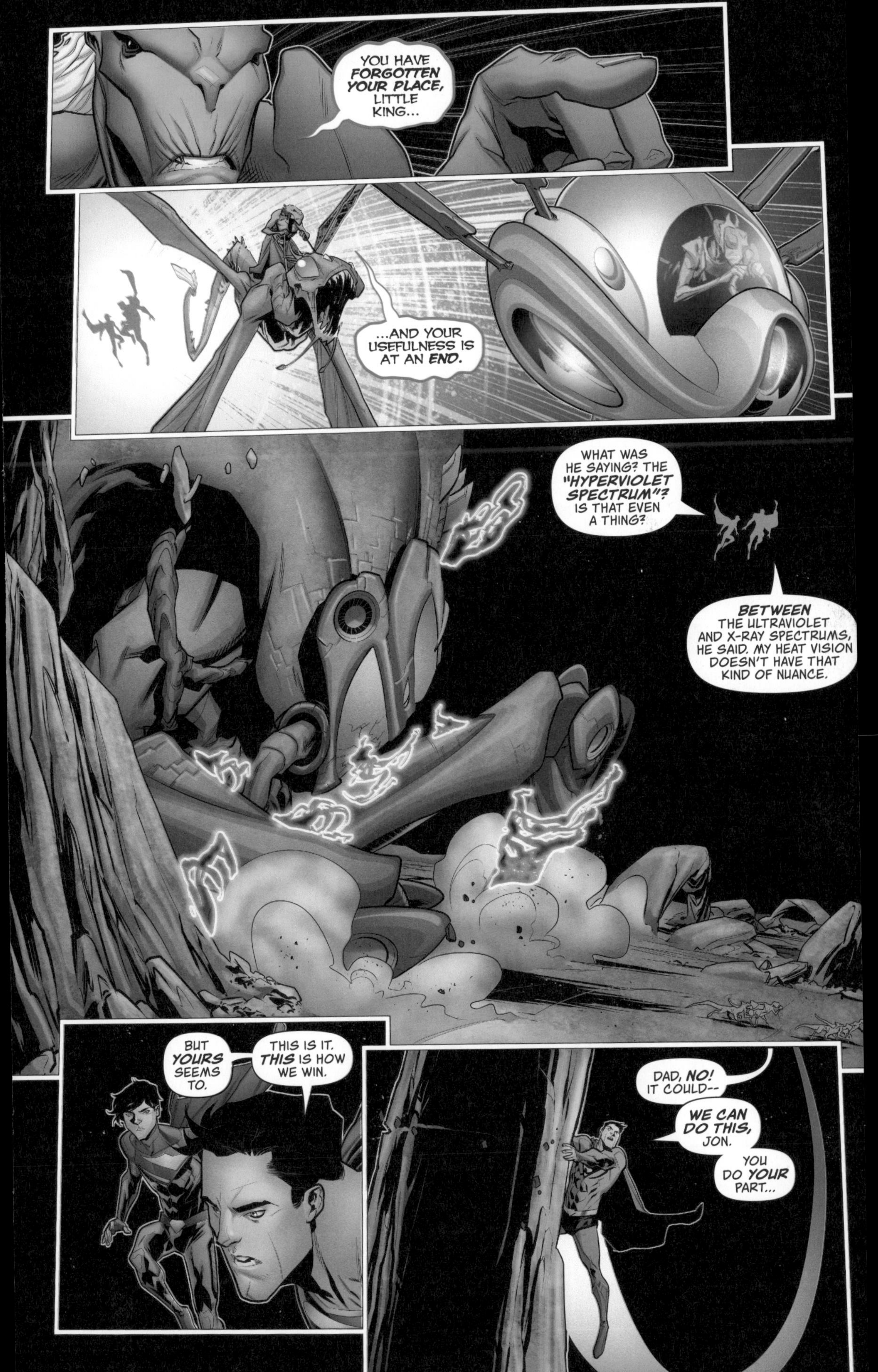

YOU HAVE FORGOTTEN YOUR PLACE, LITTLE KING...
...AND YOUR USEFULNESS IS AT AN END.
WHAT WAS HE SAYING? THE "HYPERVIOLET SPECTRUM"? IS THAT EVEN A THING?
BETWEEN THE ULTRAVIOLET AND X-RAY SPECTRUMS, HE SAID. MY HEAT VISION DOESN'T HAVE THAT KIND OF NUANCE.
BUT YOURS SEEMS TO.
THIS IS IT. THIS IS HOW WE WIN.
DAD, NO! IT COULD--
WE CAN DO THIS, JON.
YOU DO YOUR PART...

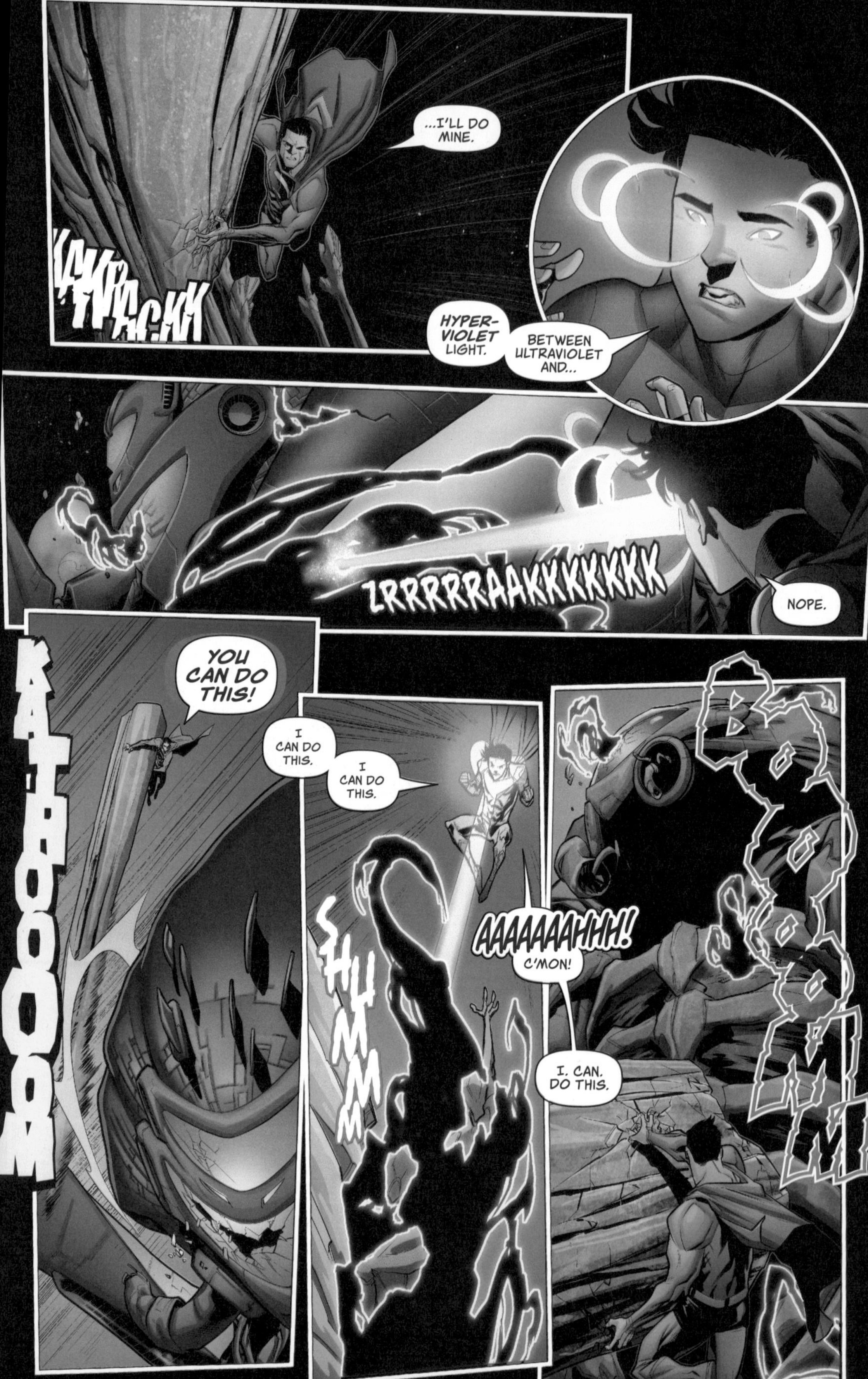
...I'LL DO MINE.
BETWEEN ULTRAVIOLET AND...
HYPER-VIOLET LIGHT.
ZRRRRRAAKKKKKKK
NOPE.
YOU CAN DO THIS!
I CAN DO THIS.
I CAN DO THIS.
AAAAAAAHHH!
C'MON!
I. CAN. DO THIS.

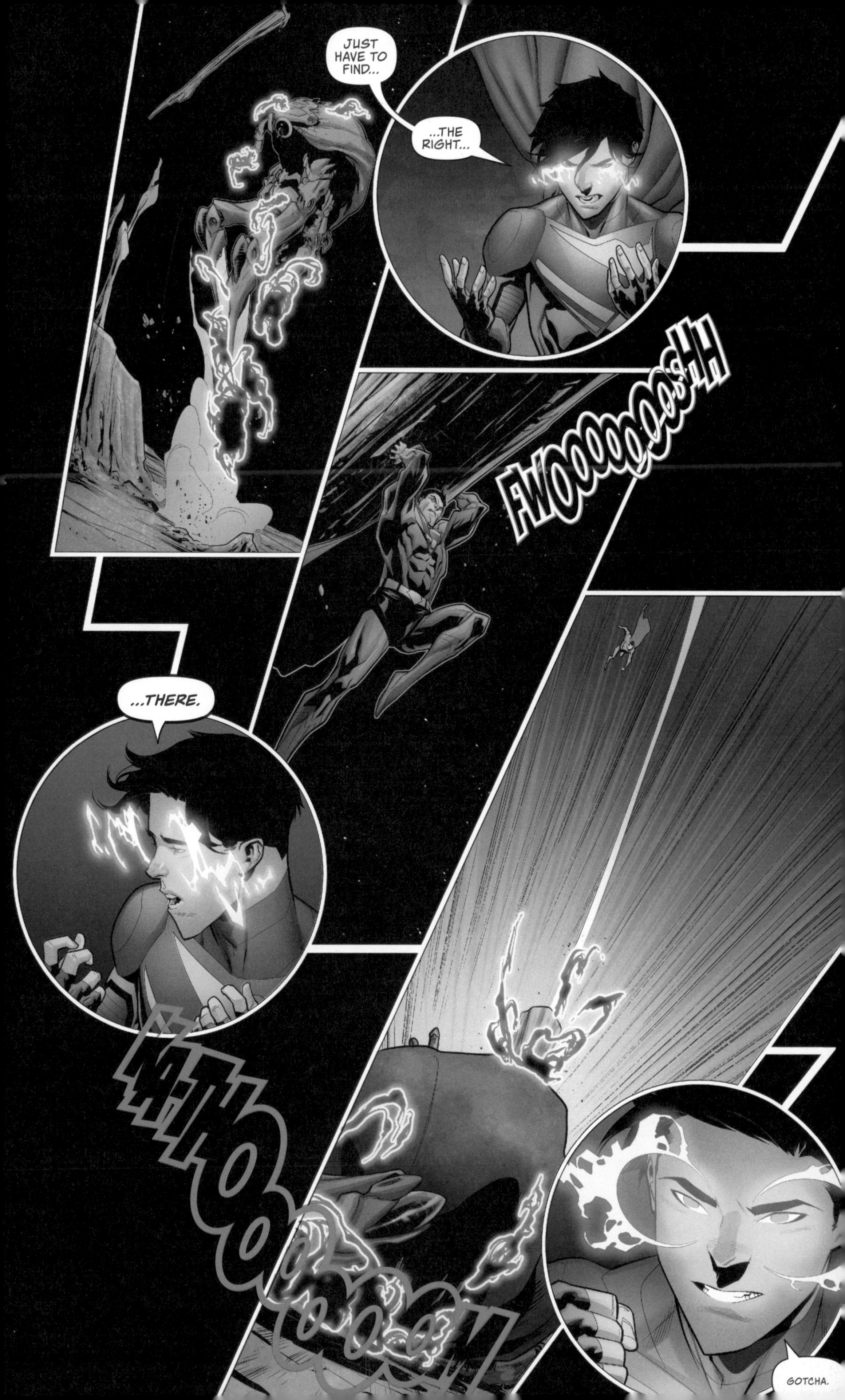
JUST HAVE TO FIND...
...THE RIGHT...
FWOOOOOOOSHH
...THERE.
WHOOOOOOOM
GOTCHA.

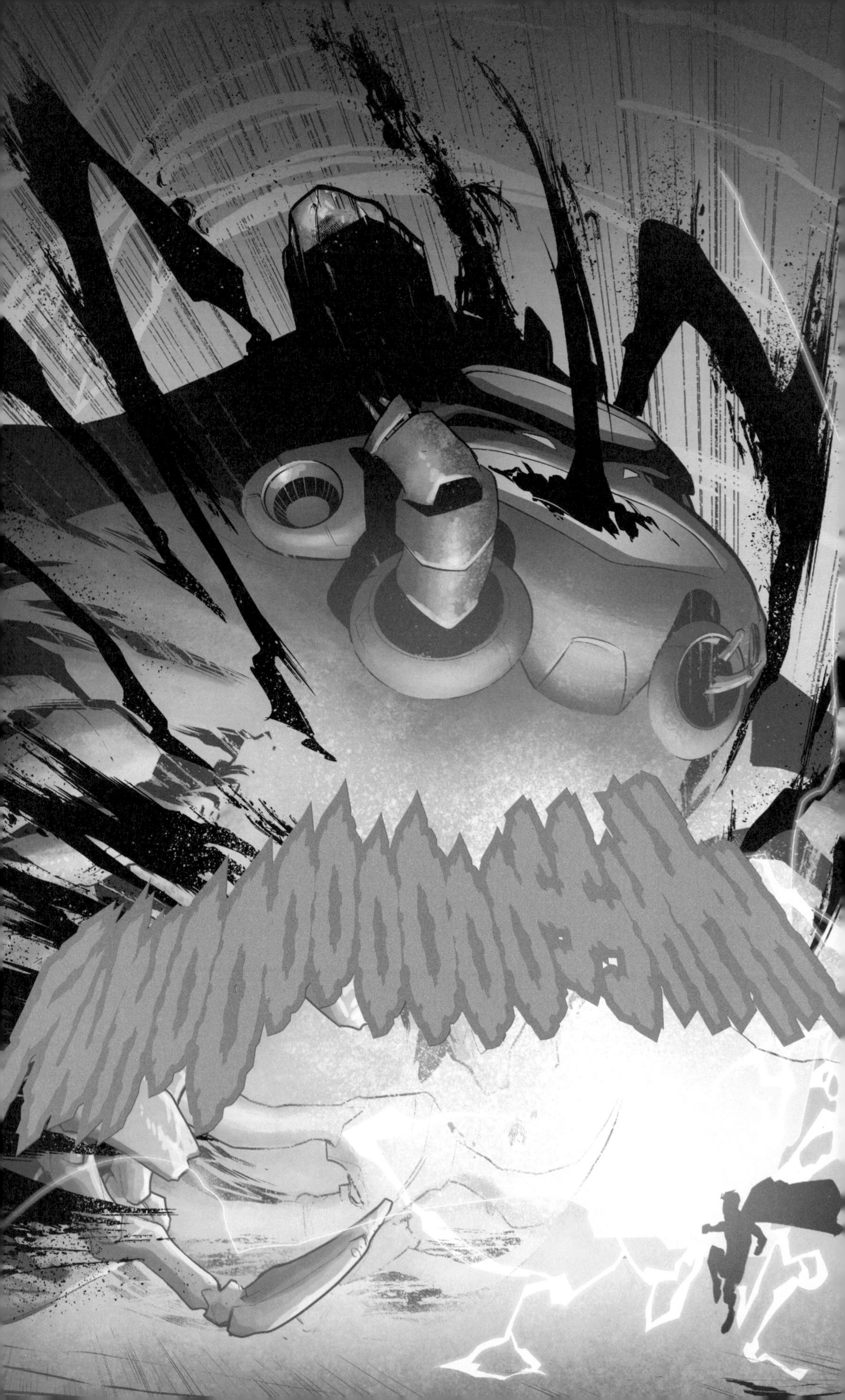

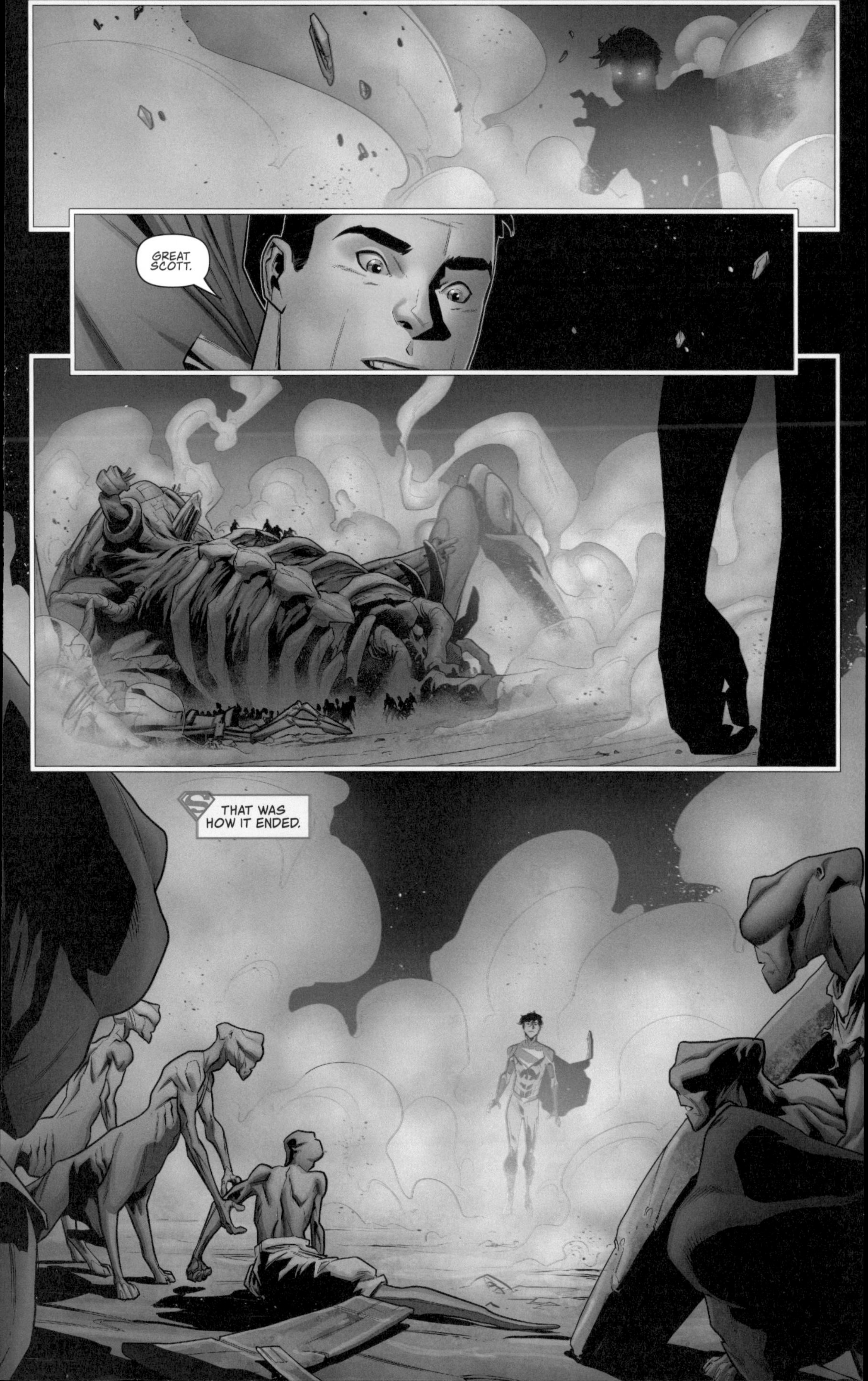
GREAT SCOTT.
THAT WAS HOW IT ENDED.

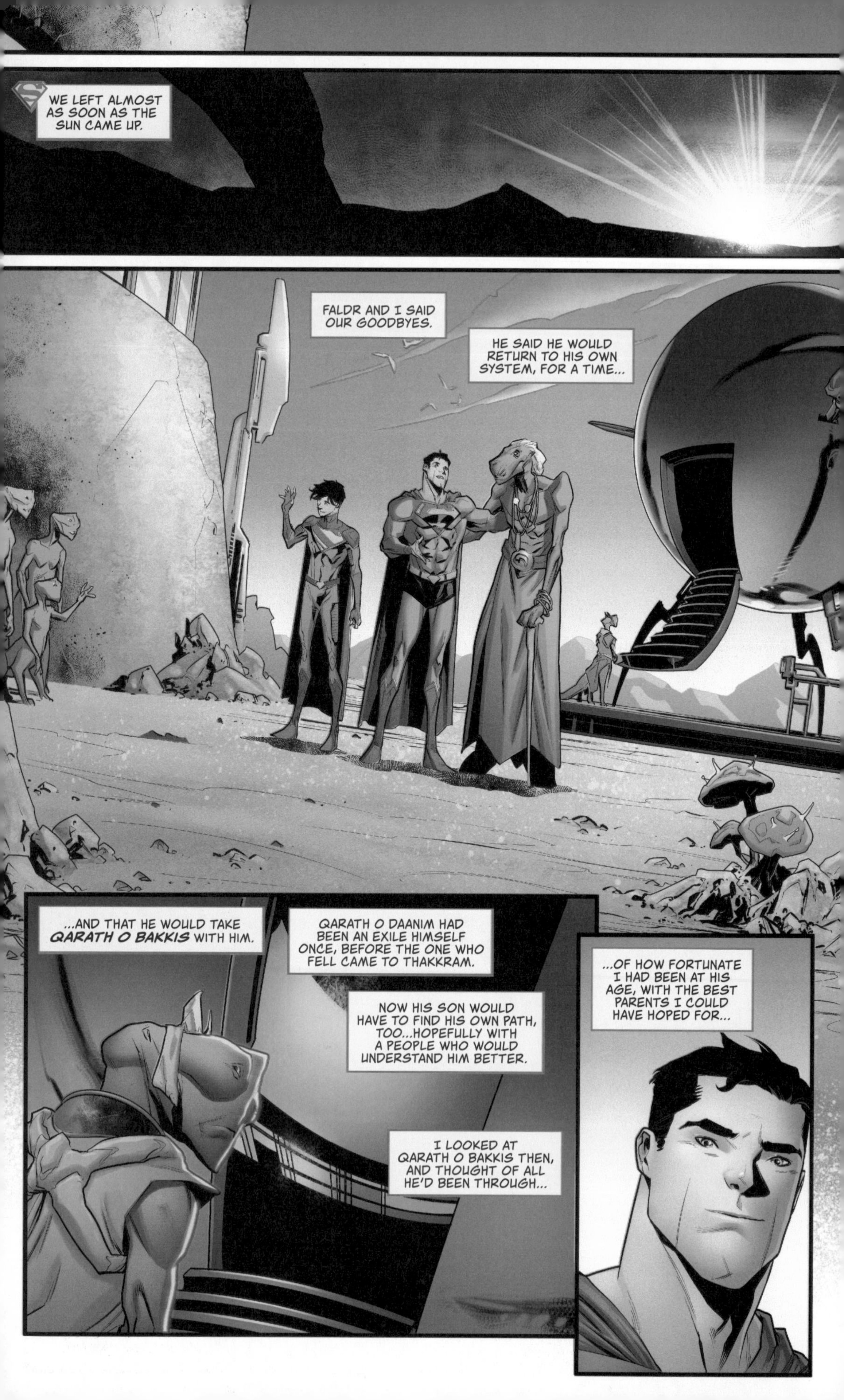

WE LEFT ALMOST AS SOON AS THE SUN CAME UP.
FALDR AND I SAID OUR GOODBYES.
HE SAID HE WOULD RETURN TO HIS OWN SYSTEM, FOR A TIME...
...AND THAT HE WOULD TAKE QARATH O BAKKIS WITH HIM.
QARATH O DAANIM HAD BEEN AN EXILE HIMSELF ONCE, BEFORE THE ONE WHO FELL CAME TO THAKKRAM.
NOW HIS SON WOULD HAVE TO FIND HIS OWN PATH, TOO...HOPEFULLY WITH A PEOPLE WHO WOULD UNDERSTAND HIM BETTER.
I LOOKED AT QARATH O BAKKIS THEN, AND THOUGHT OF ALL HE'D BEEN THROUGH...
...OF HOW FORTUNATE I HAD BEEN AT HIS AGE, WITH THE BEST PARENTS I COULD HAVE HOPED FOR...

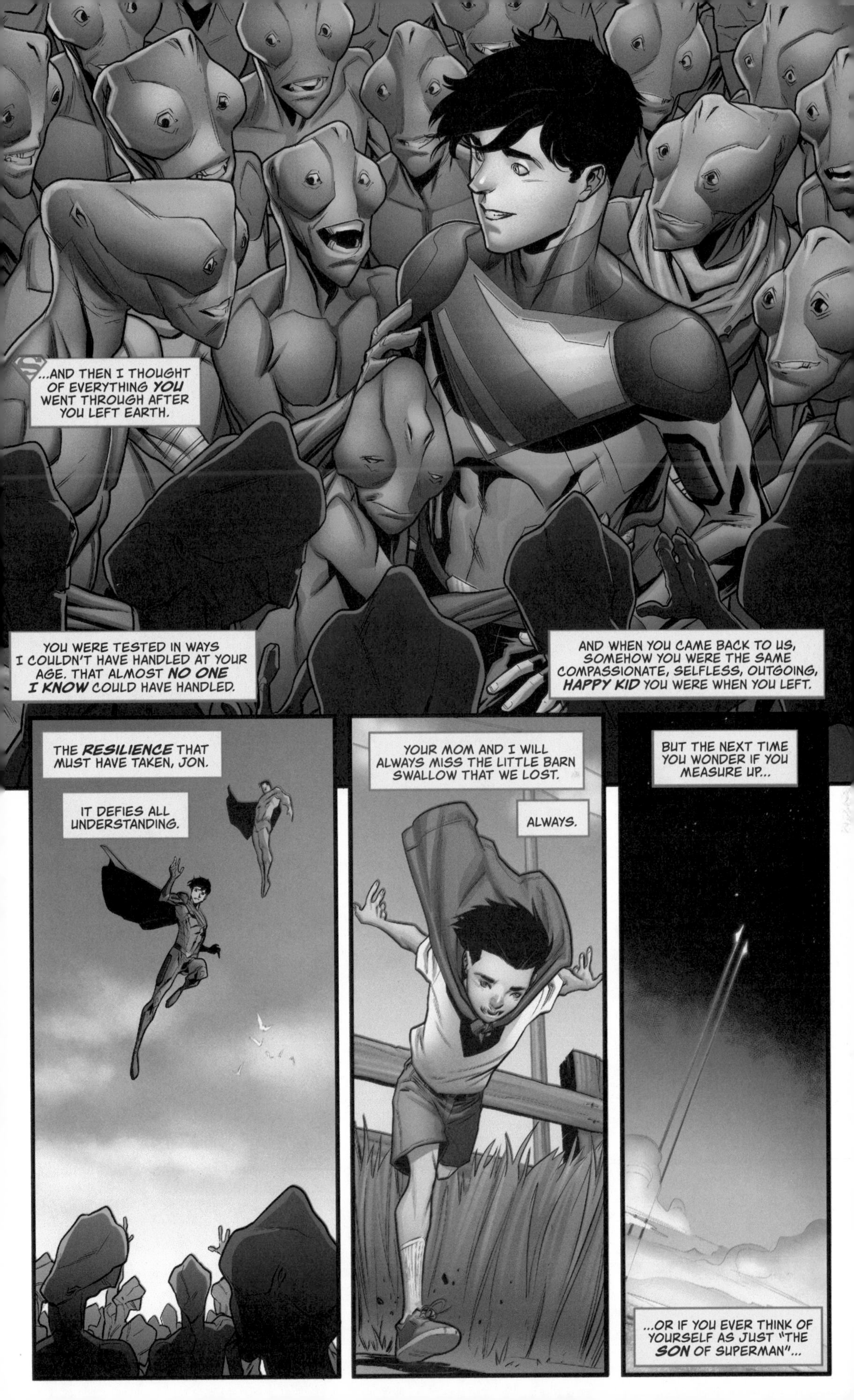
...AND THEN I THOUGHT OF EVERYTHING YOU WENT THROUGH AFTER YOU LEFT EARTH.
YOU WERE TESTED IN WAYS I COULDN'T HAVE HANDLED AT YOUR AGE. THAT ALMOST NO ONE I KNOW COULD HAVE HANDLED.
AND WHEN YOU CAME BACK TO US, SOMEHOW YOU WERE THE SAME COMPASSIONATE, SELFLESS, OUTGOING, HAPPY KID YOU WERE WHEN YOU LEFT.
THE RESILIENCE THAT MUST HAVE TAKEN, JON.
IT DEFIES ALL UNDERSTANDING.
YOUR MOM AND I WILL ALWAYS MISS THE LITTLE BARN SWALLOW THAT WE LOST.
ALWAYS.
BUT THE NEXT TIME YOU WONDER IF YOU MEASURE UP...
...OR IF YOU EVER THINK OF YOURSELF AS JUST "THE SON OF SUPERMAN"...

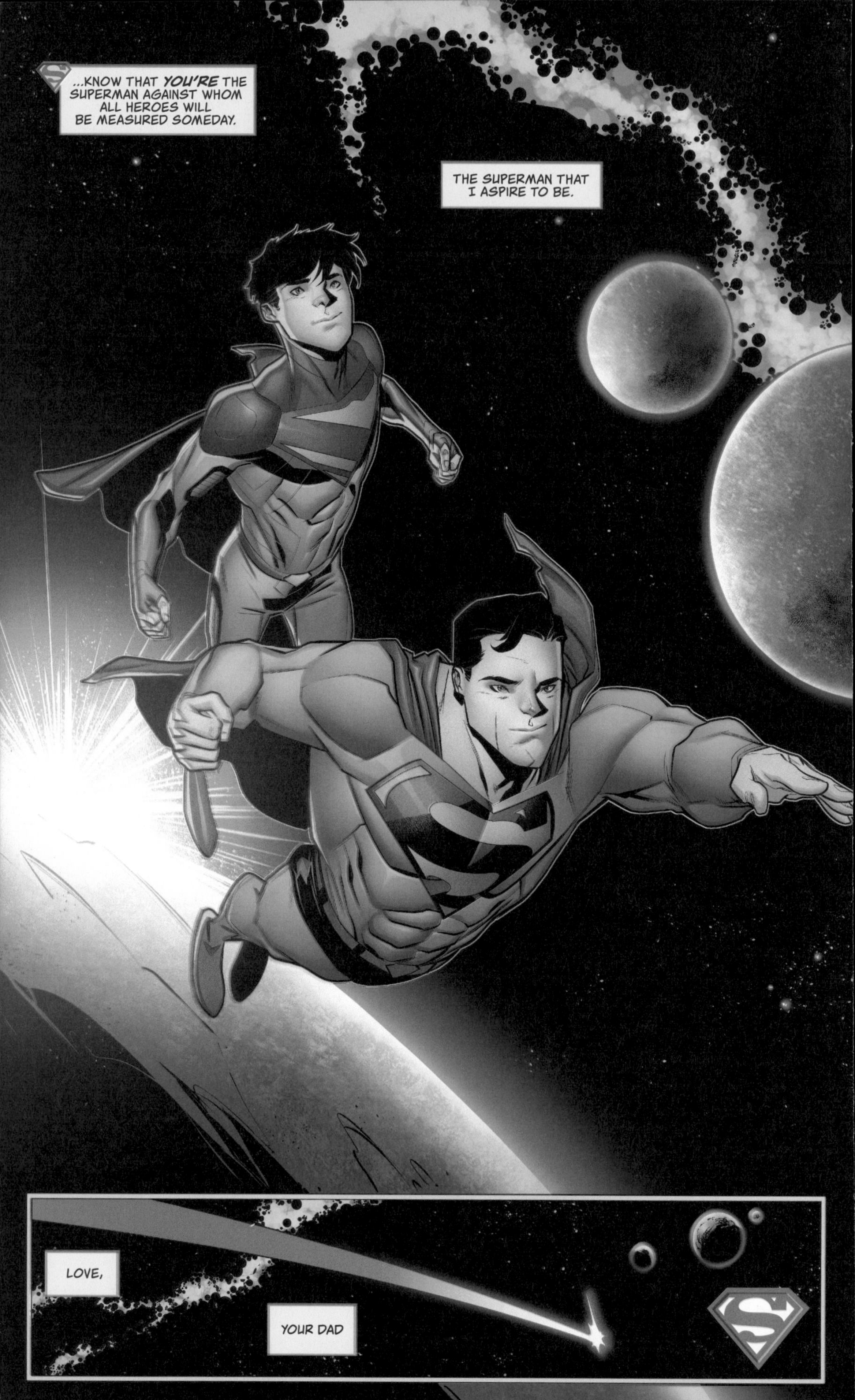
...KNOW THAT YOU'RE THE SUPERMAN AGAINST WHOM ALL HEROES WILL BE MEASURED SOMEDAY.
THE SUPERMAN THAT I ASPIRE TO BE.
LOVE,
YOUR DAD

VARIANT COVERS and SKETCH GALLERY

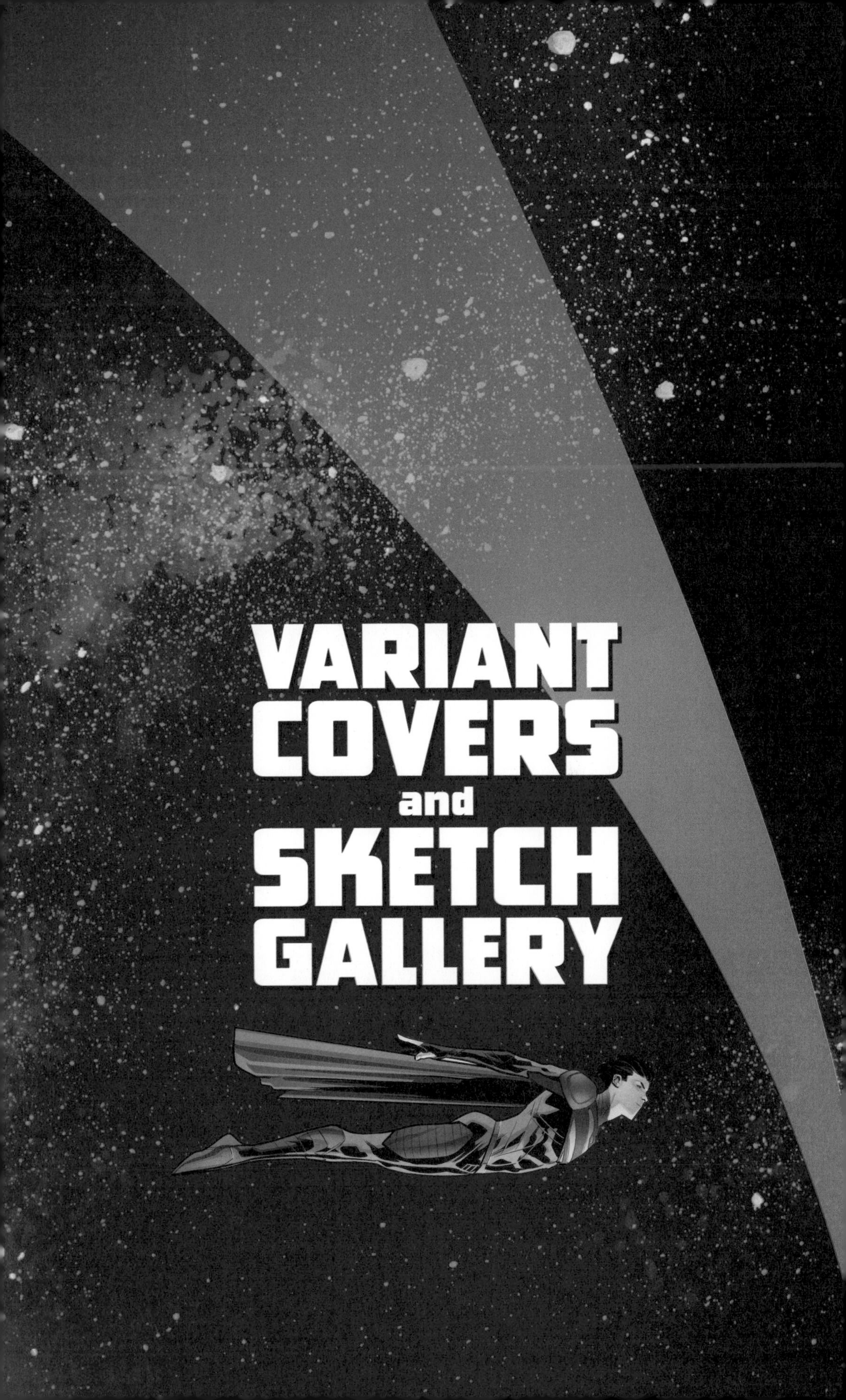

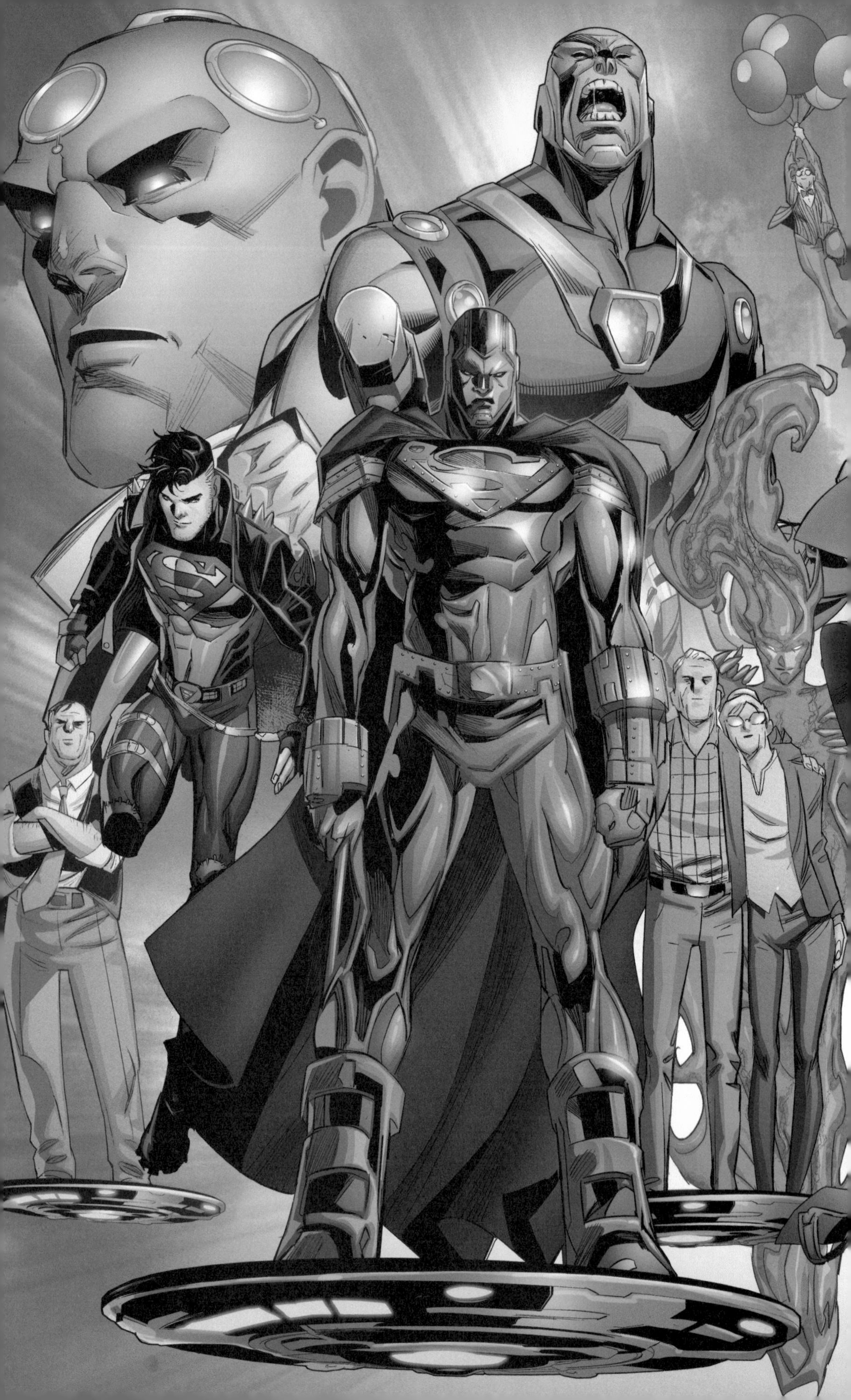

Superman #29 variant cover art by **JOHN TIMMS** & **GABE ELTAEB**

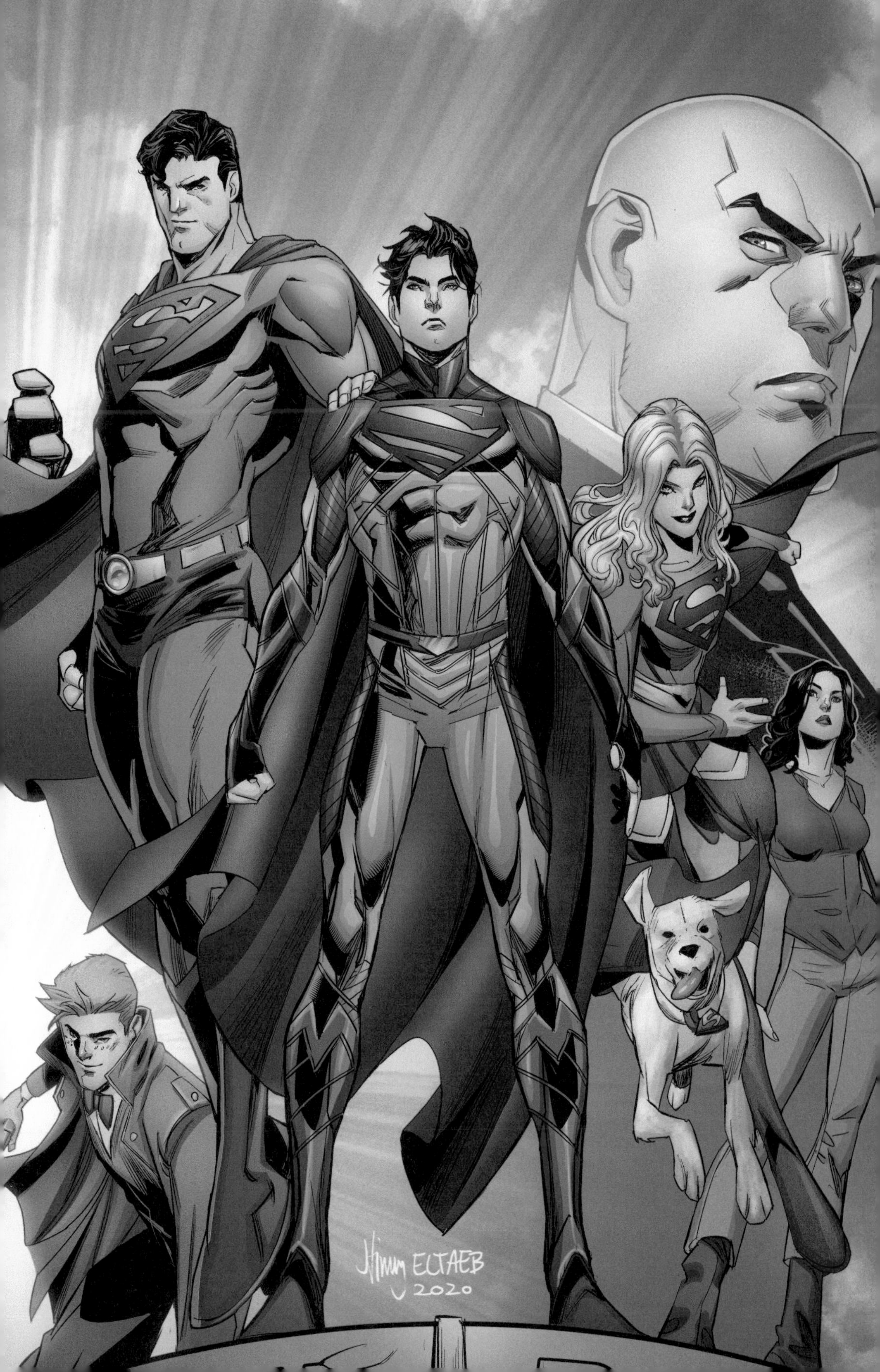
ELTAEB
2020

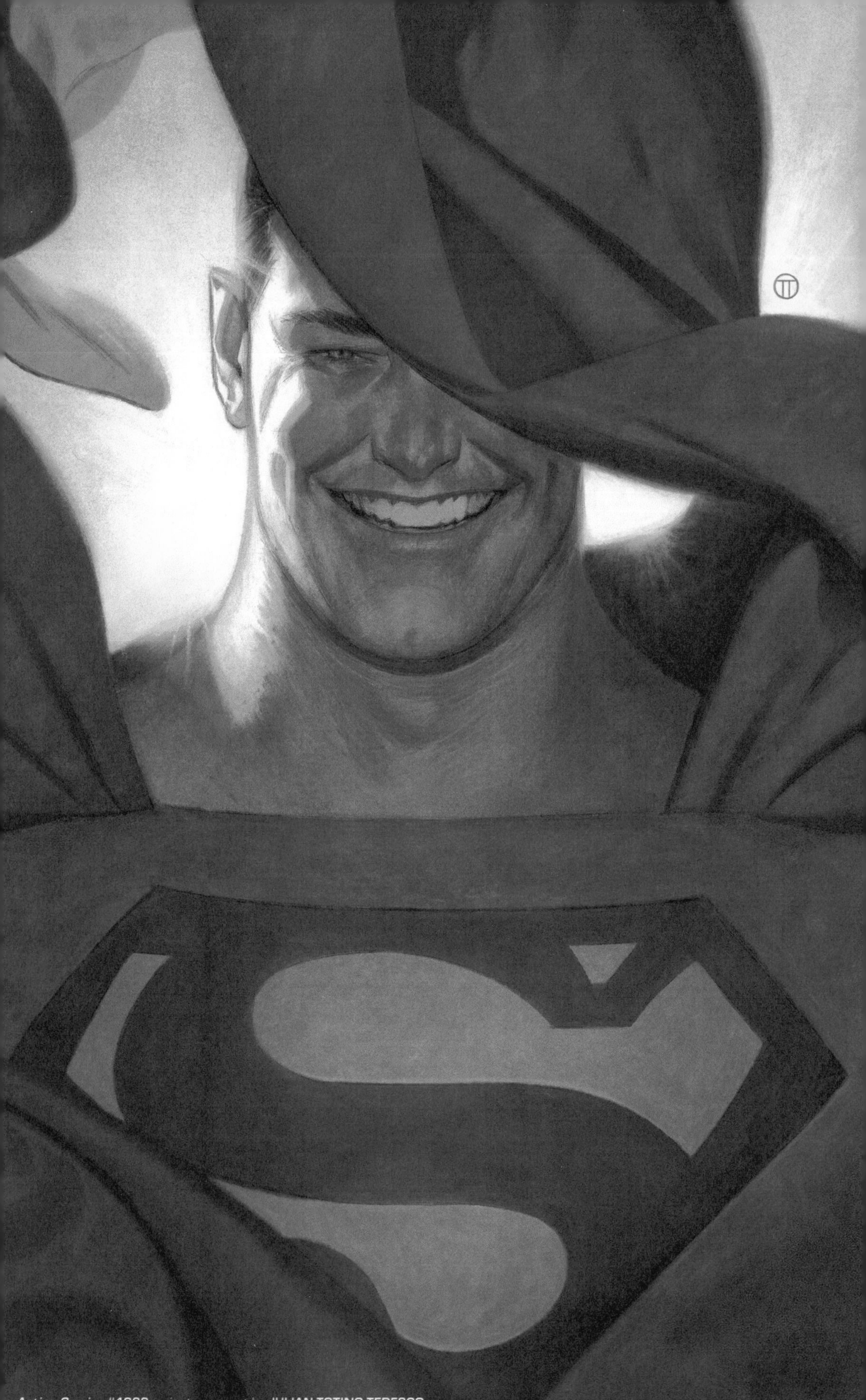
TT

Action Comics #1029 variant cover art by JULIAN TOTINO TEDESCO

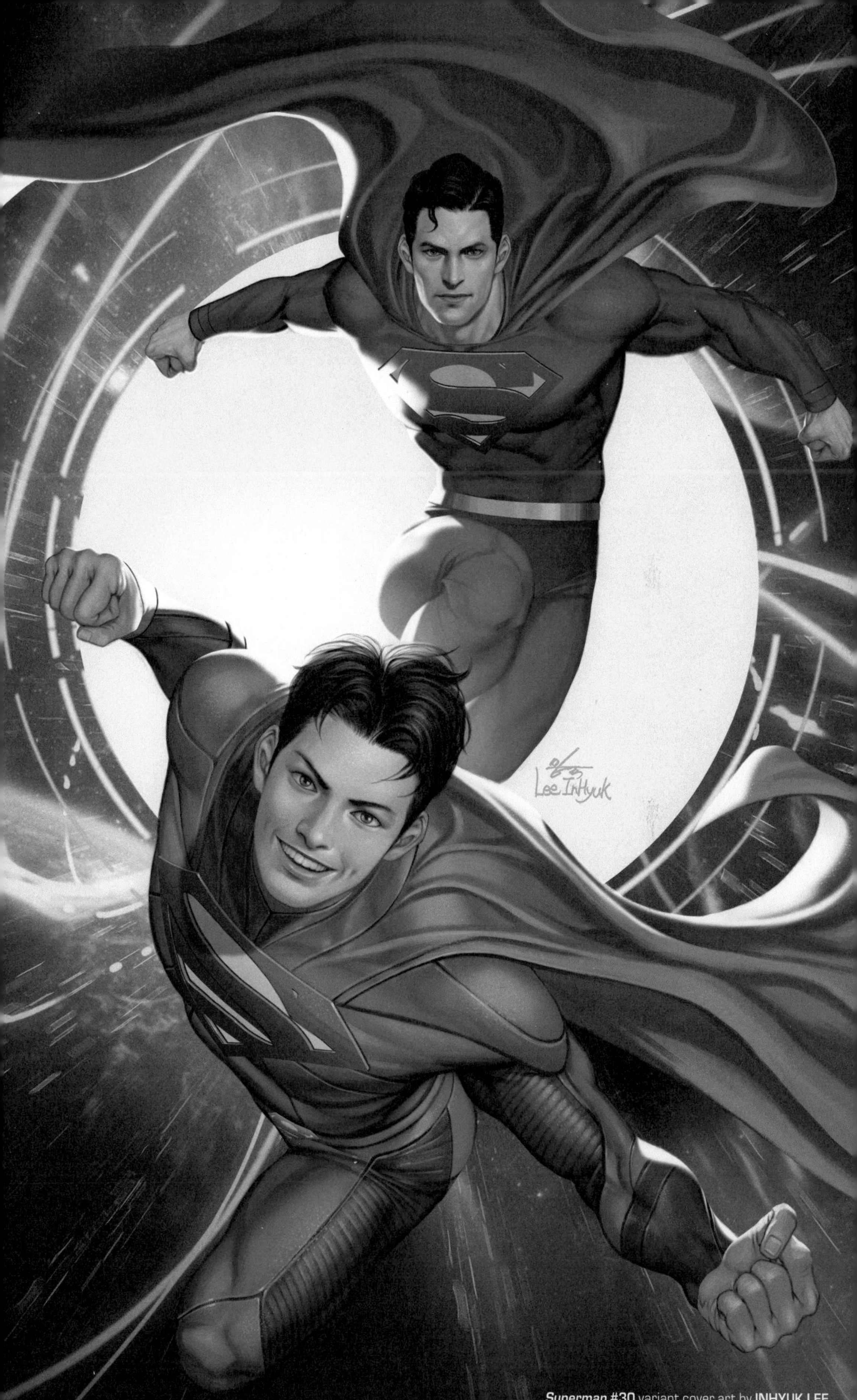
Lee InHyuk

Superman **#30** variant cover art by **INHYUK LEE**

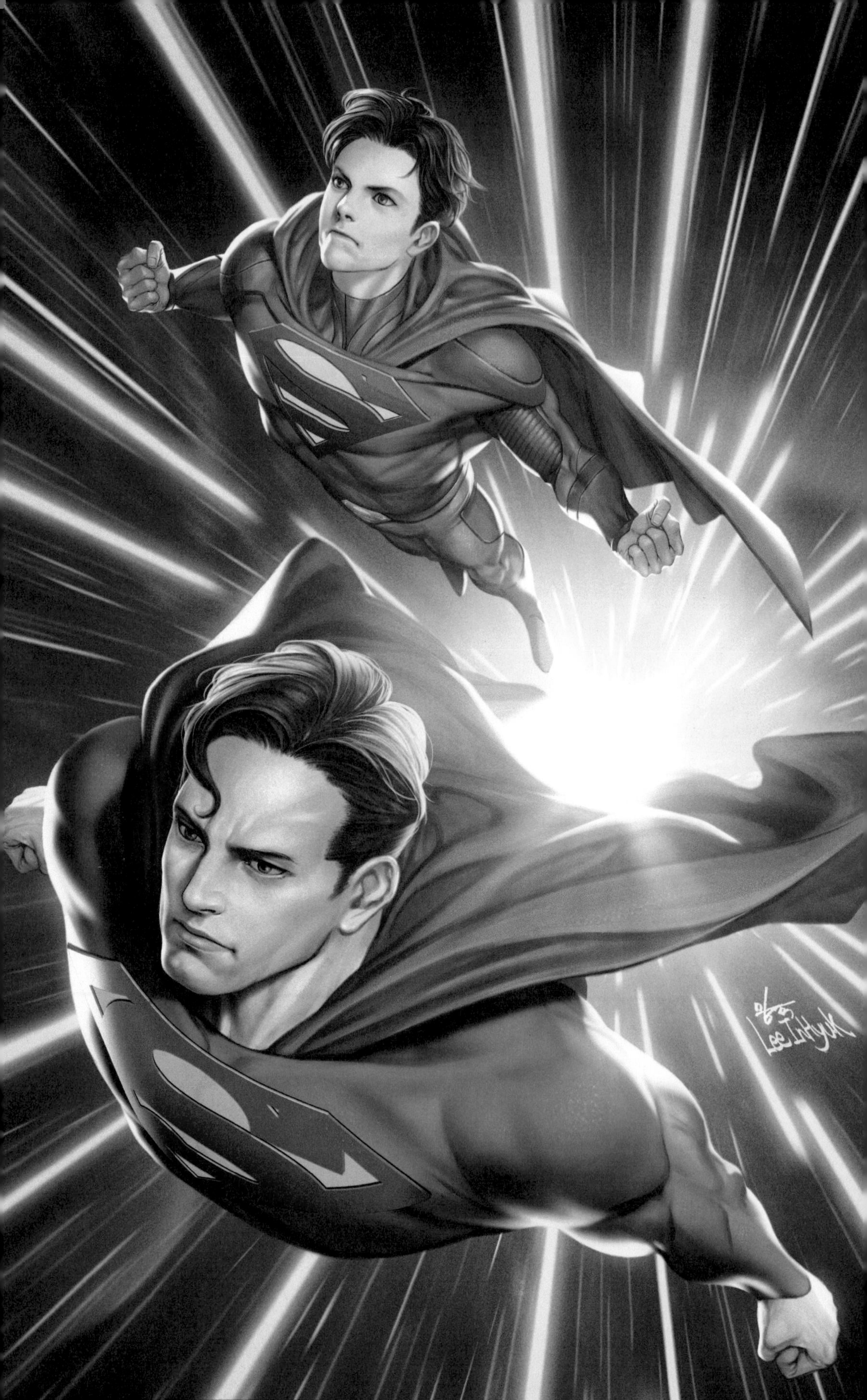
Lee InHyuk

Superman **#31** variant cover art by **INHYUK LEE**

Superman #32 variant cover art by **INHYUK LEE**

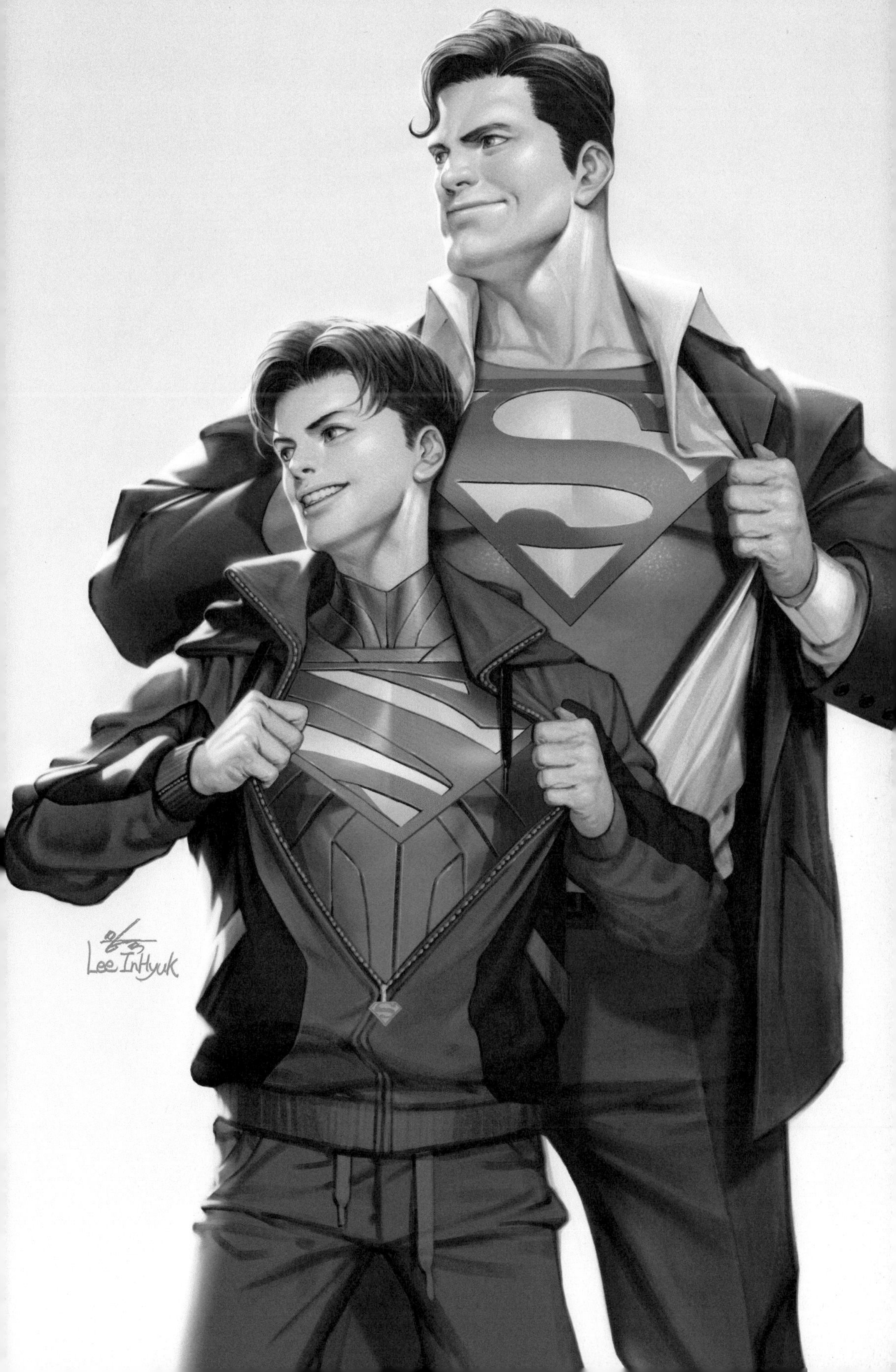
Lee InHyuk

***Superman* #32** Pride variant cover art by **DAVE TALASKI**

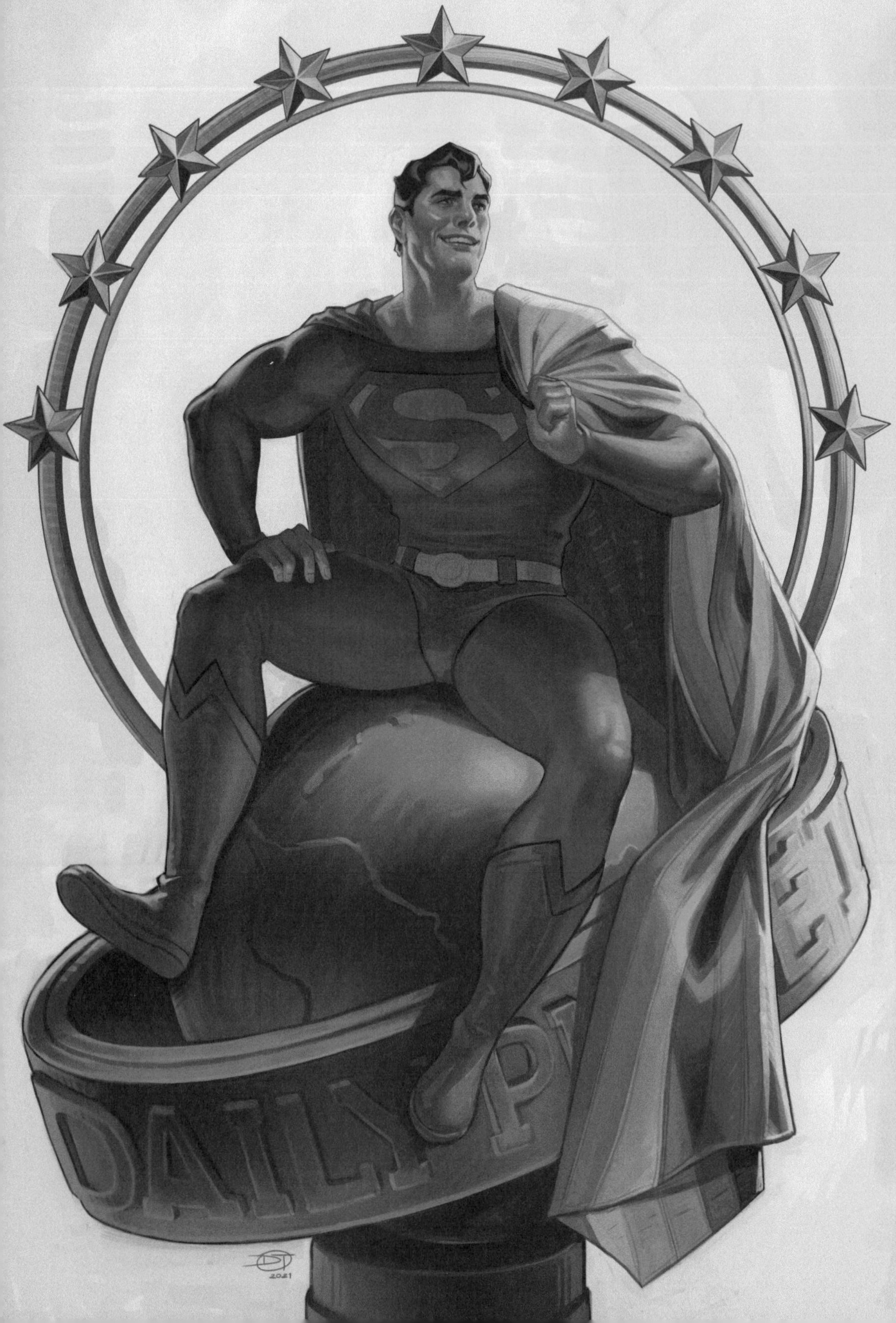
DAILY

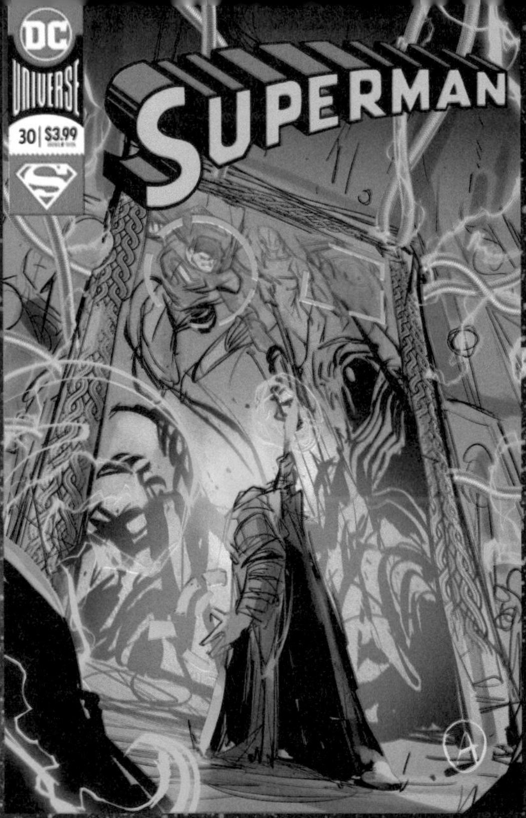
DC UNIVERSE
30 | $3.99
SUPERMAN

Superman #30
cover sketches by
JOHN TIMMS

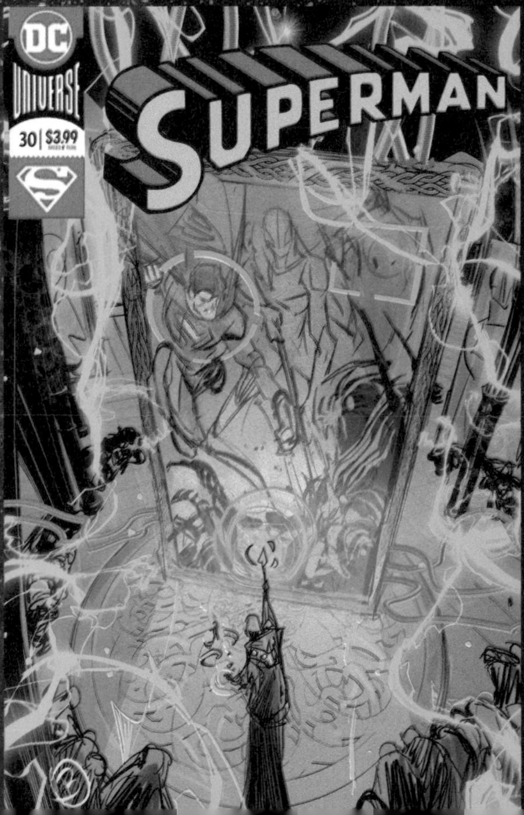
DC UNIVERSE
30 | $3.99
SUPERMAN

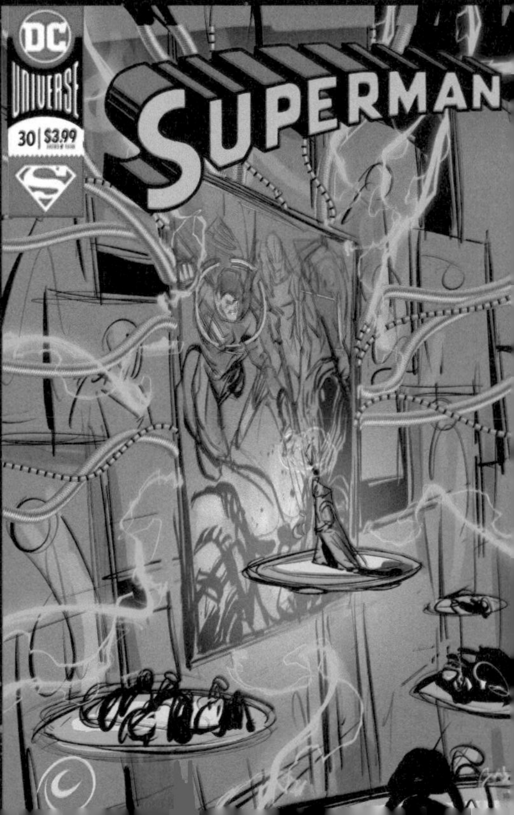
DC UNIVERSE
30 | $3.99
SUPERMAN

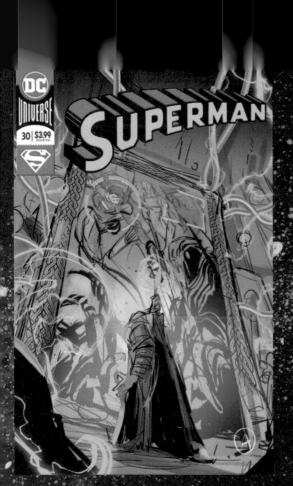

Superman #31
cover sketches by
JOHN TIMMS

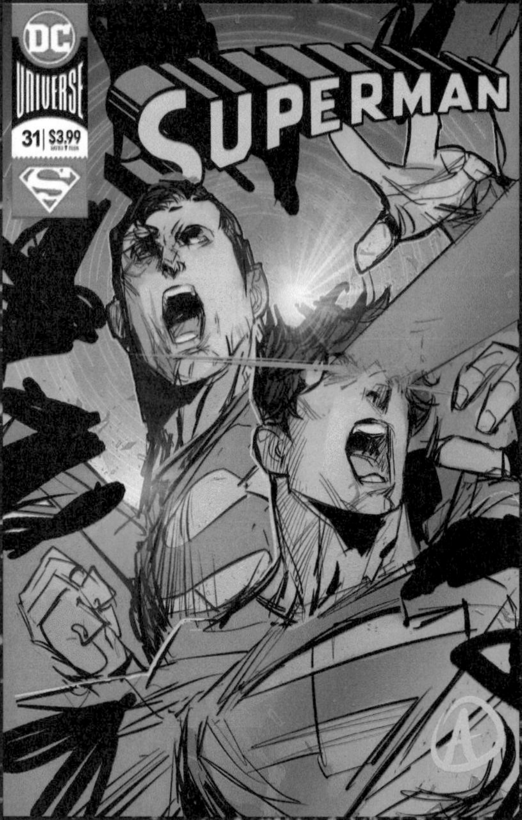
DC
UNIVERSE
31 | $3.99
SUPERMAN
A

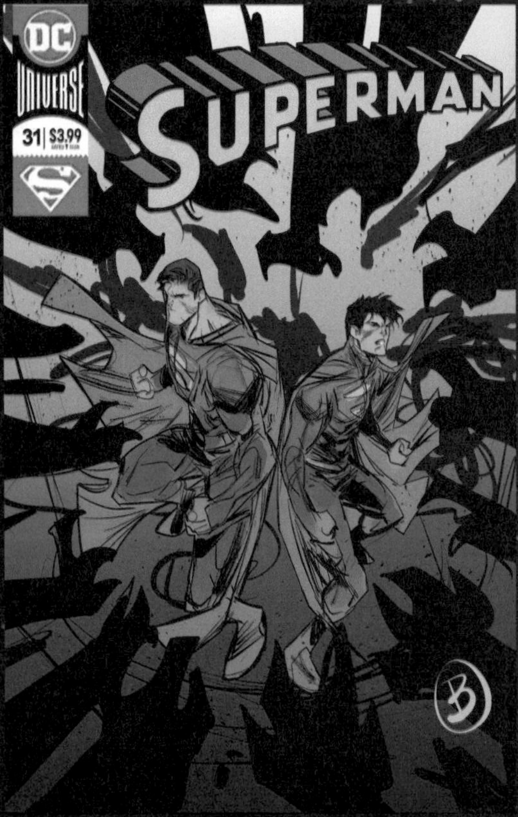
DC
UNIVERSE
31 | $3.99
SUPERMAN
B

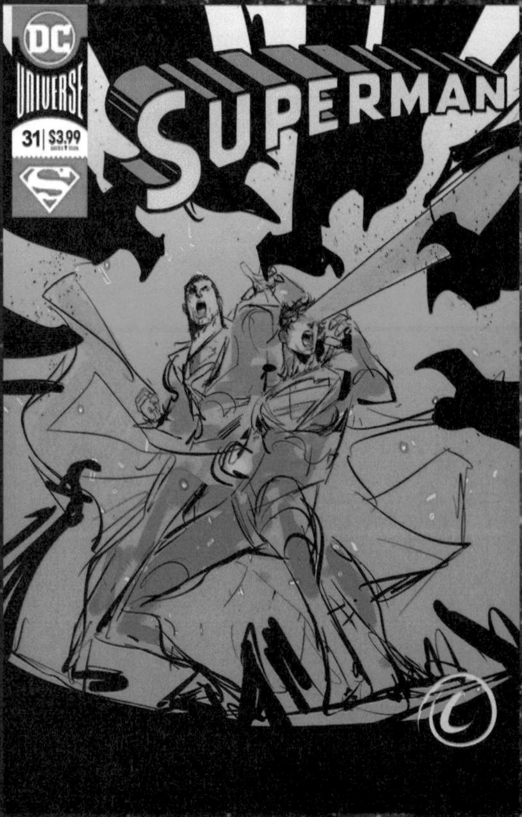
DC
UNIVERSE
31 | $3.99
SUPERMAN
C

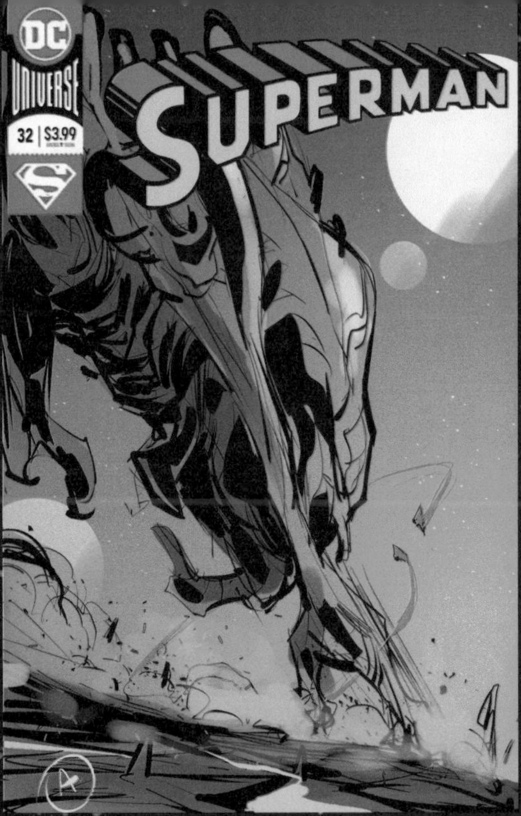
DC
UNIVERSE
32 | $3.99
SUPERMAN

Superman #32
cover sketches by
JOHN TIMMS

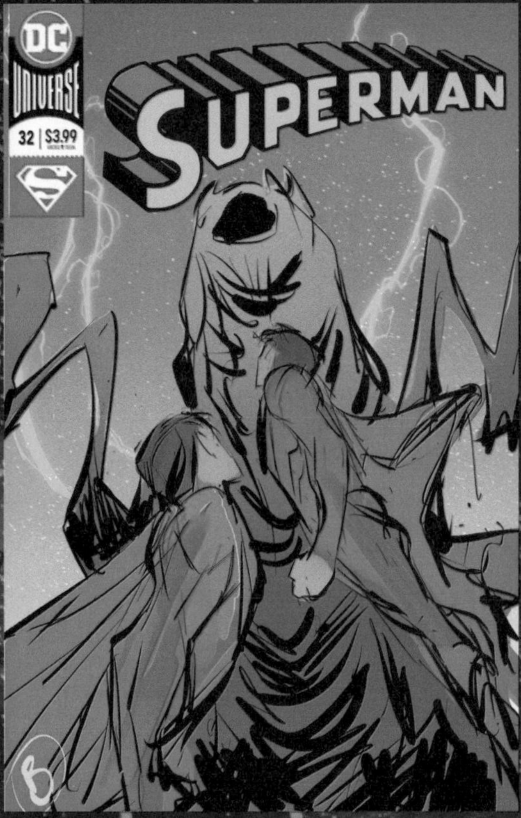
DC
UNIVERSE
32 | $3.99
SUPERMAN

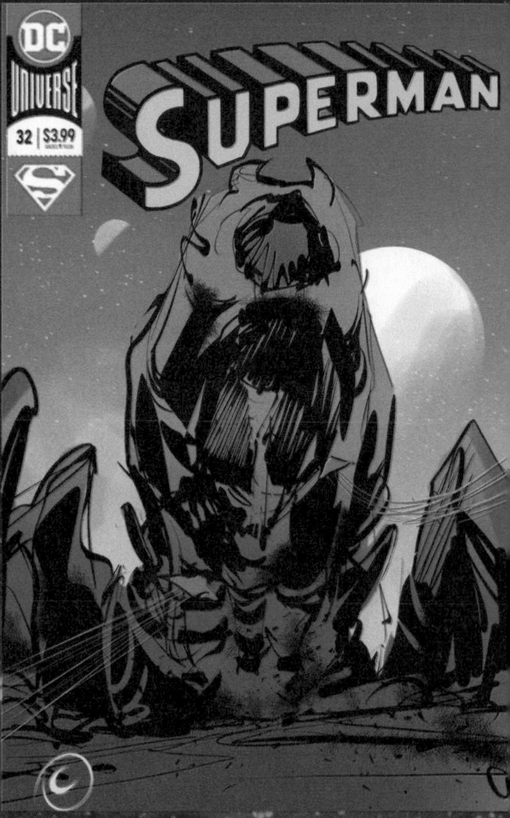
DC
UNIVERSE
32 | $3.99
SUPERMAN

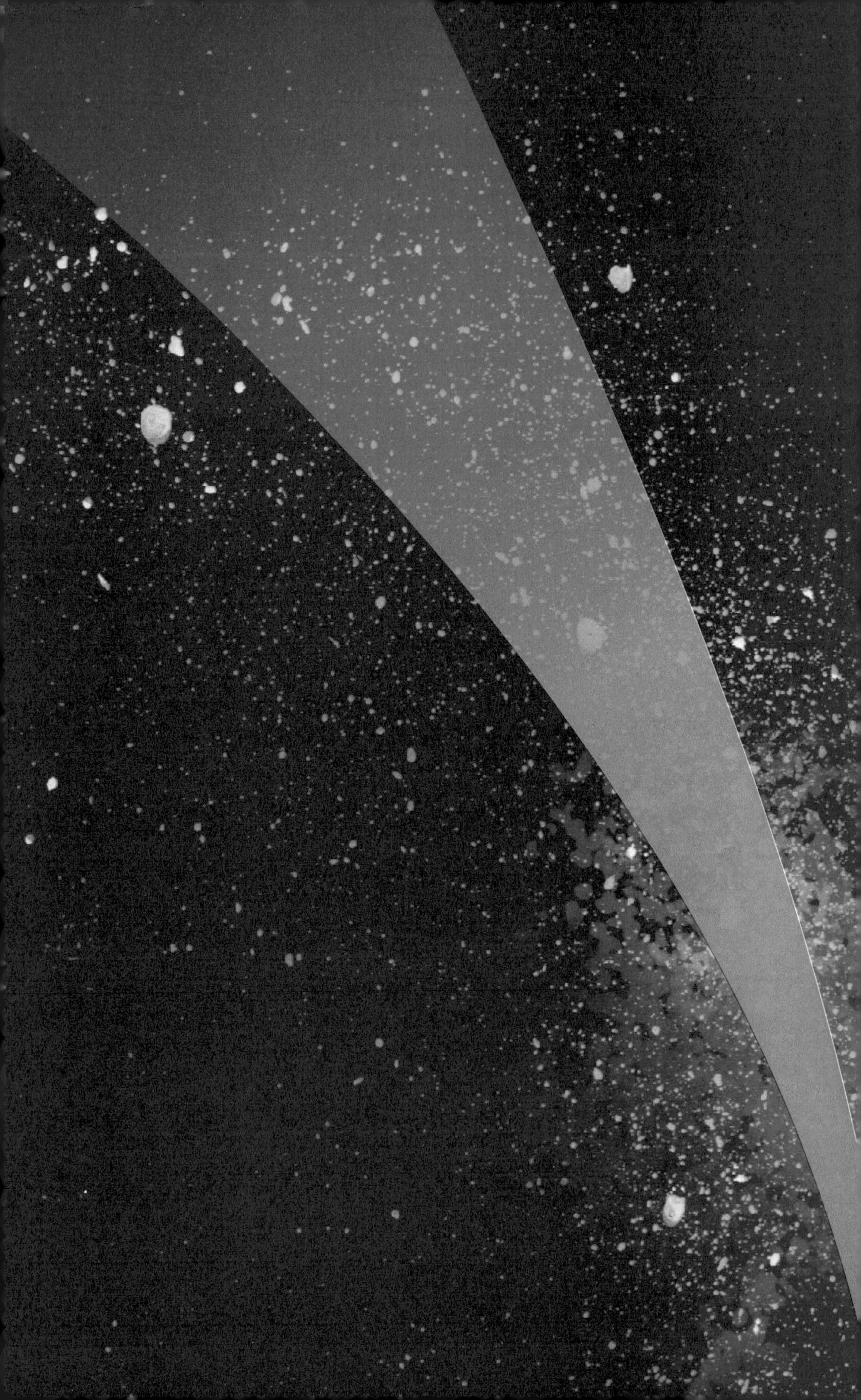